The Self in Society

Edited by Leslie Irvine
University of Colorado, Boulder

cognella™
San Diego, CA

First published in the United States of America in 2013 by Cognella, Inc.

Printed in the United States of America

ISBN: 978-1-60927-867-0 (pbk)

www.cognella.com 800.200.3908

Contents

CHAPTER 3: NEW DIRECTIONS IN THE STUDY OF THE SELF

Preface

PURPOSE AND THEME OF THE BOOK

For many years, I have had the privilege to teach a course called "The Self in Modern Society" at the University of Colorado at Boulder. My syllabus opens with the statement that "Few ideas in modern societies are as taken for granted as the idea that people possess selves." The self, as a concept, is an important starting point for many areas of study within sociology and other disciplines. It is a pleasure and a challenge to entice students not to take this idea for granted. This book represents what, in my experience teaching the course, has been most helpful in that endeavor. Thus, the book offers thought-provoking readings on a range of topics related to the self, from its socio-cultural roots, to the methods used to study it, to the challenges recently presented by neuroscience and research on other species. Throughout, the readings are intended to show how the self is important for many sociological subfields, including deviance, race and ethnicity, gender and sexuality, and inequalities, just to list a few.

BOOK DESIGN AND FORMAT

This book is designed to work as either an alternative or a supplement to a traditional textbook, depending on the course and its scope. It would stand alone in courses that focus on the self, and it would provide useful readings for courses in which the self is one topic among many. The collection of articles gives students exposure to what scholars of the self would consider the "classics," while also providing a sample of more current research. I have organized the contents around seven themes, each in its own chapter. Within most chapters, the readings "speak to" one another, but they could be used separately, too. An introduction to each chapter helps students understand the main issues under discussion. At the end of each chapter, I have provided discussion questions and suggestions for further reading.

Acknowledgments

I want to thank the editors and staff at University Readers, especially Becky Smith and Brent Hannify. I thank the Department of Sociology and the University of Colorado for offering "The Self in Modern Society" and providing me the opportunity to teach it regularly. My thanks also go to Jim Downton for creating the course and passing it on to me. I thank Robert Zussman for a graduate seminar on the self, many years ago, which fostered my interest in the topic. And I thank Marc Krulewitch, most of all, for being himself.

CHAPTER 1

†

Classic perspectives on the self

INTRODUCTION

This section introduces the major sociological perspectives on the self. We begin with some history. It is perhaps more appropriate, and more important, to say that this section introduces the major sociological perspectives on the *social* self. As Holstein and Gubrium explain in their selection, "Formulating a Social Self," the sociological perspective is unique in conceptualizing the self as grounded in everyday experiences. Until the nineteenth century, philosophers had set the terms for the discussion of the self. In philosophical conceptualizations, the self existed beyond the grasp of ordinary people. It was something we could speculate about, but not study empirically. The self, like the soul or spirit, was considered inaccessible. Holstein and Gubrium trace this image of the self to René Descartes (1596–1650), although traces of it appear in the work of other scholars, too. Because the relevance of Descartes for our discussion of the self is both important and complex, I will provide a bit of background that might enrich your understanding of Holstein and Gubrium's chapter.

During the seventeenth century, Descartes made his famous statement, "I think, therefore I am." This statement is often referred to as the *cogito*, from the Latin, *cogito ergo sum*. Descartes was engaged in a deep exploration of how we can really know anything. This was not just a strange preoccupation of his, but a growing concern among many scholars in his time. The end of the Middle Ages had made social, political, and moral order uncertain. Scientific research held promise of producing real knowledge. But so many "truths" had been discarded that many thinkers were deeply skeptical about how we could claim anything as "true." Descartes wanted to build a reliable foundation for knowledge. To get to the root of the problem of uncertainty, he systematically doubted every source of knowledge. He rejected any source that could potentially be false. He rejected opinions because we can often hold false views. He rejected knowledge gained through the senses because even the hands and eyes can be deceived. He rejected everyday experience because he could not know he was not dreaming when he thought he was awake. He proposed that an all-powerful God, if one did exist, or an "Evil Genius," would have the power to deceive him. He doubted his own memory, because he could deceive himself. As he was reaching total uncertainty, and had convinced himself that nothing existed for sure, Descartes asked whether that meant that he himself did not exist. He realized that his ongoing capacity to be deceived held a clue. The capacity for deception existed whenever he was thinking. Whatever thinks must exist. Even when he was being deceived, then he must exist. Thus, existence is the only thing that is certain. Descartes could not be certain of *your* existence, or *mine*. But anyone who thinks can be certain that he or she exists.

With the statement "I think, therefore I am," Descartes situated the self in the mind. As the source of thought, it was the source of the self. This conceptualization of the self is referred to as "transcendental" because it exists apart from everyday experience. In the Cartesian framework, this self is the precondition for all existence that comes after it. In these lofty, philosophical terms, the self cannot be studied; it can only be assumed to exist. The scholars known as the *pragmatists* changed all this, starting in the nineteenth century. As Holstein and Gubrium explain, the term *pragmatism* in this sense does not mean "practical," as it does in everyday vocabulary. In this context, it refers to the belief that what we call "reality" is not some mysterious quality that exists outside of the everyday world. In the pragmatist view, we create "reality" as we go about the matters of ordinary living. We solve problems and, as we continue to use solutions that have worked for us, we consider them "real." The pragmatists' grounding of knowledge in everyday life would provide the foundation for a self that would become increasingly social.

The American psychologist and philosopher William James (1842–1910) introduced a concept that became highly influential in the sociological view of the self. Specifically, he proposed a two-part self: One that has experiences and one that reflects on these experiences. These are not actually separate parts of the self, but are capacities or dimensions of the self. When we think about ourselves, for example, there is a source of that thinking, which James called the "I," and the object of our thought, which James called the "me." You might think of it as the "knower" and the "known." Although this might seem similar to the Cartesian image of the self as situated in thought, for James, this self is rooted in everyday experiences. He presents a self that is not transcendental, but is deeply influenced and shaped by ordinary social life.

Sociologist Charles Horton Cooley (1864–1929) expanded on James's idea that the self could reflect on itself. He, too, was critical of transcendental notions of the self. He pointed out that we not only reflect on ourselves, but we reflect using the perspectives of others. Cooley spelled out this framework in the concept of the "looking glass self." In the reading included here, Cooley reflects on how we sense the "I," focusing on the feeling of self.

George Herbert Mead (1863–1931), another key thinker in the sociological study of the self, had studied with William James at Harvard University. He made use of James's notion of the dual self; again, not as actual, separate parts of the self, but as different phases that allow the self to be an object to itself. He was also influenced by Cooley's "looking glass self." Mead explained how we develop a self through interaction, with language playing an essential part in the process. He showed how we learn to "take the role of the other" in interactions beginning in childhood. Our interactions "call out," in Mead's words, responses from our stockpile of knowledge about roles. This knowledge constitutes a structure—a highly *social* structure—that is the self.

Finally, the excerpt from Erving Goffman's book, *The Presentation of Self in Everyday Life,* offers a dramaturgical perspective on the self. Goffman is often identified as a symbolic interactionist, but his work also builds on the functionalist work of Emile Durkheim by emphasizing the ritual and moral dimensions of social life. Using the analogy of the theater, he illustrates how the self is the product of the performances we enact in ordinary interactions. To grasp the moral dimension of Goffman's work, as you read it, ask yourself what keeps us from leading others to believe we are not really who they think we are.

Formulating a Social Self

BY JAMES A. HOLSTEIN AND JABER F. GUBRIUM

The story of the social self is a big one, a blockbuster of its genre. Our version begins with the American pragmatists William James, Charles Horton Cooley, and George Herbert Mead, who wrote and taught philosophy and sociology during the late nineteenth and early twentieth centuries.[1] As pragmatists, they oriented to the working features of experience, focusing on the provisional truths and knowledge of everyday life. Andrew Feffer (1993, p. 3) explains that "the pragmatist theory of truth [is] that knowledge is [not universal, but] relative to social behavioral 'situations'... evolving as an instrument in the ongoing process of problem solving." One of the pragmatists' most significant conceptual breakthroughs along these lines came with what James (1961[1892], p. 43) called an "empirical" understanding of the self. By this, he meant that the self should be conceived as an entity whose existence in the world, knowledge of itself, and sense of well-being derived from experience. This use of the term *empirical* is rather different from what it has come to mean for many in the social and behavioral sciences today. While the term is now often associated with particular research methods, privileging measurement, quantification, and statistical analysis, the pragmatists used it to reference experience in general.

The social self the pragmatists envisioned was anything but cosmic, extraordinary, or otherwise transcendental.[2] Bringing it down to earth, so to speak, they situated the self in daily living; one could see and hear it unfolding in the social interactions of ordinary individuals, which stood in marked contrast to a European heritage of philosophical commentary. Terms of reference hearkened the commonplace: I, me, mine, you, them, us, other. Most simply, this was to be the story of the grounded, workaday self, whose plots and characters emerged as much from the persons and situations under consideration as from the authors and philosophers who added to the storyline in their own right. This story begins to unravel at twentieth-century's end when it is eclipsed by another, radically

James A. Holstein and Jaber F. Gubrium, "Formulating a Social Self," from *The Self We Live By: Narrative Identity in a Postmodern World*, Pp. 17-37. Copyright © 1999 by Oxford University Press. Permission to reprint granted by the publisher.

different, even destructive account that replaces the experiencing self with mere images of itself.

In this chapter, we trace the story through key texts, starting with James's, Cooley's, and Mead's classic contributions. Their work provided the impetus for related treatments that developed at mid-century. We emphasize, above all, how the pragmatist contribution to the story served as a basis for rejecting the existing transcendental or philosophical status of the self, offering up in its place a social self derived from, formed by, and changing with everyday life.

TURNING AWAY FROM THE TRANSCENDENTAL SELF

Perhaps the quintessential image of the transcendental self resides in René Descartes's famous seventeenth-century dictum, "I think, therefore I am." With this pronouncement, Descartes established a *logical* place for the self, which virtually preoccupied Western philosophical commentary for the centuries to come. Whether called the "I" or the "self," Descartes's is the cognitive entity—the cogito—that he claims presents itself through philosophical reflection. As if to argue, "I know I am thinking, therefore the entity that thinks behind my thoughts exists as 'I,'" Descartes locates the self at thought's ostensible origin. The source of his thoughts, in other words, is an entity that is centered where thought begins.

This is a philosophical, not an empirical, exercise in self discovery. Self isn't derived from experience, as the pragmatists would later insist. Nor is it used to comment on the resulting vicissitudes of everyday life. Indeed, as Robert Solomon (1988) points out, this self is existentially thin, certainly not as morally rich and substantial as the entity Descartes's compatriot Jean-Jacques Rousseau discovers decades later strolling through the forests of St. Germain in France: "Self as such, the soul of humanity … the self that he shared with all men and women the world over" (p. 1).

Logically thin or morally rich, this self nonetheless transcended ordinary social life. It didn't extend empirically to ordinary working men or women and certainly was far removed from those at the margins of society such as the ostensibly crazed or stigmatized. It was, rather, a philosophical position from which social matters were considered and argued. Whether it was Descartes's Enlightenment cogito, which had decidedly rational leanings, or Rousseau's more romantic counterpart, it was a self placed prior to, or above, "the artifices and superficialities of the social whirl," as Solomon puts it. If Descartes thought and therefore was, the position from which he did so was detached from the swirl of social life. This transcendental self was disembodied, separated, and distinguished from the very corporeal body upon which it otherwise philosophically mused and cast judgment. If anything, social life and the body spoiled the logically envisioned, transcendental self; they certainly didn't participate in inventing or producing it.

While the cogito stood its philosophical ground for years, its experiential fragility is highlighted in a contemporary joke that casts empirical doubt on Descartes's assertion. As the joke goes, Descartes was once invited to a regal English tea party, where he was to be introduced with a flourish as the famous purveyor of "I think, therefore I am." Appreciating the attention, Descartes accepted the invitation, despite his strong distaste for English tea. As the party got under way, an unknowing waiter approached the great philosopher and dutifully asked him if he would like a cup of tea. Haughtily, Descartes responded, "I think not!"— whereupon he vanished into thin air. So much for the disembodied self!

Joking aside, as experientially fragile as this position later proved to be, what Descartes suggested about the self was nonetheless epoch-making, setting the retrospective and prospective terms for centuries of debate. While some, such as Rousseau, may have romanticized a fuller self, and others, such as Augustine hundreds of years before that, painfully explored inwardness in relation to other-worldliness, it was Descartes who placed a separate and logically distinct self at the center of philosophy. This was a fully reasoned, not other-worldly, fulcrum for ensuing deliberation over the meaning of existence and the moral order (Taylor 1989). As Charles Taylor explains, "the change [effected by Descartes] might be described by saying that Descartes situates the moral sources within us" (p. 143), not somewhere else in the cosmos.

But as Solomon (1988) also points out, the self Descartes logically derived was never purely philosophical; it had ideological bearing. According to Solomon, Descartes spawned a "transcendental pretense." The story of modern continental philosophy, which stems from Descartes's *Meditations,* is not just about specialized problems in metaphysics and epistemology, but is also a dramatic narrative of the European self-image. The transcendental self was an equally compelling fulcrum for a Eurocentric view of the world, one that was at the time being explored, colonized, and hegemonically interpreted. In this narrative, Solomon adds, "… science and knowledge play an important role but only alongside the romantic imagination, unprecedented cosmic arrogance, continual reaction and rebellion, and the ultimate collapse of a bloated cosmopolitan self-confidence" (p. 3).

Solomon explains that the leading theme of the narrative was the rise and fall of "an extraordinary concept of the self." It served its adherents and national interests in a variety of ways, not the least of which was to provide a hugely successful logical context for understanding human nature, experience, others, and their relation to the cosmos. Its philosophers assumed that they could change the world, which, indeed, they sometimes succeeded in doing. And, Solomon notes, it was done with an extravagant lack of modesty, one that took for granted that the European scale for weighing reason and the sentiments was also the world's standard. The assumption was that the cogito or philosophically reflecting self not only had knowledge of itself, but, in that knowledge, knew any and all possible selves. What followed from this transcendental pretense was that everyone, everywhere, was principally the same. As Solomon (p. 4) comments,

The self that becomes the star performer in modern European philosophy is the transcendental self, or transcendental ego, whose nature and ambitions were unprecedentedly arrogant, presumptuously cosmic, and consequently mysterious. The transcendental self was *the* self—timeless, universal, and in each one of us around the globe and throughout history. Distinguished from our individual idiosyncrasies, this was the self we shared. In modest and ordinary terms it was called "human nature." In much less modest, extraordinary terminology, the transcendental self was nothing less than God, the Absolute Self, the World Soul.

Solomon goes on to say:

The transcendental pretense is no innocent philosophical thesis, but a political weapon of enormous power. Even as it signaled a radical egalitarianism, and suggested a long-awaited global sensitivity, it also justified unrestricted tolerance for paternalism and self-righteousness—"the white philosopher's burden." Philosophers who never left their home town declared themselves experts on "human nature," and weighed the morals of civilization and "savages" thousands of miles beyond their ken. (P. 6)

The critique suggests what the early pragmatists were up against as they began to formulate the self in more mundane terms. Broadly speaking, they envisioned a contrasting kind of self, one enmeshed in the diverse activities and circumstances of daily life. This self was to mirror the reflexive consciousness of ordinary men and women in the world. While the pragmatists did not ignore the social self's logical relation to nature and the universe, theirs was not some idealized or abstract position from which one contemplated nature, the cosmos, and our place in relation to them. Rather, they were more interested in how selves operate *in* the world, especially how individuals managed their relations with each other as they reflected upon themselves and upon those with whom they interacted.

As the term *pragmatism* implies, adherents turned their attention to the *practice* of everyday life, an important concern of which was the nature of the workaday self. While the social and behavioral sciences now take this for granted, we cannot overemphasize how radical this reaction turned out to be. The pragmatist turnabout did not so much mean being realistic or expedient in consideration of the issues in question, which is a common enough interpretation of the term *pragmatist*. Rather, it meant considering issues in the context of ordinary living, not the transcendental world of traditional philosophical commentary.

While James, Cooley, and Mead often refer to the self in the singular—as the self or Self—its lived presence in the world of everyday life needed to be plural. James (1961[1892], p. 46), for example, called attention to the socially manifold self when he emphatically stated, "Properly speaking, *a man has as many social selves as there are individuals who recognize him* and carry an image of him in their mind" (emphasis in the original). For the pragmatists, references to the self or Self were more a manner of speaking than they were representations of a state of being. In contrast, it was much more likely for the European philosophers to refer to the self or Self in the singular, tellingly signaling that self's transcendental character. James's, Cooley's, and Mead's self was plural because their attention was concertedly empirical, focused as it was on the varied "we's," "us's," and "them's" we are to one another as we go about our daily lives. The social self was always the self-at-hand, the socially operative sense of who we are to ourselves and to others.

James, Cooley, and Mead also had a more politically modest self in mind than did their philosophical forebears. Their formulation coincided with an empirically democratic, some say distinctly American, view that selves belong to all of us and take their shape and import their substance in our everyday relations with each other. It was a decidedly non-European view. Several commentators have suggested that the pragmatists were in the unwitting "business," so to speak, of formulating a version of the self suitable to American bourgeois interests, less centered on imperial, universal reason than on a progressive, democratically dispersed working agency appropriate to the times (see Reynolds 1990). But, as William Skidmore (1975) cautions,

> Some say it [pragmatism] was a peculiarly American philosophy because it took a disapproving view of pure abstraction for its own sake and because it put considerable emphasis on action, as opposed to thinking and logic, and in general, the mind. ... But pragmatism, to its philosophical adherents, did not mean simply "If it works, it's good," as is sometimes said ... pragmatism was a movement which used the traditional concerns of philosophy as a point of departure from which to defend a somewhat novel way of looking at these problems. (P. 201)

Whether or not the early pragmatists' self was intentionally formulated to resonate with distinctly American interests, their view did establish the grounds for a different approach. The selves that resulted could not be transcendent nor arrogant, simply because they were commonplace. They had no empirical warrant for being anything other than the ordinary subjectivities they were within the whirl of everyday life. According to Norbert Wiley (1994), this whirl was no more evident than in the vibrant and growing metropolitan cities of the time, where the fantastic diversity of immigrants and religious affiliations virtually demanded a conception of the self that could encompass the differences. If existing philosophical formulations were too conceptually distant, the popular psychological understanding of the self as a configuration of traits or "faculties" was also sorely lacking empirically. The pragmatists' social self, in contrast, was up to the challenge of the broad range of experiences.

Lest this sound too triumphant, it's important to remember that the pragmatists' formulation would itself be challenged in due course, both on the home front by commentators on the state of the self in American life (see Chapter 3) and by dissenting European heirs to the transcendental pretense (see Chapter 4). But, for now, let's consider in greater detail the social self in the pragmatists' chapter of the story.

WILLIAM JAMES'S EMPIRICAL SELF

In their discussion of the development of symbolic interactionism from pragmatist thought, Bernard Meitzer, John Petras, and Larry Reynolds (1975, p. 6) indicate that "a significant advance made by James was the removal of the concept of self from the purely metaphysical realm to the view of at least some aspect of it as derived from interaction processes in the social environment." Commenting on James's ideas, philosopher George Santayana (1957) refers to the European transcendental tradition's "genteel" intrusion into American philosophy, which James argued against because it stood removed from the commonplace experiences of social life. In particular, Santayana applauds the pragmatists' turn away from Hegel's absolute self.[3] In a speech given in 1911 to the Philosophical Union of the University of California, Santayana describes James's effort, emphasizing the value of taking into account the experiences of common men and women.

> William James kept his mind and heart wide open to all that might seem, to polite minds, odd, personal, or visionary in religion and philosophy. He gave a sincerely respectful hearing to sentimentalists, mystics, spiritualists, wizards, cranks, quacks, and impostors—for it is hard to draw the line, and James was not willing to draw it prematurely. He thought, with his usual modesty, that any of these might have something to teach him. The lame, the halt, the blind, and those speaking with tongues could come to him with the certainty of finding sympathy. (P. 205)

According to Santayana, James's pragmatism "broke the spell of the genteel tradition," grounding intelligence and the self in the empirical world. Referring to James's views, Santayana writes:

> Intelligence has its roots and its issues in the context of events; it is one kind of practical adjustment, an experimental act, a form of vital tension. It does not essentially serve to picture other parts of reality but to connect them. (P. 206)

James's (1961[1892]) discussion of the empirical self begins simply, not with a philosophical problem, but with the self he and others experience in everyday life—the self of daily awareness that is formed in reflection upon itself. Using personal pronouns, he explains that awareness senses a source—"I"—and an object of awareness—"me"—of whom I am aware. While James's "logic" is reminiscent of Descartes's, it is important to note that its object of reference is intentionally empirical. James puts it this way in his book *Psychology: The Briefer Course* (1961[1892]):

> Whatever I may be thinking of, I am always at the same time more or less aware of *myself,* of my *personal existence.* At the same time it is I who am aware; so that the total self of me, being as it were duplex, partly known and partly knower, partly object and partly subject, must have two aspects discriminated in it, of which for shortness we may call one the *Me* and the other the *I.* I call these "discriminated aspects" and not separate things, because the identity of *I* with *me,* even in the very act of their discrimination, is perhaps the most ineradicable dictum of common-sense, and must not be undermined by a terminology here at the outset, whatever we may come to think of its validity at our inquiry's end. (P. 43, emphasis in the original)

From the start, James sets an "everyday" tone. In his very first sentence, he describes something each of us might well refer to "personally" and, more or less, be aware of. James wants to emphasize the commonplace, "an ineradicable dictum of common-sense." This individual reflexivity—a personal awareness of oneself—is so plain and simple, it seems, that its discussion needn't even be bogged down by a special terminology. As if to say that each and every one of us has and uses the words—words we carry around with us all the time: *I, me,* and *myself* in particular—James hesitates to insinuate himself into his text as an author, a philosopher, or a psychologist with a language of his own. Rather, he suggests that he is merely commenting on what each of us, more or less, already possesses.

The self, according to James, is not to be hastily objectified; it must wait for experience to do its work before it is realized. While we all use personal pronouns to refer to ourselves, and the point of origin of our self awareness (I) can be discriminated from the object of that awareness (me), James warns us that the "ineradicable" identity or unity of *I* with *me* must not be undermined by this terminology- James cautions us that to have words for things, such as the *I* and the *me* of the self, risks reifying them rather than sustaining their referential status as simultaneous facets of the selves we are. James is suggesting that the terms he, and we, use to refer to aspects of ourselves are just that, namely, terms of reference, not separate and distinct experiential objects. When we think ("whatever I may be thinking of"), we can—in mind's discourse—think of ourselves thinking. In that sense, we become objects to ourselves. Similarly, James informs us that when we communicate with others about who we are, we again inadvertently convey both subjectivity and objectivity. That is, we distinguish between the *I* and *me,* even while James admits that, empirically, "between what a man calls *me* and what he simply calls *mine* the line is difficult to draw"

(p. 43). This referential entity we call *me* is not clearly distinct from what we and others claim to own, including our bodies and possessions.

Whether James is discussing thought or speech, he is careful to point out that the self and its referential facets are aspects of communication, either the inner practice of self-awareness in thought or the allocations of subjectivity evident in open references to personal characteristics—to you and yours or to me and mine. Self is part and parcel of the process of referring to ourselves, to others, and to the world, however that is accomplished. It doesn't exist separate from, or over and above, communication. James's aspirations for a psychological science, however, do lead him to concentrate on the interior of the communication process. As we will see later, it is George Herbert Mead who concertedly takes the self outside of itself, locating it within what he calls "social behavior." Still, while James develops a psychology, his discussion of the empirical self isn't mentalistic. His focus is always practical, beginning with people in their worlds, surrounded by others, whoever they might be, referring to each other and involved in the concrete affairs of daily living.

James concentrates on the empirical self, which he subdivides into the material me, the social me, and the spiritual me. His discussion of the social me formulates a decidedly social self. Emphasizing its everyday endowments and embodiment, James introduces the empirical self or "me" in the following way:

> We feel and act about certain things that are ours very much as we feel and act about ourselves. Our fame, our children, the work of our hands, may be as dear to us as our bodies are, and arouse the same feelings and the same acts of reprisal if attacked. And our bodies themselves, are they simply ours, or are they *us?* Certainly men have been ready to disown their very bodies and to regard them as mere vestures, or even as prisons of clay from which they should some day be glad to escape. (Pp. 43–44)

It's evident that James doesn't want to sharply distinguish the body and other material markers of who we are from the selves we, and others, consider ourselves to be. Indeed, this very lack of demarcation typifies pragmatist thought. The self is viewed as a working point of reference for ourselves and others that arises and gets designated within the course of embodied interaction. Our bodies and the material aspects of social interaction are important features as well as signs of who we and others are and, as such, feature our identities in practice.

Because the self is plunked down in everyday life, it shifts and is bandied about in the course of social interaction. It is formed locally, not universally. The social self emerges, grows, and is altered, within our daily affairs; it doesn't transcend them. If this self is at all extraordinary, it's extraordinarily mundane. If it has constancy, it is as stable as the patterns and accompanying material signs of our relationships. This returns us to James's comment that *"a man has as many social selves as there are individuals who recognize him and that carry an image of him in their minds."* This social self is not fixed, analytically or philosophically, nor is it finalized to accord with an idealized state of being. Rather, as James puts it, whether "me" or "mine," it is

> … fluctuating material; the same object being sometimes treated as a part of me, at other times as simply mine, and then again as if I had nothing to do with it at all. *In its widest possible sense,* however, *a man's Me is the sum total of all that he* CAN *call his,* not only his body and his psychic powers, but his clothes and his house, his wife and children, his ancestors and friends, his reputation and works, his lands and horses, and yacht and bank-account. All these things give him the same emotions. If they wax, and prosper, he feels triumphant; if they dwindle and die away he feels cast down—not necessarily in the same degree for each thing, but in much the same way for all. [I understand] the *Me* in this widest sense. (P. 44, emphasis in the original)

CHARLES HORTON COOLEY'S LOOKING-GLASS SELF

Paralleling James, Cooley devotes two chapters of his book *Human Nature and the Social Order* (1964[1902]) to this empirical or social self. Like James, he begins with the leading personal pronouns. Terms of reference such as "I," "me," "my," and "myself" signal more than points of view; they are the commonplace communicative markers of the experiencing self. In the following extract from the introduction to the first chapter, Cooley almost desperately aims to leave aside ideas of a transcendental self. He clearly wants to locate his concern in the realm of everyday life, in the world of "common speech," set forth as a "self that can be apprehended or verified by ordinary observation," not in terms of what he thereafter refers to as the "abstruseness" of metaphysical discussion.

> It is well to say at the outset that by the word "self" in this discussion is meant simply that which is designated in common speech by the pronouns of the first person singular, "I," "me," "my," "mine," and "myself." "Self" and "ego" are used by metaphysicians and moralists in many other senses, more or less remote from the "I" of daily speech and thought, and with these I wish to have as little to do as possible. What is here discussed is what psychologists call the empirical self, the self that can be apprehended or verified by ordinary observation. I qualify it by the word social not as implying the existence of a self that is not social— for I think that the "I" of common language always has more or less distinct reference to other people as well as the speaker—but because I wish to emphasize and dwell upon the social aspect of it. (Pp. 168–69)

In one fell swoop, Cooley locates the object of his interest and, following that, designates a procedure for investigating it. The self he wishes to discuss is possessed by each and every one of us. It doesn't belong to metaphysicians or moralists. Yet, because it belongs to everyone, it also would include the object of metaphysicians' and moralists' own ordinary references to themselves.[4] Cooley notes that he's interested in what psychologists refer to as the "empirical self," but he qualifies this, explaining that what he calls the *social* self" is the same entity, but with an emphasis on "the social aspect of it." Cooley thus formulates an object of study he believes to be natural and distinct from philosophy's counterpart transcendental entity, but which clearly registers a reality shared with psychology.

Cooley goes on to indicate that his way of viewing the self will not be philosophical. He throws his lot in with the scientific method, in particular, with what "can be apprehended or verified by ordinary observation." While Cooley's subsequent development of introspection is scientifically suspect, he nonetheless intends to proceed empirically, in relation to concrete experiences. His systematic observations of his two children's self-references at play are exemplary. Together with other observations, this serves as evidence for his claims and hypotheses. Consider how "factual" and perhaps somewhat snide Cooley is about this in the following extract:

> Although the topic of the self is regarded as an abstruse one, this abstruseness belongs chiefly, perhaps, to the metaphysical discussion of the "pure ego"— whatever that may be—while the empirical self should not be very much more difficult to get hold of than other facts of the mind. At any rate, it may be assumed that the pronouns of that first person have a substantial, important, and not very recondite meaning, otherwise they would not be in constant and intelligible use by simple people and young children the world over. And since they have such a meaning why should it not be observed and reflected upon like any other matter of fact? (P. 169)

Dismissing metaphysical and moral offerings, Cooley declares that the core of the empirical self is self-feeling, not philosophical categories. Self-feeling, of course, implicates the body. While originary self-feeling is hardly the social self envisioned as developing out of group relations, the body is the grounds of everyday self-awareness and self-control, according to Cooley. Appealing to James and Hiram Stanley, Cooley puts this directly:

> The distinctive thing in the idea for which the pronouns of the first person are names is apparently a characteristic kind of feeling which may be called the my-feeling or sense of appropriation. Almost any sort of ideas may be associated with this feeling, and so come to be named "I" or "mine," but the feeling and that alone it would seem, is the determining factor in the matter. As Professor James says in his admirable discussion of the self, the words "me" and "self"

designate "all the things which have the power to produce in a stream of con-sciousness excitement of a certain peculiar sort." This view is very fully set forth by Professor Hiram M. Stanley, whose work, "The Evolutionary Psychology of Feeling," has an extremely suggestive chapter on self-feeling. (Pp. 169–70)

Reflecting pragmatists' Darwinian heritage, Cooley then explains:

> The emotion or feeling of self may be regarded as instinctive, and has doubtless evolved in connection with its important function in stimulating and unifying the special activities of individuals. It is thus very profoundly rooted in the history of the human race and apparently indispensable to any plan of life at all similar to ours. It seems to exist in a vague though vigorous form at the birth of each individual, and, like other instinctive ideas or germs of ideas, to be defined and developed by experience, becoming associated, or rather incorporated, with muscular, visual, and other sensations; with perceptions, apperceptions, and conceptions of every degree of complexity and of infinite variety of content; and, especially, with personal ideas. Meantime the feeling itself does not remain unaltered, but undergoes differentiation and refinement just as does any other sort of crude innate feeling. (Pp. 170–71)

To Cooley, crude feelings of self are instinctive, but are also shaped and transformed with our experience in the world. The self is embodied and visceral from the start, part of our natural human endowment. But it isn't immutable; original self-feeling is built up into innumerable self sentiments. With experience, self-feeling forms into the social self, with all the nuances and variety that experience can muster. The empirical self adds meaning, direction, and control to self-feeling. What is original for us as human beings, then, are the visceral sensations of our individuality, according to Cooley, and this provides the bodily underpinnings for stimulating our activities as social entities.

These are pretty solid empirical groundings, distinctly different from those offered by transcendental philosophy. How does Cooley convince us that this is a compelling source of the self, one that rivals the offerings of metaphysicians and moralists? For this, he turns to matters that would ostensibly be evident to anyone who cared to think about them. While Cooley indicates the empirical self by pointing to the common pronouns we use to refer to ourselves, he also asserts that there "can be no final test of the self except the way we feel; the self is that toward which we have a 'my' attitude." Cooley claims that "a formal definition of self-feeling, or indeed of any sort of feeling, must be as hollow as a formal definition of the taste of salt, or the color red; we can expect to know what it is only by experiencing it," again implicating the body (p. 172). The empirical self, Cooley argues, is most evident in the various actions we take, in response to events or conduct that cast aspersions on self-feeling, revealing the "my" attitude. Cooley puts this plainly:

But as this feeling is quite as familiar to us and as easy to recall as the taste of salt or the color red, there should be no difficulty in understanding what is meant by it. One need only imagine some attack on his "me," say ridicule of his dress or an attempt to take away his property or his child, or his good name by slander, and self-feeling immediately appears. Indeed, we need only pronounce, with strong emphasis, one of the self-words, like "I" or "my," and self-feeling will be recalled by association. (Pp. 172–73)

Whether or not we agree, Cooley is nonetheless presenting a story of the self that contrasts materially with those he "wishes to have as little to do [with] as possible." If he were inclined to make a related point about how to study the self, he would say that we must turn to metaphysicians and moralists' actual objects of concern, not the concern in its own right, in order to understand the selves we are. To emphasize this, Cooley recalls several literary examples of self-assertion, implicating both experience and self-feeling, which again prods his philosophical nemesis. This is followed by yet another illustration from everyday life to make his point:

We all have thoughts of the same sort as these, and yet it is possible to talk so coldly or mystically about the self that one begins to forget that there is, really, any such thing. But, perhaps the best way to realize the naive meaning of "I" is to listen to the talk of children playing together, especially if they do not agree very well. They use the first person with none of the conventional self-repression of their elders, but with much emphasis and variety of inflection, so that its emotional animus is unmistakable. (P. 174)

In a much quoted passage, Cooley suggests that the self, while rooted in self-feeling, nonetheless operates in the imagination, drawing from, reflecting upon, and responding to real and imagined others. This forms Cooley's well-known "looking-glass self," which has three principal components: "The imagination of our appearance to the other person; the imagination of his judgment of that appearance, and some sort of self-feeling, such as pride or mortification" (p. 184). It is responsive not simply to itself, and certainly not to some transcendental category of meaning or morality, but to how it imagines itself from the standpoint of another. Here again, we glimpse the penetrating richness of Cooley's self, an entity that draws both from what it makes of itself from the point of view of the other and from the resulting self-feeling.

GEORGE HERBERT MEAD'S INTERACTING SELF

The self becomes less instinctive and more socially interactive when Mead takes up the narrative. With telling reference to both James and Cooley, Mead (1934, p. 173) discusses the place of cognition, feeling, and interaction in the formation of the self. He begins by noting that "emphasis should be laid on the central position of thinking." Self-consciousness, rather than feelings, "provides the core and primary structure of the self," according to Mead. But, most importantly, self-consciousness is the inner representation of what is otherwise an *external conversation* of significant gestures. Mead avoids a strict line of demarcation between inner life and social interaction; in his view, they are both forms of communication. Thinking is an inner conversation with oneself; social interaction is an external conversation with others. Both are socially symbolic and reflexively interactive. The empirical self is neither more nor less a part of internal or external life. Rather, it is an integral part of a working subjectivity, wherever that is experientially located.

Mead disagrees with James and Cooley's emphasis on self-feeling, because a focus on self-feeling viscerally essentializes the self, leaving it only secondarily social.

> The thinking or intellectual process—the internalization and inner dramatization, by the individual, of the external conversation of significant gestures which constitutes his chief mode of interaction with other individuals belonging to the same society—is the earliest experiential phase in the genesis and development of the self. (P. 173)

He then explains:

> Cooley and James, it is true, endeavor to find the basis of the self in reflexive affective experiences, i.e., experiences involving "self-feeling"; but the theory that the nature of the self is to be found in such experiences does not account for the origin of the self, or of the self-feeling which is supposed to characterize such experiences. The individual need not take the attitudes of others toward himself in these experiences, since these experiences merely in themselves do not necessitate his doing so, and unless he does so, he cannot develop a self; and he will not do so in these experiences unless his self has already originated otherwise, namely, in the way we have been describing. The *essence* of the self, as we have said, is cognitive: it lies in the internalized conversation of gestures which constitutes thinking, or in terms of which thought or reflection proceeds. And hence the origin and foundations of the self, like those of thinking, are social. (P. 173)

Mead turns skeptically to Cooley's looking-glass self, which Cooley claims to operate in the imagination. Mead's concern here is that—contrary to the title of Cooley's book—Cooley's project is more about an oddly unsocial human nature than it is about social order. Contrasting biological and social origins, Mead comments on the "advantage" of a more clearly social perspective. According to Mead, his own social approach, which locates self in ongoing social interaction,

> enables us to give a detailed account and actually to explain the genesis and development of mind; whereas the view that mind is a congenital biological endowment of the individual organism does not really enable us to explain its nature and origin at all: neither what sort of biological endowment it is, nor how organisms *at* a certain level of evolutionary progress come to possess it. (P. 224)

In a footnote, Mead succinctly discusses Cooley's looking-glass self. It's evident here that Mead is still astutely the philosopher, yet one who espouses a distinctly nontranscendental view. He focuses on Cooley's implicit solipsism, accusing Cooley of placing social interaction within the imagination of the individual, rather than the reverse. Mead pulls no punches.

> According to the traditional assumption of psychology, the content of experience is entirely individual and not in any measure to be primarily accounted for in social terms, even though its setting or context is a social one. And for a social psychology like Cooley's—which is founded on precisely this same assumption—all social interactions depend upon the imaginations of the individuals involved, and take place in terms of their direct conscious influences upon one another in the processes of social experience. Cooley's social psychology, as found in his *Human Nature and the Social Order,* is hence inevitably introspective, and his psychological method carries with it the implication of complete solipsism: society really has no existence except in the individual's mind, and the concept of the self as in any sense intrinsically social is a product of imagination. Even for Cooley the self presupposes experience, and experience is a process within which selves arise; but since that process is for him primarily internal and individual rather than external and social, he is committed in his psychology to a subjectivistic and idealistic, rather than an objectivistic and naturalistic, metaphysical position. (P. 224)

Interestingly, Mead's terminology for the empirical self is the same as James's and Cooley's, even while it is decidedly more interactional. Before Mead discusses the "I" and the "me," he considers the social foundation of the self, again toeing the line between the philosopher and the empiricist. From the start, he locates the self's foundation in language. For Mead, the self is *part* of the process of communication. It doesn't exist before it, nor does it develop and come to be expressed through it. These would categorically separate the self from the social, from language and communication. Instead, Mead begins by locating the self *within* communicative action. Self is that part of communicative action that reflects on itself, either in the course of the inner conversation called thinking or as an openly reflexive product of social interaction.

Mead goes on to distinguish the self from the mere body.

> The self has a character which is different from that of the physiological organism proper. The self is something which has a development; it is not initially there, at birth, but arises in the process of social experience and activity, that is, develops in the given individual as a result of his relations to that process as a whole and to other individuals within that process. (P. 135)

Then he differentiates the self as an object from other objects of experience.

> It is the characteristic of the self as an object to itself that I want to bring out. This characteristic is represented in the word "self," which is a reflexive, and indicates that which can be both subject and object. This type of object is essentially different from other objects, and in the past it has been distinguished as conscious, a term which indicates an experience with, an experience of, one's self. It was assumed that consciousness in some way carried this capacity of being an object to itself. In giving a behavioristic statement of consciousness we have to look for some sort of experience in which the physical organism can become an object to itself. (Pp. 136–37)

Mead seems to be saying that in a Cartesian framework ("in the past"), consciousness in its own right was taken to constitute the self. In contrast, he argues that consciousness per se cannot be the self's own object without substantive experiences to reflect upon, and from which we indicate to itself who it is. Experience provides the means and the meanings through which one becomes conscious of what one is. Consciousness, in effect, is always consciousness *of something*, including consciousness of oneself as meaningfully something (some thing) or another.

In practice, the answer to the question of who we are to ourselves requires that we first behave in the world. The "I" who eventually tells itself or others *"that's* me," needs the communicative resources of experience to make this designation. The very "I" that is presumed to do so, itself only exists in reflexive relation to the "me" it indicates and specifies in the course of social interaction. Both "I" and "me" must wait, as it were, for the activity of everyday life to unfold in order to exist empirically. Mead's interacting self is in this sense an integral part of society; indeed, it *can't* be imagined, even described, without the meanings drawn from experience. To attempt to imagine or describe a self separate from experience would be tantamount to communicating without meaning. Such a self would be literally meaning-less, unrecognizable and nonexistent.

Because the self is "essentially a social structure" (p. 140) that arises in social interaction, it is an "object" that is dynamic, elastic, and manifold. If the self has unity, it is a unity derived from patterns of experience with others. Mead provides examples from everyday life.

> We realize in everyday conduct and experience that an individual does not mean a great deal of what he is doing and saying. We frequently say that such an individual is not himself. We come away from an interview with a realization that we have left out important things, that there are parts of the self that did not get into what was said. What determines the amount of the self that gets into communication is the social experience itself. Of course, a good deal of the self does not need to get expression. We carry on a whole series of different relationships to different people. We are one thing to one man and another thing to another. There are parts of *the* self which exist only for the self in relationship to itself. We divide ourselves up in all sorts of different selves with reference to our acquaintances. We discuss politics with one and religion with another. There are all sorts of different selves answering to all sorts of different social reactions. It is the social process itself that is responsible for the appearance of the self; it is not there as a self apart from this type of experience. (P. 142)

In this context, Mead then speaks of the normality of a multiple personality: if we think of the self as an integral part of social relations, it is reasonable to consider its separate personas. As Mead reminds us, "We are one thing to one man and another thing for another." In the course of everyday life, we become— separately and distinctly—the varied selves that we present in relation to whomever regularly participates in our affairs. The regularities of home, say, or the work place, provide contexts for the production and reproduction of particular selves. The indulgent and affectionate father of home life can normally reside alongside the strait-laced martinet who commands the office. Being a social structure, self is formulated in relation to the very conditions it responds to and, in this regard, it normally divides into different selves.

How does this manifold self develop out of social experience in the first place? Mead views the formation of the social self in relation to play and organized games. He describes the play of children with imaginary others to make his point. In the early stage of self development, Mead argues, children literally practice selves as they actively play out who and what they are with imaginary others, taking roles such as mother, father, teacher, and policeman. Mead refers to this as a kind of "doubling," in which one both plays a role and responds to it. We can actually hear doubling in operation as the child now plays the mother and then responds as a child to what transpired in the role of mother. The child, in effect, rehearses a pair of social structures—a set of roles and selves—and in the process learns how to "do" the mother-child dyad, in effect, doing interacting identities. In familiar phrasing, Mead refers to stimuli that "call out" such socially meaningful responses.

> In the play period the child utilizes his own responses to these stimuli which he makes use of in building a self. The response which he has a tendency to make to these stimuli organizes them. He plays that he is, for instance, offering himself something, and he buys it; he gives a letter to himself and takes it away; he addresses himself as a parent, as a teacher; he arrests himself as a policeman. He has a set of stimuli which call out in himself the sort of responses they call out in others. He takes this group of responses and organizes them into a certain whole. Such is the simplest form of being another to one's self. ... A certain organized structure arises in him and in his other which replies to it, and these carry on the conversation of gestures between themselves. (Pp. 150–51)

His reference to "a certain organized structure" leads Mead directly to the games in which we experience and articulate varied selves at a later stage. He is referring to a socially shared kind of game plan, which can be played out once it is identified. Mead argues that whether it is playing cops-and-robbers or playing dolls, the organized structures of such games form particular selves. In turn, such game-activated selves reflexively direct and manage their related social actions. Once we learn the game, our selves and related actions are structured to elicit certain performances and not others, making us distinctly accountable to ourselves and each other. A child who knows the game can play its various roles, thus coordinating his or her actions in relation to other players. Mead contrasts simple play with what develops from playing games:

> In that early stage he passes from one role to another just as a whim takes him. But in a game where a number of individuals are involved, then the child taking one role must be ready to take the role of everyone else. ... In the game, then, there is a set of responses of such others so organized that the attitude of one calls out the appropriate attitudes in the other. (P. 151)

> The fundamental difference between the game and play is that in the [former] the child must have the attitude of all the others *involved* in that game. ... We get then an "other" which is an organization of the attitudes of those involved in the same process. The organized community or social group which gives to the individual his unity of self may be called "the generalized other." (Pp. 153–54)

Thus Mead leads us to a fully social self. While Mead isn't clear about just how gamelike the self is in practice, the term *game* is there, connoting selves that are collectively, not individually, structured. Together with the idea of the generalized other, Mead gives us an empirical self that is reflexively conscious of the working organization of roles that constitute it as a social structure.[5]

SYMBOLIC INTERACTIONIST CONTRIBUTIONS

Following the early pragmatists' formulations, the story of the social self we are recounting becomes increasingly sociological. In the 1930s and 1940s, Herbert Blumer (1969), one of Mead's students at the University of Chicago, began to organize Mead's notions about mind, self, and society into a distinct perspective that he almost casually labeled "symbolic interactionism" (Blumer 1969, p. 1). In time, the label itself contributed immensely to the unfolding storyline. Just as the term *pragmatism* both reflected and, in turn, conceptually secured a body of American philosophical thought around James, Cooley, Mead, and others, *symbolic interactionism* became a rubric for disciplinary identity within sociology. As the label gained currency, it became the hallmark of a particular set of ideas about human nature and social order and, especially, about the relationship of the individual to society. As Stephen and Jonathan Turner (1990, p. 169) note, symbolic interactionism became "a vocabulary that could be used to give quick, novel descriptions of [such] familiar material in a manner beyond common sense."

Symbolic interactionism orients to the principle that individuals respond to the meanings they construct as they interact with one another. Individuals are active agents in their social worlds, influenced, to be sure, by culture and social organization, but also instrumental in producing the culture, society, and meaningful conduct that influences them (Hewitt 1997, 1998; Lindesmith, Strauss, and Denzin 1988; Manis and Meitzer 1967; Rose 1962; Stone and Farberman 1970; Stryker 1980). The self is never far behind in this scheme of things. It is the agent that serves as the reflexive beacon of social interaction, not existing separate from, or otherwise transcending, social life.

The focus on the social self in an increasingly scientized environment inexorably led to the question of whether the self could be studied by methods of social science research. If the early pragmatists concentrated on formulating the *idea* of a social self, symbolic interactionists became as interested in systematically documenting its empirical manifestations. Over the years, two streams of symbolic interactionist thinking—the so-called Chicago and Iowa schools—took this in different directions.[6] Blumer (1969), who taught at the University of Chicago, became the central figure of the more process-oriented Chicago school, while Manford Kuhn (1960, 1964) and his associates (Couch 1962; Kuhn and McPartland 1954; McPartland and Cumming 1958; McPartland, Cumming, and Garretson 1961; Mulford and Salisbury 1964; Vernon 1962) at the University of Iowa were the leading proponents of the more structured Iowa school (see Denzin 1970 and Joas 1987). Their respective methodological emphases on firsthand qualitative observation versus quantitative measurement served to define the scientific meaning of the social self to both followers and outsiders for years to come (see Fine 1995).

Blumer (1969) summarizes his methodological position in what he refers to as "three simple premises" (p. 2), belying their complexity. While the premises are meant to convey his view of symbolic interaction in general, by extension they would also apply to the construction of the self. The first premise is "that human beings act toward things on the basis of the meanings that the things have for them" (p. 2). Blumer explains that whatever those things are—physical objects, other human beings, social roles, activities, or situations—it is not the things in their own right that mediate human beings' actions, but what they mean for them. If symbolic interactionists emphasize the "meanings" component of the premise, it is important to note that the meanings at stake are human beings' *own* meanings. It's not some independent or transcendent source of meaning that effects action, but what ordinary human beings themselves, in the course of social interaction, consider meaningful. Again, we can take this as applying with equal significance to the meanings attached to the self.

Blumer's second premise is that "the meaning of such things is derived from, or arises out of, the social interaction that one has with one's fellows" (p. 2). This draws from Mead's view that the social self is an integral part of social interaction, not an entity which stands separately from it. The self, as Mead puts it, is a social structure. The premise has methodological implications, suggesting that to know and document the shape and content of the self, one must observe the self in action. Secondary reports will not do. Nor will idealized or socially distant representations. If we are to study lives, including selves in social interaction, we must study them from *within* the social contexts they unfold, not separate from them. Blumer instructs his reader to study what is natural to the self, to view it and document its place within the actual process of social interaction.

Blumer's third premise is that "meanings are handled in, and modified through, an interpretive process used by the person in dealing with the things he encounters." This is cautionary. While Blumer directs us to human beings' own meanings and to the everyday interaction within which meanings arise, he also warns us not to take those meanings for granted. Human beings don't settle their affairs with meaning once and for all. Rather, they continually engage the interpretive process, including the interpretation of what they mean to themselves.

The caution is explicitly directed at those symbolic interactionists who, while they would accept the first two premises, are remiss on the third, employing highly structured methods that don't permit the interpretive process to continually show through.[7] Blumer urges us to view the human being in social interaction as incessantly involved in meaning-making. The methodological directive here is to document the articulation and emergence of meaning in rich detail as it unfolds, not in lifeless analytic categories and statistical tables. Blumer explains:

> The actor selects, checks, suspends, regroups, and transforms the meanings in the light of the situation in which he is placed and the direction of his action. Accordingly, interpretation should not be regarded as a mere automatic application of established meanings but as a formative process in which meanings are used and revised as [indigenous] instruments for the guidance and formation of action. (P. 5)

In other words, symbolic interactionists should describe how people form and revise what is meaningful to them, which we assume would include meanings that define the self.

Adherents of the Iowa school developed a more structured approach. While Blumer and those who followed in his footsteps emphasized naturalistic inquiry, Kuhn and his Iowa school associates were concerned with measurement. Certainly, for them, as for all symbolic interactionists, the self was a social entity par excellence. But Kuhn and his associates also believed they needed to precisely pin down the meanings of the self before moving on to consider its relationship to other aspects of social life.

In a seminal paper, Kuhn and McPartland (1954) argue that, while the self has been a key concept in the symbolic interactionist approach to social psychology, "little, if anything, has been done to employ it directly in empirical research." Here, the term *empirical* veers away from having an experiential connotation and, instead, takes on a distinctly quantitative tone. From Kuhn and McPartland's discussion, it's clear that the emphasis is on the self as a meaningful object, not on the self as interactively meaningful. The aim is to designate concisely what each specific self under consideration is to itself, a goal that works against Blumer's third premise. This leads directly to the formulation of a method to assess self-attitudes, as Kuhn and McPartland explain.

> If, as we suppose, human behavior is *organized* and *directed,* and if, as we further suppose, the organization and direction are supplied by the individual's *attitudes toward himself,* it ought to be of crucial significance to social psychology to be able to identify and measure self-attitudes. (P. 68, emphasis in the original)

The emphasis on the words *organized, directed,* and *attitudes toward himself* is conceptually and procedurally telling. The terms are part of the vocabulary of a more standardized and ostensibly "scientific" approach to the social self than Blumer could abide. Kuhn and McPartland refer to human behavior as organized and directed, implying causation. Human behavior does not just simply form, develop, and respond to itself, but is organized and directed *by something*. Inasmuch as "the organization and direction are supplied by the individual's *attitudes toward himself,*" self-attitudes can be viewed as causal agents. In other words, one's behavior will vary according to one's self-attitudes. From here, it is a short step to arguing that other aspects of human behavior also provide organization and direction, affecting self-attitudes in their own right. The working vocabulary stands in opposition to

Blumer's language, which comprises terms such as *act, meaning, interpretation,* and *process.* The latter are part of a language stressing descriptive intelligibility and understanding, which eschews the logic of causation. Virtually specifying alternate empirical horizons and related research procedures, the respective vocabularies could not help but contribute to the development of opposing "schools" of the social self.

In perhaps its most significant methodological invention, the Iowa group developed the Twenty Statements Test (TST). As Kuhn and McPartland (1954) reasoned, "The obvious first step in the application of self-theory to empirical research is the construction and standardization of a test which will identify and measure self-attitudes" (p. 68). Reflecting the post-World War II trend toward quantification in the social and behavioral sciences, the term *empirical* also was being appropriated for the increasingly popular preference for "hard" scientific procedure. It was taken for granted that the Twenty Statements Test would indeed serve to "[do something] to employ [the self] directly in empirical research."

Described in numerous articles, and employed in countless research projects, the TST consists of a single sheet of paper, with twenty numbered spaces, directing respondents to do the following:

> There are twenty numbered blanks on the page below. Please write twenty answers to the simple question "Who am I" in the blanks. Just give twenty different answers to this question. Answer as if you were giving the answers to yourself, not to somebody else. Write the answers in the order that they occur to you. Don't worry about logic or "importance." Go along fairly fast, for time is limited. (Kuhn and McPartland 1954, p. 69)

Over the years, the exact wording of the TST varied somewhat, mainly becoming less specific in its instructions, but the format remained much the same.

Some researchers focused on the alleged causes of the resulting self-attitudes, hypothesizing that independent variables such as class, educational background, and age "organized and directed" self-attitudes (see, for example, Kuhn 1960 and McPartland and Cumming 1958). Others examined the behavioral consequences of particular attitudes, hypothesizing that self-attitudes "organize and direct" conduct (see, for instance, McPartland, Cumming, and Garretson 1961 and Waisanen 1962). In hindsight, it's amazing what a single research instrument produced in the context of times that stressed the scientifically rigorous study of social life (see Kuhn 1964). Perhaps as much as any research development, the TST objectified and concretized the formulation of the social self. It showed just how far adherents could turn away from the transcendental self and what could be scientifically accomplished in the name of the "empirical."

ERVING GOFFMAN'S SOCIALLY SITUATED SELF

If symbolic interactionists document the condition of the self in social interaction, it is Erving Goffman (1959) who takes the self full-tilt into the situations of everyday life. Goffman's self takes on meaning in interpersonal relations and, in that sense, Goffman agrees with symbolic interactionists. But he is also deeply concerned with the situated contingencies and rituals of interaction. As Goffman puts it, "[the] self itself does not derive from its possessor, but from the whole scene of his action" (p. 252).

Goffman would not object to Blumer's three methodological premises as they apply to the self, but he adds his own twist to the story by way of a theatrical language composed of terms such as *scenes, scripts, front stage, back stage,* and *performances.*[8] The language highlights the "dramaturgic" or scenic features of the social self, suggesting that self and social interaction are more patterned than Blumer's premises would give them credit for being. In Goffman's view, the self is not just social in that it develops from and responds to others in the course of daily living. Circumstances being what they are, actors take account of the setting where, and occasion when, self formation occurs. For Goffman, there is always more at stake for the self than ongoing social interaction; there's an "interaction order" (1967). Traditional terms of reference such as "I," "other," and "role" provide an important analytic initiative, but these are not situated enough to take account of localized contingencies such as who, in particular, might be cooperating with the actor in question to define the self. For example, one would think that it might make a great deal of difference if those cooperating were a loosely organized as opposed to a well-coordinated team, or whether they were responsible for appreciating or degrading the actor in question. If negative purposes have negative implications for self-attitudes and coordination makes a difference, then a disciplined team effort could very well be, say, situationally devastating (see Goffman 1961).

It's important to point out that while Goffman stresses the situated contingencies of social interaction, he does not lose sight of the working self. Like the early pragmatists, Goffman preserves a self formulated as both "I" and "me," performatively placed in the world of everyday life. If the interaction order is center stage, the self that is articulated in the varied scripts of social life nonetheless has room for improvisation. The self is not just a role player, a mere puppet of its staging, but works with others at its dramatic realization.

Goffman's self is dramaturgic in two senses of the term. First, it *presents* itself to others. It is actively engaged in its dramatic performances, mustering what it is capable of presenting in light of the social scripts of various occasions. Its engagement is moral in the sense that it commits itself, or is committed to, the ongoing interaction order of the varied scenes within which experience unfolds, and its performance is evaluated in those terms. As such, the selves presented are not simply given, but are "given off," as Goffman puts it, further revealing the effort that is put into its accountable production. Goffman introduces his approach this way in *The Presentation of Self in Everyday Life* (1959):

The perspective employed in this report is that of the theatrical performance; the principles derived are dramaturgical ones. I shall consider the way in which the individual in ordinary work situations presents himself and his activity to others, the ways in which he guides and controls the impression they form of him, and the kinds of things he may and may not do while sustaining his performance before them. (P. xi)

The self is also dramaturgic in that it is *staged* to accomplish particular moral ends. It manages and successfully performs both small and large everyday dramas, whether they are as simple as a greeting on the street or as complex as international diplomacy. The self not only works to dramatically realize itself, but simultaneously engages in particular performances, which to some extent have a life of their own. Just as a theatrical performance has roles, a play, and the stage upon which actors develop their roles, everyday life more or less realizes its own moral scripts.

While the differences between the theater and real life should not be overlooked, for Goffman their similarities are vast.

I assume that when an individual appears before others he will have many motives for trying to control the impression they receive of the situation. This report is concerned with some of the common techniques that persons employ to sustain such impressions and with some of the contingencies associated with the employment of these techniques. The specific content of any activity presented by the individual participant, or the role it plays in the interdependent activities of an on-going social system, will not be at issue; I shall be concerned only with the participant's dramaturgical problems of presenting the activity before others. The issues dealt with by stagecraft and stage management are sometimes trivial but they are quite general; they seem to occur everywhere in social life, providing a clear-cut dimension for formal sociological analysis. (P. 15)

In many respects, Goffman fleshes out the project that the early pragmatists began. The self, in his chapter of the story, is not only social and empirical, but circumstantially realized. It is a locally interactive beacon of experience and it takes shape within, not separate from, the various situations of everyday life. Time and again, Goffman reveals that each and every one of us has many selves, pertinent to the purposes of daily living, always part of, yet also reflexively separate from, the moral orders we share with others.

The Social Self—the Meaning of "I"

BY CHARLES HORTON COOLEY

I t is well to say at the outset that by the word "self" in this discussion is meant simply that which is designated in common speech by the pronouns of the first person singular, "I," "me," "my," "mine," and "myself." "Self" and "ego" are used by metaphysicians and moralists in many other senses, more or less remote from the "I" of daily speech and thought, and with these I wish to have as little to do as possible. What is here discussed is what psychologists call the empirical self, the self that can be apprehended or verified by ordinary observation. I qualify it by the word social not as implying the existence of a self that is not social—for I think that the "I" of common language always has more or less distinct reference to other people as well as the speaker—but because I wish to emphasize and dwell upon the social aspect of it.

Although the topic of the self is regarded as an abstruse one this abstruseness belongs chiefly, perhaps, to the metaphysical discussion of the "pure ego"—whatever that may be—while the empirical self should not be very much more difficult to get hold of than other facts of the mind. At any rate, it may be assumed that the pronouns of the first person have a substantial, important, and not very recondite meaning, otherwise they would not be in constant and intelligible use by simple people and young children the world over. And since they have such a meaning why should it not be observed and reflected upon like any other matter of fact? As to the underlying mystery, it is no doubt real, important, and a very fit subject of discussion by those who are competent, but I do not see that it is a *peculiar* mystery. I mean that it seems to be simply a phase of the general mystery of life, not pertaining to "I" more than to any other personal or social fact; so that here as elsewhere those who are not attempting to penetrate the mystery may simply ignore it. If this is a just view of the matter, "I" is merely a fact like any other.

The distinctive thing in the idea for which the pronouns of the first person are names is apparently a characteristic kind of feeling which may be called the my-feeling or sense of appropriation. Almost any sort of ideas may be associated with this feeling, and so come to be named "I" or "mine," but the feeling, and that alone it would seem, is the determining factor in the matter. As Professor James says in his admirable discussion of the self, the words "me" and "self" designate "all the things which have the power to produce in a stream of consciousness excitement of a certain peculiar sort."[1] This view is very fully set forth by Professor Hiram M. Stanley, whose work, *The Evolutionary Psychology of Feeling*, has an extremely suggestive chapter on self-feeling.

I do not mean that the feeling aspect of the self is necessarily more important than any other, but that it is the immediate and decisive sign and proof of what "I" is; there is no appeal from it; if we go behind it. It must be to study its history and conditions, not to question its authority. But, of course, this study of history and conditions may be quite as profitable as the direct contemplation of self-feeling. What I would wish to do is to present each aspect in its proper light.

The emotion or feeling of self may be regarded as instinctive, and was doubtless evolved in connection with its important function in stimulating and unifying the special activities of individuals.[2] It is thus very profoundly rooted in the history of the human race and apparently indispensable to any plan of life at all similar to ours. It seems to exist in a vague though vigorous form at the birth of each individual, and, like other instinctive ideas or germs of ideas, to be defined and developed by experience, becoming associated, or rather incorporated, with muscular, visual, and other sensations; with perceptions, apperceptions, and conceptions of every degree of complexity and of infinite variety of content; and, especially, with personal ideas. Meantime the feeling itself does not remain unaltered, but undergoes differentiation and refinement just as does any other sort of crude innate feeling. Thus, while retaining under every phase its characteristic tone or flavor, it breaks up into innumerable self-sentiments. And concrete self-feeling, as it exists in mature persons, is a whole made up of these various sentiments, along with a good deal of primitive emotion not thus broken up. It partakes fully of the general development of the mind, but never loses that peculiar

---

1   "The words *me,* then, and *self,* so far as they arouse feeling and connote emotional worth, are *objective* designations meaning *all the things* which have the power to produce in a stream of consciousness excitement of a certain peculiar sort" (William James, *Psychology,* i, p. 319). A little earlier he says. "In its widest possible sense, however, a man's self is the sum total of all he *can* call his, not only his body and his psychic powers, but his clothes and his house, his wife and children, his ancestors and friends, his reputation and works, his lands and horses and yacht and bank-account. All these things give him the same emotions" *(Idem,* p. 291).

So Wun1p2 says of "Ich": "Es ist ein *Gefühl,* nicht eine Vorstellung, wie es häufig genannt wird" *(Grundriss der Psychologie,* 4 Auflage, S. 265).

2   It is, perhaps, to be thought of as a more general instinct, of which anger, etc., are differentiated forms, rather than as standing by itself.

gusto of appropriation that causes us to name a thought with a first-personal pronoun. The other contents of the self-idea are of little use, apparently, in defining it, because they are so extremely various. It would be no more futile, it seems to me, to attempt to define fear by enumerating the things that people are afraid of, than to attempt to define "I" by enumerating the objects with which the word is associated. Very much as fear means primarily a state of feeling, or its expression, and not darkness, fire, lions, snakes, or other things that excite it, so "I" means primarily self-feeling, or its expression, and not body, clothes, treasures, ambition, honors, and the like, with which this feeling may be connected. In either case it is possible and useful to go behind the feeling and inquire what ideas arouse it and why they do so, but this is in a sense a secondary investigation.

Since "I" is known to our experience primarily as a feeling, or as a feeling-ingredient in our ideas, it cannot be described or defined without suggesting that feeling. We are sometimes likely to fall into a formal and empty way of talking regarding questions of emotion, by attempting to define that which is in its nature primary and indefinable. A formal definition of self-feeling, or indeed of any sort of feeling, must be as hollow as a formal definition of the taste of salt, or the color red; we can expect to know what it is only by experiencing it. There can be no final test of the self except the way we feel; it is that toward which we have the "my" attitude. But as this feeling is quite as familiar to us and as easy to recall as the taste of salt or the color red, there should be no difficulty in understanding what is meant by it. One need only imagine some attack on his "me," say ridicule of his dress or an attempt to take away his property or his child, or his good name by slander, and self-feeling immediately appears. Indeed, he need only pronounce, with strong emphasis, one of the self-words, like "I" or "my," and self-feeling will be recalled by association. Another good way is to enter by sympathy into some self-assertive state of mind depicted in literature; as, for instance, into that of Coriolanus when, having been sneered at as a "boy of tears," he cries out:

> Boy! …
> If you have writ your annals true, 'tis there,
> That, like an eagle in a dovecote, I
> Fluttered your Volscians in Corioli;
> Alone I did it.—Boy!

Here is a self indeed, which no one can fail to feel, though he might be unable to describe it. What a ferocious scream of the outraged ego is that "I" at the end of the second line!

So much is written on this topic that ignores self-feeling and thus deprives "self" of all vivid and palpable meaning, that I feel it permissible to add a few more passages in which this feeling is forcibly expressed. Thus in Lowell's poem, "A Glance Behind the Curtain," Cromwell says:

> "I, perchance,
> Am one raised up by the Almighty arm
> To witness some great truth to all the world.

And his Columbus, on the bow of his vessel, soliloquizes:

> "Here am I, with no friend but the sad sea,
> The beating heart of this great enterprise,
> Which, without me, would stiffen in swift death."

And so the "I am the way" which we read in the New Testament is surely the expression of a sentiment not very different from these. In the following we have a more plaintive sentiment of self:

> *Philoctetes.*—And know'st thou not, O boy, whom thou dost see?
> *Neoptolemus.*—How can I know a man I ne'er beheld?
> *Philoctetes.*—And didst thou never hear my name, nor fame Of these my ills, in which I pined away?
> *Neoptolemus.*—Know that I nothing know of what thou ask'st.
> *Philoctetes.*—O crushed with many woes, and of the Gods Hated am I, of whom, in this my woe, No rumor travelled homeward, nor went forth Through any clime of Hellas.[3]

We all have thoughts of the same sort as these, and yet it is possible to talk so coldly or mystically about the self that one begins to forget that there is, really, any such thing.

But perhaps the best way to realize the naïve meaning of "I" is to listen to the talk of children playing together, especially if they do not agree very well. They use the first person with none of the conventional self-repression of their elders, but with much emphasis and variety of inflection, so that its emotional animus is unmistakable.

Self-feeling of a reflective and agreeable sort, an appropriative zest of contemplation, is strongly suggested by the word "gloating." To gloat, in this sense, is as much as to think "mine, mine, mine," with a pleasant warmth of feeling. Thus a boy gloats over something he has made with his scroll-saw, over the bird he has brought down with his gun, or over his collection of stamps or eggs; a girl gloats over her new clothes, and over the approving

---

3   Plumptre's Sophocles, p. 352.

words or looks of others; a farmer over his fields and his stock; a business man over his trade and his bank-account; a mother over her child; the poet over a successful quatrain; the self-righteous man over the state of his soul; and in like manner every one gloats over the prosperity of any cherished idea.

I would not be understood as saying that self-feeling is clearly marked off in experience from other kinds of feeling; but it is, perhaps, as definite in this regard as anger, fear, grief, and the like. To quote Professor James, "The emotions themselves of self-satisfaction and abasement are of a unique sort, each as worthy to be classed as a primitive emotional species as are, for example, rage or pain."[4] It is true here, as wherever mental facts are distinguished, that there are no fences, but that one thing merges by degrees into another. Yet if "I" did not denote an idea much the same in all minds and fairly distinguishable from other ideas, it could not be used freely and universally as a means of communication.

As many people have the impression that the verifiable self, the object that we name with "I," is usually the material body, it may be well to say that this impression is an illusion, easily dispelled by any one who will undertake a simple examination of facts. It is true that when we philosophize a little about "I" and look around for a tangible object to which to attach it, we soon fix upon the material body as the most available *locus;* but when we use the word naively, as in ordinary speech, it is not very common to think of the body in connection with it; not nearly so common as it is to think of other things. There is no difficulty in testing this statement, since the word "I" is one of the commonest in conversation and literature, so that nothing is more practicable than to study its meaning at any length that may be desired. One need only listen to ordinary speech until the word has occurred, say, a hundred times, noting its connections, or observe its use in a similar number of cases by the characters in a novel. Ordinarily it will be found that in not more than ten cases in a hundred does "I" have reference to the body of the person speaking. It refers chiefly to opinions, purposes, desires, claims, and the like, concerning matters that involve no thought of the body. I think or feel so and so; *I* wish or intend so and so; *I* want this or that; are typical uses, the self-feeling being associated with the view, purpose, or object mentioned. It should also be remembered that "my" and "mine" are as much the names of the self as "I," and these, of course, commonly refer to miscellaneous possessions.

I had the curiosity to attempt a rough classification of the first hundred "I's" and "me's" in *Hamlet,* with the following results. The pronoun was used in connection with perception, as "I hear," "I see," fourteen times; with thought, sentiment, intention, etc., thirty-two times; with wish, as "I pray you," six times; as speaking— "I'll speak to it"—sixteen times; as spoken to, twelve times; in connection with action, involving perhaps some vague notion of the body, as "I came to Denmark," nine times; vague or doubtful, ten

---

4   William James, *Psychology,* i, p. 307.

times; as equivalent to bodily appearance—"No more like my father than I to Hercules"—once. Some of the classifications are arbitrary, and another observer would doubtless get a different result; but he could not fail, I think, to conclude that Shakespeare's characters are seldom thinking of their bodies when they say "I" or "me." And in this respect they appear to be representative of mankind in general.

As already suggested, instinctive self-feeling is doubtless connected in evolution with its important function in stimulating and unifying the special activities of individuals. It appears to be associated chiefly with ideas of the exercise of power, of being a cause, ideas that emphasize the antithesis between the mind and the rest of the world. The first definite thoughts that a child associates with self-feeling are probably those of his earliest endeavors to control visible objects—his limbs, his playthings, his bottle, and the like. Then he attempts to control the actions of the persons about him, and so his circle of power and of self-feeling widens without interruption to the most complex objects of mature ambition. Although he does not say "I" or "my" during the first year or two, yet he expresses so clearly by his actions the feeling that adults associate with these words that we cannot deny him a self even in the first weeks.

The correlation of self-feeling activity is easily seen by observing the course of any productive enterprise. If a boy sets about making a boat, and has any success, his interest in the matter waxes, he gloats over it, the keel and stem are dear to his heart, and its ribs are more to him than those of his own frame. He is eager to call in his friends and acquaintances, saying to them, "See what I am doing! Is it not remarkable?" feeling elated when it is praised, and resentful or humiliated when fault is found with it. But so soon as he finishes it and turns to something else, his self-feeling begins to fade away from it, and in a few weeks at most he will have become comparatively indifferent. We all know that much the same course of feeling accompanies the achievements of adults. It is impossible to produce a picture, a poem, an essay, a difficult bit of masonry, or any other work of art or craft, without having self-feeling regarding it, amounting usually to considerable excitement and desire for some sort of appreciation; but this rapidly diminishes with the activity itself, and often lapses into indifference after it ceases.

It may perhaps be objected that the sense of self, instead of being limited to times of activity and definite purpose, is often most conspicuous when the mind is unoccupied or undecided, and that the idle and ineffectual are commonly the most sensitive in their self-esteem. This, however, may be regarded as an instance of the principle that all instincts are likely to assume troublesome forms when denied wholesome expression. The need to exert power, when thwarted in the open fields of life, is the more likely to assert itself in trifles.

The social self is simply any idea, or system of ideas, drawn from the communicative life, that the mind cherishes as its own. Self-feeling has its chief scope *within* the general life, not outside of it; the special endeavor or tendency of which it is the emotional aspect finds its principal field of exercise in a world of personal forces, reflected in the mind by a world of personal impressions.

As connected with the thought of other persons the self idea is always a consciousness of the peculiar or differentiated aspect of one's life, because that is the aspect that has to be sustained by purpose and endeavor, and its more aggressive forms tend to attach themselves to whatever one finds to be at once congenial to one's own tendencies and at variance with those of others with whom one is in mental contact. It is here that they are most needed to serve their function of stimulating characteristic activity, of fostering those personal variations which the general plan of life seems to require. Heaven, says Shakespeare, doth divide and self-feeling is one of the means by which this diversity is achieved.

The state of man in divers functions
Setting endeavor in continual motion

Agreeably to this view we find that the aggressive self manifests itself most conspicuously in an appropriativeness of objects of common desire, corresponding to the individual's need of power over such objects to secure his own peculiar development, and to the danger of opposition from others who also need them. And this extends from material objects to lay hold, in the same spirit, of the attentions and affections of other people, of all sorts of plans and ambitions, including the noblest special purposes the mind can entertain, and indeed of any conceivable idea which may come to seem a part of one's life and in need of assertion against some one else. The attempt to limit the word self and its derivatives to the lower aims of personality is quite arbitrary; at variance with common sense as expressed by the emphatic use of "I" in connection with the sense of duty and other high motives, and unphilosophical as ignoring the function of the self as the organ of specialized endeavor of higher as well as lower kinds.

That the "I" of common speech has a meaning which includes some sort of reference to other persons is involved in the very fact that the word and the ideas it stands for are phenomena of language and the communicative life. It is doubtful whether it is possible to use language at all without thinking more or less distinctly of some one else, and certainly the things to which we give names and which have a large place in reflective thought are almost always those which are impressed upon us by our contact with other people. Where there is no communication there can be no nomenclature and no developed thought. What we call "me," "mine," or "myself" is, then, not something separate from the general life, but the most interesting part of it, a part whose interest arises from the very fact that it is both general and individual. That is, we care for it just because it is that phase of the mind that is living and striving in the common life, trying to impress itself upon the minds of others. "I" is a militant social tendency, working to hold and enlarge its place in the general current of tendencies. So far as it can it waxes, as all life does. To think of it as apart from society is a palpable absurdity of which no one could be guilty who really *saw* it as a fact of life.

> Der Mensch erkennt sich nur im Menschen, nur
> Das Leben lehret jedem was er sei.[5]

If a thing has no relation to others of which one is conscious he is unlikely to think of it at all, and if he does think of it he cannot, it seems to me, regard it as emphatically *his*. The appropriative sense is always the shadow, as it were, of the common life, and when we have it we have a sense of the latter in connection with it. Thus, if we think of a secluded part of the woods as "ours," it is because we think, also, that others do not go there. As regards the body I doubt if we have a vivid my-feeling about any part of it which is not thought of, however vaguely, as having some actual or possible reference to some one else. Intense self-consciousness regarding it arises along with instincts or experiences which connect it with the thought of others. Internal organs, like the liver, are not thought of as peculiarly ours unless we are trying to communicate something regarding them, as, for instance, when they are giving us trouble and we are trying to get sympathy.

"I," then, is not all of the mind, but a peculiarly central, vigorous, and well-knit portion of it, not separate from the rest but gradually merging into it, and yet having a certain practical distinctness, so that a man generally shows clearly enough by his language and behavior what his "I" is as distinguished from thoughts he does not appropriate. It may be thought of, as already suggested, under the analogy of a central colored area on a lighted wall. It might also, and perhaps more justly, be compared to the nucleus of a living cell, not altogether separate from the surrounding matter, out of which indeed it is formed, but more active and definitely organized.

The reference to other persons involved in the sense of self may be distinct and particular, as when a boy is ashamed to have his mother catch him at something she has forbidden, or it may be vague and general, as when one is ashamed to do something which only his conscience, expressing his sense of social responsibility, detects and disapproves; but it is always there. There is no sense of "I," as in pride or shame, without its correlative sense of you, or he, or they. Even the miser gloating over his hidden gold can feel the "mine" only as he is aware of the world of men over whom he has secret power; and the case is very similar with all kinds of hid treasure. Many painters, sculptors, and writers have loved to withhold

---

5   "Only in man does man know himself, life alone teaches each one what he is" (Goethe, *Tasso,* act 2, sc. 3).

their work from the world, fondling it in seclusion until they were quite done with it; but the delight in this, as in all secrets, depends upon a sense of the value of what is concealed. I remarked above that we think of the body as "I" when it comes to have social function or significance, as when we say "I am looking well to-day," or "I am taller than you are." We bring it into the social world, for the time being, and for that reason put our self-consciousness into it. Now it is curious, though natural, that in precisely the same way we may call any inanimate object "I" with which we are identifying our will and purpose. This is notable in games, like golf or croquet, where the ball is the embodiment of the player's fortunes. You will hear a man say, "I am in the long grass down by the third tee," or "I am in position for the middle arch." So a boy flying a kite will say "I am higher than you," or one shooting at a mark will declare that he is just below the bullseye.

In a very large and interesting class of cases the social reference takes the form of a some-what definite imagination of how one's self—that *is any idea he appropriates*—*appears* in a particular mind, and the kind of self-feeling one has is determined by the attitude toward this attributed to that other mind. A social self of this sort might be called the reflected or looking-glass self:

> Each to each a looking-glass
> Reflects the other that doth pass.

As we see our face, figure, and dress in the glass, and are interested in them because they are ours, and pleased or otherwise with them according as they do or do not answer to what we should like them to be; so in imagination we perceive in another's mind some thought of our appearance, manners, aims, deeds, character, friends, and so on, and are variously affected by it.

A self-idea of this sort seems to have three principal elements: the imagination of our appearance to the other person; the imagination of his judgment of that appear-ance; and some sort of self-feeling, such as pride or mortification. The comparision with a looking-glass hardly suggests the second element, the imagined judgment, which is quite essential. The thing that moves us to pride or shame is not the mere mechanical reflection of ourselves, but an imputed sentiment, the imagined effect of this reflection upon another's mind. This is evident from the fact that the character and weight of that other, in whose mind we see ourselves, makes all the difference with our feeling. We are ashamed to seem evasive in the presence of a straightforward man, cowardly in the presence of a brave one, gross in the eyes of a refined one, and so on. We always imagine, and in imagining share, the judgments of the other mind. A man will boast to one person of an action— say some sharp transaction in trade—which he would be ashamed to own to another.

It should be evident that the ideas that are associated with self-feeling and form the intellectual content of the self cannot be covered by any simple description, as by saying that the body has such a part in it, friends such a part, plans so much, etc., but will vary indefinitely with particular temperaments and environments. The tendency of the self, like every aspect of personality, is expressive of far-reaching hereditary and social factors, and is not to be understood or predicted except in connection with the general life. Although special, it is in no way separate—speciality and separateness are not only different but contradictory, since the former implies connection with a whole. The object of self-feeling is affected by the general course of history, by the particular development of nations, classes, and professions, and other conditions of this sort.

The truth of this is perhaps most decisively shown in the fact that even those ideas that are most generally associated or colored with the "my" feeling, such as one's idea of his visible person, of his name, his family, his intimate friends, his property, and so on, are not universally so associated, but may be separated from the self by peculiar social conditions. Thus the ascetics, who have played so large a part in the history of Christianity and of other religions and philosophies, endeavored not without success to divorce their appropriative thought from all material surroundings, and especially from their physical persons, which they sought to look upon as accidental and degrading circumstances of the soul's earthly sojourn. In thus estranging themselves from their bodies, from property and comfort, from domestic affections—whether of wife or child, mother, brother or sister—and from other common objects of ambition, they certainly gave a singular direction to self-feeling, but they did not destroy it: there can be no doubt that the instinct, which seems imperishable so long as mental vigor endures, found other ideas to which to attach itself; and the strange and uncouth forms which ambition took in those centuries when the solitary, filthy, idle, and sense-tormenting anchorite was a widely accepted ideal of human life, are a matter of instructive study and reflection. Even in the highest exponents of the ascetic ideal, like St. Jerome, it is easy to see that the discipline, far from effacing the self, only concentrated its energy in lofty and unusual channels. The self-idea may be that of some great moral reform, of a religious creed, of the destiny of one's soul after death, or even a cherished conception of the deity. Thus devout writers, like George Herbert and Thomas à Kempis, often address *my* God, not at all conventionally as I conceive the matter, but with an intimate sense of appropriation. And it has been observed that the demand for the continued and separate existence of the individual soul after death is an expression of self-feeling, as by J. A. Symonds, who thinks that it is connected with the intense egotism and personality of the European races, and asserts that the millions of Buddhism shrink from it with horror.[6]

---

6   Symonds, *John Addington Symonds*, ed. H. F. Brown, vol. ii, p. 120.

Habit and familiarity are not of themselves sufficient to cause an idea to be appropriated into the self. Many habits and familiar objects that have been forced upon us by circumstances rather than chosen for their congeniality remain external and possibly repulsive to the self; and, on the other hand, a novel but very congenial element in experience, like the idea of a new toy, or, if you please, Romeo's idea of Juliet, is often appropriated almost immediately, and becomes, for the time at least, the very heart of the self. Habit has the same fixing and consolidating action in the growth of the self that it has elsewhere, but is not its distinctive characteristic.

As suggested in the previous chapter, self-feeling may be regarded as in a sense the antithesis, or better perhaps, the complement, of that disinterested and contemplative love that tends to obliterate the sense of a divergent individuality. Love of this sort has no sense of bounds, but is what we feel when we are expanding and assimilating new and indeterminate experience, while self-feeling accompanies the appropriating, delimiting, and defending of a certain part of experience; the one impels us to receive life, the other to individuate it. The self, from this point of view, might be regarded as a sort of citadel of the mind, fortified without and containing selected treasures within, while love is an undivided share in the rest of the universe. In a healthy mind each contributes to the growth of the other: what we love intensely or for a long time we are likely to bring within the citadel, and to assert as part of ourself. On the other hand, it is only on the basis of a substantial self that a person is capable of progressive sympathy or love.

The sickness of either is to lack the support of the other. There is no health in a mind except as it keeps expanding, taking in fresh life, feeling love and enthusiasm; and so long as it does this its self-feeling is likely to be modest and generous; since these sentiments accompany that sense of the large and the superior which love implies. But if love closes, the self contracts and hardens: the mind having nothing else to occupy its attention and give it that change and renewal it requires, busies itself more and more with self-feeling, which takes on narrow and disgusting forms, like avarice, arrogance, and fatuity. It is necessary that we should have self-feeling about a matter during its conception and execution; but when it is accomplished or has failed the self ought to break loose and escape, renewing its skin like the snake, as Thoreau says. No matter what a man does, he is not fully sane or human unless there is a spirit of freedom in him, a soul unconfined by purpose and larger than the practicable world. And this is really what those mean who inculcate the suppression of the self; they mean that its rigidity must be broken up by growth and renewal, that it must be more or less decisively "born again." A healthy self must be both vigorous and plastic, a nucleus of solid, well-knit private purpose and feeling, guided and nourished by sympathy.

The view that "self" and the pronouns of the first person are names which the race has learned to apply to an instinctive attitude of mind, and which each child in turn learns to apply in a similar way, was impressed upon me by observing my child M. at the time when she was learning to use these pronouns. When she was two years and two weeks old I was surprised to discover that she had a clear notion of the first and second persons when used possessively. When asked, "Where is your nose?" she would put her hand upon it and say "my." She also understood that when some one else said "my" and touched an object, it meant something opposite to what was meant when she touched the same object and used the same word. Now, any one who will exercise his imagination upon the question how this matter must appear to a mind having no means of knowing anything about "I" and "my" except what it learns by hearing them used, will see that it should be very puzzling. Unlike other words, the personal pronouns have, apparently, no uniform meaning, but convey different and even opposite ideas when employed by different persons. It seems remarkable that children should master the problem before they arrive at considerable power of abstract reasoning. How should a little girl of two, not particularly reflective, have discovered that "my" was not the sign of a definite object like other words, but meant something different with each person who used it? And, still more surprising, how should she have achieved the correct use of it with reference to herself which, it would seem, *could not be copied from any one else,* simply because no one else used it to describe what belonged to her? The meaning of words is learned by associating them with other phenomena. But how is it possible to learn the meaning of one which, as used by others, is never associated with the same phenomenon as when properly used by one's self? Watching her use of the first person. I was at once struck with the fact that she employed it almost wholly in a possessive sense, and that, too, when in an aggressive, self-assertive mood. It was extremely common to see R. tugging at one end of a plaything and M. at the other, screaming, "My, my." "Me" was sometimes nearly equivalent to "my," and was also employed to call attention to herself when she wanted something done for her. Another common use of "my" was to demand something she did not have at all. Thus if R. had something the like of which she wanted, say a cart, she would exclaim, "Where's *my* cart?"

It seemed to me that she might have learned the use of these pronouns about as follows. The self-feeling had always been there. From the first week she had wanted things and cried and fought for them. She had also become familiar by observation and opposition with similar appropriative activities on the part of R. Thus she not only had the feeling herself, but by associating it with its visible expression had probably divined it, sympathized with it, resented it, in others. Grasping, tugging, and screaming would be associated with the feeling in her own case and would recall the feeling when observed in others. They would constitute a language, precedent to the use of first-personal pronouns, to express the self-idea. All was ready, then, for the word to name this experience. She now observed that R., when contentiously appropriating something, frequently exclaimed, *"my" "mine"* "give it to *me"* "I want it," and the like. Nothing more natural, then, than that she should adopt these words as names for a frequent and vivid experience with which she was already familiar in her own case and had learned to attribute to others. Accordingly it appeared to me, as I recorded in my notes at the time, that "'my' and 'mine' are simply names for concrete images of appropriativeness," embracing both the appropriative feeling and its manifestation. If this is true the child does not at first work out the I-and-you idea in an abstract form. The first-personal pronoun is a sign of a concrete thing after all, but that thing is not primarily the child's body, or his muscular sensations as such, but the phenomenon of aggressive appropriation, practised by himself, witnessed in others, and incited and interpreted by a hereditary instinct. This seems to get over the difficulty above mentioned, namely, the seeming lack of a common content between the meaning of "my" when used by another and when used by one's self. This common content is found in the appropriative feeling and the visible and audible signs of that feeling. An element of difference and strife comes in, of course, in the opposite actions or purposes which the "my" of another and one's own "my" are likely to stand for. When another person says "mine" regarding something which I claim, I sympathize with him enough to understand what he means, but it is a hostile sympathy, overpowered by another and more vivid "mine" connected with the idea of drawing the object my way.

In other words, the meaning of "I" and "mine" is learned in the same way that the meanings of hope, regret, chagrin, disgust, and thousands of other words of emotion and sentiment are learned: that is, by having the feeling, imputing it to others in connection with some kind of expression, and hearing the word along with it. As to its communication and growth the self-idea is in no way peculiar that I see, but essentially like other ideas. In its more complex forms, such as are expressed by "I" in conversation and literature, it is a social sentiment, or type of sentiments, defined and developed by intercourse, in the manner suggested … previous[ly.][7]

R., though a more reflective child than M., was much slower in understanding these pronouns, and in his thirty-fifth month had not yet straightened them out, sometimes calling his father "me." I imagine that this was partly because he was placid and uncontentious in his earliest years, manifesting little social self-feeling, but chiefly occupied with impersonal experiment and reflection; and partly because he saw little of other children by antithesis to whom his self could be awakened. M., on the other hand, coming later, had R.'s opposition on which to whet her naturally keen appropriativeness. And her society had a marked effect in developing self-feeling in R., who found self-assertion necessary to preserve his playthings, or anything else capable of appropriation. He learned the use of "my," however, when he was about three years old, before M. was born. He doubtless acquired it in his dealing with his parents. Thus he would perhaps notice his mother claiming the scissors as *mine* and seizing upon them, and would be moved sympathetically to claim something in the same way—connecting the word with the act and the feeling

---

7   Compare my "Study of the Early Use of Self-Words by a Child," in the *Psychological Review,* vol. 15 (November 1908), p. 339.

rather than the object. But as I had not the problem clearly in mind at that time I made no satisfactory observations.

I imagine, then, that as a rule the child associates "I" and "me" at first only with those ideas regarding which his appropriative feeling is aroused and defined by opposition. He appropriates his nose, eye, or foot in very much the same way as a plaything—by antithesis to other noses, eyes, and feet, which he cannot control. It is not uncommon to tease little children by proposing to take away one of these organs, and they behave precisely as if the "mine" threatened were a separable object—which it might be for all they know. And, as I have suggested, even in adult life, "I," "me," and "mine" are applied with a strong sense of their meaning only to things distinguished as peculiar to us by some sort of opposition or contrast. They always imply social life and relation to other persons. That which is most distinctively mine is very private, it is true, but it is that part of the private which I am cherishing in antithesis to the rest of the world, not the separate but the special. The aggressive self is essentially a militant phase of the mind, having for its apparent function the energizing of peculiar activities, and, although the militancy may not go on in an obvious, external manner, it always exists as a mental attitude.

In some of the best-known discussions of the development of the sense of self in children the chief emphasis has been placed upon the speculative or quasi-metaphysical ideas concerning "I" which children sometimes formulate as a result either of questions from their elders, or of the independent development of a speculative instinct. The most obvious result of these inquiries is to show that a child, when he reflects upon the self in this manner, usually locates "I" in the body. Interesting and important as this juvenile metaphysics is, as one phase of mental development, it should certainly not be taken as an adequate expression of the childish sense of self, and probably President G. Stanley Hall, who has collected valuable material of this kind, does not so take it.[8] This analysis of the "I," asking one's self just where it is located, whether particular limbs are embraced in it, and the like, is somewhat remote from the ordinary, naive use of the word, with children as with grown people. In my own children I only once observed anything of this sort, and that was in the case of R., when he was struggling to achieve the correct use of his pronouns; and a futile, and as I now think mistaken, attempt was made to help him by pointing out the association of the word with his body. On the other hand, every child who has learned to talk uses "I," "me," "mine," and the like hundreds of times a day, with great emphasis, in the simple, naive way that the race has used them for thousands of years. In this usage they refer to claims upon playthings, to assertions of one's peculiar will or purpose, as "I don't want to do it that way," "I am going to draw a kitty," and so on, rarely to any part of the body. And when a part of the body is meant it is usually by way of claiming approval for it, as "Don't I look nice?" so that the object of chief interest is after all

---

8   Compare G. Stanley Hall, "Some Aspects of the Early Sense of Self," *American Journal of Psychology*, vol. 9, p. 351.

another person's attitude. The speculative "I," though a true "I," is not the "I" of common speech and workaday usefulness, but almost as remote from ordinary thought as the ego of metaphysicians, of which, indeed, it is an immature example.

That children, when in this philosophizing state of mind, usually refer "I" to the physical body, is easily explained by the fact that their materialism, natural to all crude speculation, needs to locate the self somewhere, and the body, the one tangible thing over which they have continuous power, seems the most available home for it.

The process by which self-feeling of the looking-glass sort develops in children may be followed without much difficulty. Studying the movements of others as closely as they do they soon see a connection between their own acts and changes in those movements; that is, they perceive their own influence or power over persons. The child appropriates the visible actions of his parent or nurse, over which he finds he has some control, in quite the same way as he appropriates one of his own members or a plaything, and he will try to do things with this new possession, just as he will with his hand or his rattle. A girl six months old will attempt in the most evident and deliberate manner to attract attention to herself, to set going by her actions some of those movements of other persons that she has appropriated. She has tasted the joy of being a cause, of exerting, and wishes more of it. She will tug at her mother's skirts, wriggle, gurgle, stretch out her arms, etc., all the time watching for the hoped-for effect. These performances often give the child, even at this age, an appearance of what is called affectation, that is, she seems to be unduly preoccupied with what other people think of her. Affectation, at any age, exists when the passion to influence others seems to overbalance the established character and give it an obvious twist or pose. It is instructive to find that even Darwin was, in his childhood, capable of departing from truth for the sake of making an impression. "For instance," he says in his autobiography, "I once gathered much valuable fruit from my father's trees and hid it in the shrubbery, and then ran in breathless haste to spread the news that I had discovered a hoard of stolen fruit."[9]

The young performer soon learns to be different things to different people, showing that he begins to apprehend personality and to foresee its operation. If the mother or nurse is more tender than just she will almost certainly be "worked" by systematic weeping. It is a matter of common observation that children often behave worse with their mother than with other and less sympathetic people. Of the new persons that a child sees it is evident that some make a strong impression and awaken a desire to interest and please them, while others are indifferent or repugnant. Sometimes the reason can be perceived or guessed, sometimes not; but the fact of selective interest, admiration, prestige, is obvious before the end of the second year. By that time a child already cares much for the reflection of himself

---

9 Charles Darwin, *Life and Letters of Charles Darwin,* ed. F. Darwin, p. 27.

upon one personality and little for that upon another. Moreover, he soon claims intimate and tractable persons as *mine,* classes them among his other possessions, and maintains his ownership against all comers. M., at three years of age, vigorously resented R.'s claim upon their mother. The latter was *"my* mamma," whenever the point was raised.

Strong joy and grief depend upon the treatment this rudimentary social self receives. In the case of M. , I noticed as early as the fourth month a "hurt" way of crying which seemed to indicate a sense of personal slight. It was quite different from the cry of pain or that of anger, but seemed about the same as the cry of fright. The slightest tone of reproof would produce it. On the other hand, if people took notice and laughed and encouraged, she was hilarious. At about fifteen months old she had become "a perfect little actress," seeming to live largely in imaginations of her effect upon other people. She constantly and obviously laid traps for attention, and looked abashed or wept at any signs of disapproval or indifference. At times it would seem as if she could not get over these repulses, but would cry long in a grieved way, refusing to be comforted. If she hit upon any little trick that made people laugh she would be sure to repeat it, laughing loudly and affectedly in imitation. She had quite a repertory of these small performances, which she would display to a sympathetic audience, or even try upon strangers. I have seen her at sixteen months, when R. refused to give her the scissors, sit down and make-believe cry, putting up her under lip and snuffling, meanwhile looking up now and then to see what effect she was producing.[10]

In such phenomena we have plainly enough, it seems to me, the germ of personal ambition of every sort. Imagination co-operating with instinctive self-feeling has already created a social "I," and this has become a principal object of interest and endeavor.

Progress from this point is chiefly in the way of a greater definite-ness, fulness, and inwardness in the imagination of the other's state of mind. A little child thinks of and tries to elicit certain visible or audible phenomena, and does not go back of them; but what a grownup person desires to produce in others is an internal, invisible condition which his own richer experience enables him to imagine, and of which expression is only the sign. Even adults, however, make no separation between what other people think and the visible expression of that thought. They imagine the whole thing at once, and their idea differs from that of a child chiefly in the comparative richness and complexity of the elements that accompany and interpret the visible or audible sign. There is also a progress from the naive to the subtle in socially self-assertive action. A child obviously and simply, at first, does things for effect. Later there is an endeavor to suppress the appearance of doing so; affection, indifference, contempt, etc., are simulated to hide the real wish to affect the self-image. It is perceived that an obvious seeking after good opinion is weak and disagreeable.

---

10   This sort of thing is very familiar to observers of children. See, for instance, Miss Shinn's *Notes on the Development of a Child,* p. 153.

I doubt whether there are any regular stages in the development of social self-feeling and expression common to the majority of children. The sentiments of self develop by imperceptible gradations out of the crude appropriative instinct of new-born babes, and their manifestations vary indefinitely in different cases. Many children show "self-consciousness" conspicuously from the first half-year; others have little appearance of it at any age. Still others pass through periods of affectation whose length and time of occurrence would probably be found to be exceedingly various. In childhood, as at all times of life, absorption in some idea other than that of the social self tends to drive "self-consciousness" out.

Nearly every one, however, whose turn of mind is at all imaginative goes through a season of passionate self-feeling during adolescence, when, according to current belief, the social impulses are stimulated in connection with the rapid development of the functions of sex. This is a time of hero-worship, of high resolve, of impassioned revery, of vague but fierce ambition, of strenuous imitation that seems affected, of *gêne* in the presence of the other sex or of superior persons, and so on.

Many autobiographies describe the social self-feeling of youth which, in the case of strenuous, susceptible natures, prevented by weak health or uncongenial surroundings from gaining the sort of success proper to that age, often attains extreme intensity. This is quite generally the case with the youth of men of genius, whose exceptional endowment and tendencies usually isolate them more or less from the ordinary life about them. In the autobiography of John Addington Symonds we have an account of the feelings of an ambitious boy suffering from ill-health, plainness of feature—peculiarly mortifying to his strong aesthetic instincts—and mental backwardness. "I almost resented the attentions paid me as my father's son... I regarded them as acts of charitable condescension. Thus I passed into an attitude of haughty shyness which had nothing respectable in it except a sort of self-reliant, world-defiant pride, a resolution to effectuate myself, and to win what I wanted by my exertions. ... I vowed to raise myself somehow or other to eminence of some sort. ... I felt no desire for wealth, no mere wish to cut a figure in society. But I thirsted with intolerable thirst for eminence, for recognition as a personality. ... The main thing which sustained me was a sense of self—imperious, antagonistic, unmalleable. ... My external self in these many ways was being perpetually snubbed, and crushed, and mortified. Yet the inner self hardened after a dumb, blind fashion. I kept repeating, 'Wait, wait. I will, I shall, I must.' " At Oxford he overhears a conversation in which his abilities are depreciated and it is predicted that he will not get his "first." "The sting of it remained in me; and though I cared little enough for first classes, I then and there resolved that I would win the best first of my year. This kind of grit in me has to be notified. Nothing aroused it so much as a seeming slight, exciting my rebellious manhood." Again he exclaims, "I look 'round me and find nothing in which I excel. ... I fret because I do not realize ambition, because I have no active work, and cannot win a position of importance like other men."[11]

This sort of thing is familiar in literature, and very likely in our own experience. It seems worthwhile to recall it and to point out that this primal need of self-effectuation, to adopt Mr. Symonds's phrase, is the essence of ambition, and always has for its object the production of some effect upon the minds of other people. We feel in the quotations above the indomitable surging up of the individualizing, militant force of which self-feeling seems to be the organ.

---

11   Symonds, *John Addington Symonds,* ed. H. F. Brown, vol. i, pp. 63, 70, 74, 120, 125, 348.

THE SOCIAL SELF

By George Herbert Mead

R ECOGNIZING that the self can not appear in consciousness as an "I," that it is always an object, *i. e.*, a "me," I wish to suggest an answer to the question, What is involved in the self being an object? The first answer may be that an object involves a subject. Stated in other words, that a "me" is inconceivable without an "I." And to this reply must be made that such an "I" is a presupposition, but never a presentation of conscious experience, for the moment it is presented it has passed into the objective case, presuming, if you like, an "I" that observes—but an "I" that can disclose himself only by ceasing to be the subject for whom the object "me" exists. It is, of course, not the Hegelism of a self that becomes another to himself in which I am interested, but the nature of the self as revealed by introspection and subject to our factual analysis. This analysis does reveal, then, in a memory process an attitude of observing oneself in which both the observer and the observed appear. To be concrete, one remembers asking himself how he could undertake to do this, that, or the other, chiding himself for his shortcomings or pluming himself upon his achievements. Thus, in the redintegrated self of the moment passed, one finds both a subject and an object, but it is a subject that is now an object of observation, and has the same nature as the object self whom we present as in intercourse with those about us. In quite the same fashion we remember the questions, admonitions, and approvals addressed to our fellows. But the subject attitude which we instinctively take can be presented only as something experienced—as we can be conscious of our acts only through the sensory processes set up after the act has begun.

The contents of this presented subject, who thus has become an object in being presented, but which still distinguish him as the subject of the passed experience from the "me" whom he addressed, *are* those images which initiated the conversation and the motor sensations which accompany the expression, plus the organic sensations and the response of the whole system to the activity initiated. In a word, just those contents which go to

George H. Mead, "The Social Self," from *The Journal of Philosophy, Psychology and Scientific Methods*, Vol. 10 No. 14, July 3, 1913, Pp. 374-377. Copyright © 1913 by Journal of Philosophy, Inc.. Permission to reprint granted by the publisher.

make up the self which is distinguished from the others whom he addresses. The self appearing as "I" is the memory image of the self who acted toward himself and is the same self who acts toward other selves.

On the other hand, the stuff that goes to make up the "me" whom the "I" addresses and whom he observes, is the experience which is induced by this action of the "I." If the "I" speaks, the "me" hears. If the "I" strikes, the "me" feels the blow. Here again the "me" consciousness is of the same character as that which arises from the action of the other upon him. That is, it is only as the individual finds himself acting with reference to himself as he acts towards others, that he becomes a subject to himself rather than an object, and only as he is affected by his own social conduct in the manner in which he is affected by that of others, that he becomes an object to his own social conduct.

The differences in our memory presentations of the "I" and the "me" are those of the memory images of the initiated social conduct and those of the sensory responses thereto.

It is needless, in view of the analysis of Baldwin, of Royce and of Cooley and many others, to do more than indicate that these reactions arise earlier in our social conduct with others than in introspective self-consciousness, *i. e.*, that the infant consciously calls the attention of others before he calls his own attention by affecting himself and that he is consciously affected by others before he is conscious of being affected by himself.

The "I" of introspection is the self which enters into social relations with other selves. It is not the "I" that is implied in the fact that one presents himself as a "me." And the "me" of introspection is the same "me" that is the object of the social conduct of others. One presents himself as acting toward others—in this presentation he is presented in indirect discourse as the subject of the action and is still an object,—and the subject of this presentation can never appear immediately in conscious experience. It is the same self who is presented as observing himself, and he affects himself just in so far and only in so far as he can address himself by the means of social stimulation which affect others. The "me" whom he addresses is the "me," therefore, that is similarly affected by the social conduct of those about him.

This statement of the introspective situation, however, seems to overlook a more or less constant feature of our consciousness, and that is that running current of awareness of what we do which is distinguishable from the consciousness of the field of stimulation, whether that field be without or within. It is this "awareness" which has led many to assume that it is the nature of the self to be conscious both of subject and of object—to be subject of action toward an object world and at the same time to be directly conscious of this subject as subject,—"Thinking its non-existence along with whatever else it thinks." Now, as Professor James pointed out, this consciousness is more logically conceived of as sciousness—the thinker being an implication rather than a content, while the "me" is but a bit of object content within the stream of sciousness. However, this logical statement does not do justice to the findings of consciousness. Besides the actual stimulations and responses and the memory images of these, within which lie perforce the organic sensations and responses which make up the "me," there accompanies a large part of our conscious experience, indeed all that we call self-conscious, an inner response to what we may be doing, saying, or thinking. At the back of our heads we are a large part of the time more or less clearly conscious of our own replies to the remarks made to others, of innervations which would lead to attitudes and gestures answering our gestures and attitudes towards others.

The observer who accompanies all our self-conscious conduct is then not the actual "I" who is responsible for the conduct in *propria persona*—he is rather the response which one makes to his own conduct. The confusion of this response of ours, following upon our social stimulations of others with the implied subject of our action, is the psychological ground for the assumption that the self can be directly conscious of itself as acting and acted upon. The actual situation is this: The self acts with reference to others and is immediately conscious of the objects about it. In memory it also redintegrates the self acting as well as the others acted upon. But besides these contents, the action with reference to the others calls out responses in the individual himself—there is then another "me" criticizing, approving, and suggesting, and consciously planning, *i. e.*, the reflective self.

It is not to all our conduct toward the objective world that we thus respond. Where we are intensely preoccupied with the objective world, this accompanying awareness disappears. We have to recall the experience to become aware that we have been involved as selves, to produce the self-consciousness which is a constituent part of a large part of our experience. As I have indicated elsewhere, the mechanism for this reply to our own social stimulation of others follows as a natural result from the fact that the very sounds, gestures, especially vocal gestures, which man makes in addressing others, call out or tend to call out responses from himself. He can not hear himself speak without assuming in a measure the attitude which he would have assumed if he had been addressed in the same words by others.

The self which consciously stands over against other selves thus becomes an object, an other to himself, through the very fact that he hears himself talk, and replies. The mechanism of introspection is therefore given in the social attitude which man necessarily assumes toward himself, and the mechanism of thought, in so far as thought uses symbols which are used in social intercourse, is but an inner conversation.

Introduction and Conclusion

BY ERVING GOFFMAN

When an individual enters the presence of others, they commonly seek to acquire information about him or to bring into play information about him already possessed. They will be interested in his general socio-economic status, his conception of self, his attitude toward them, his competence, his trustworthiness, etc. Although some of this information seems to be sought almost as an end in itself, there are usually quite practical reasons for acquiring it. Information about the individual helps to define the situation, enabling others to know in advance what he will expect of them and what they may expect of him. Informed in these ways, the others will know how best to act in order to call forth a desired response from him.

For those present, many sources of information become accessible and many carriers (or "sign-vehicles") become available for conveying this information. If unacquainted with the individual, observers can glean clues from his conduct and appearance which allow them to apply their previous experience with individuals roughly similar to the one before them or, more important, to apply untested stereotypes to him. They can also assume from past experience that only individuals of a particular kind are likely to be found in a given social setting. They can rely on what the individual says about himself or on documentary evidence he provides as to who and what he is. If they know, or know of, the individual by virtue of experience prior to the interaction, they can rely on assumptions as to the persistence and generality of psychological traits as a means of predicting his present and future behavior.

However, during the period in which the individual is in the immediate presence of the others, few events may occur which directly provide the others with the conclusive information they will need if they are to direct wisely their own activity. Many crucial

Erving Goffman, "Introduction; Performances; and Conclusion," from *The Presentation of Self in Everyday Life*, Pp. 1-21, 252-255. Published by Doubleday and Company Inc., 1959. Copyright by Random House Inc.. Permission to reprint granted by the rights holder..

facts lie beyond the time and place of interaction or lie concealed within it. For example, the "true" or "real" attitudes, beliefs, and emotions of the individual can be ascertained only indirectly, through his avowals or through what appears to be involuntary expressive behavior. Similarly, if the individual offers the others a product or service, they will often find that during the interaction there will be no time and place immediately available for eating the pudding that the proof can be found in. They will be forced to accept some events as conventional or natural signs of something not directly available to the senses. In Ichheiser's terms,[1] the individual will have to act so that he intentionally or unintentionally *expresses* himself, and the others will in turn have to be *impressed* in some way by him.

The expressiveness of the individual (and therefore his capacity to give impressions) appears to involve two radically different kinds of sign activity: the expression that he *gives*, and the expression that he *gives off*. The first involves verbal symbols or their substitutes which he uses admittedly and solely to convey the information that he and the others are known to attach to these symbols. This is communication in the traditional and narrow sense. The second involves a wide range of action that others can treat as symptomatic of the actor, the expectation being that the action was performed for reasons other than the information conveyed in this way. As we shall have to see, this distinction has an only initial validity. The individual does of course intentionally convey misinformation by means of both of these types of communication, the first involving deceit, the second feigning.

Taking communication in both its narrow and broad sense, one finds that when the individual is in the immediate presence of others, his activity will have a promissory character. The others are likely to find that they must accept the individual on faith, offering him a just return while he is present before them in exchange for something whose true value will not be established until after he has left their presence. (Of course, the others also live by inference in their dealings with the physical world, but it is only in the world of social interaction that the objects about which they make inferences will purposely facilitate and hinder this inferential process.) The security that they justifiably feel in making inferences about the individual will vary, of course, depending on such factors as the amount of information they already possess about him, but no amount of such past evidence can entirely obviate the necessity of acting on the basis of inferences. As William L. Thomas suggested:

> It is also highly important for us to realize that we do not as a matter of fact lead our lives, make our decisions, and reach our goals in everyday life either statistically or scientifically. We live by inference. I am, let us say, your guest. You do not know, you cannot determine scientifically, that I will not steal your

---

1 Gustav Ichheiser, "Misunderstandings in Human Relations," Supplement to *The American Journal of Sociology*, LV (September, 1949), pp. 6–7.

money or your spoons. But inferentially I will not, and inferentially you have me as a guest.[2]

Let us now turn from the others to the point of view of the individual who presents himself before them. He may wish them to think highly of or to think that he thinks highly of them, or to perceive how in fact he feels toward them, or to obtain no clear-cut impression; he may wish to ensure sufficient harmony so that the interaction can be sustained, or to defraud, get rid of, confuse, mislead, antagonize, or insult them. Regardless of the particular objective which the individual has in mind and of his motive for having this objective, it will be in his interests to control the conduct of the others, especially their responsive treatment of him.[3] This control is achieved largely by influencing the definition of the situation which the others come to formulate, and he can influence this definition by expressing himself in such a way as to give them the kind of impression that will lead them to act voluntarily in accordance with his own plan. Thus, when an individual appears in the presence of others, there will usually be some reason for him to mobilize his activity so that it will convey an impression to others which it is in his interests to convey. Since a girl's dormitory mates will glean evidence of her popularity from the calls she receives on the phone, we can suspect that some girls will arrange for calls to be made, and Willard Waller's finding can be anticipated:

> It has been reported by many observers that a girl who is called to the telephone in the dormitories will often allow herself to be called several times, in order to give all the other girls ample opportunity to hear her paged.[4]

Of the two kinds of communication—expressions given and expressions given off—this report will be primarily concerned with the latter, with the more theatrical and contextual kind, the non-verbal, presumably unintentional kind, whether this communication be purposely engineered or not. As an example of what we must try to examine, I would like to cite at length a novelistic incident in which Preedy, a vacationing Englishman, makes his first appearance on the beach of his summer hotel in Spain:

But in any case he took care to avoid catching anyone's eye. First of all, he had to make it clear to those potential companions of his holiday that they were of no concern to him

---

2   Quoted in E. H. Volkart, editor, *Social Behavior and Personality*, Contributions of W. I. Thomas to Theory and Social Research (New York: Social Science Research Council, 1951), p. 5.

3   Here I owe much to an unpublished paper by Tom Burns of the University of Edinburgh. He presents the argument that in all interaction a basic underlying theme is the desire of each participant to guide and control the responses made by the others present. A similar argument has been advanced by Jay Haley in a recent unpublished paper, but in regard to a special kind of control, that having to do with defining the nature of the relationship of those involved in the interaction.

4   Willard Waller, "The Rating and Dating Complex," *American Sociological Review*, II, p. 730.

whatsoever. He stared through them, round them, over them—eyes lost in space. The beach might have been empty. If by chance a ball was thrown his way, he looked surprised; then let a smile of amusement lighten his face (Kindly Preedy), looked round dazed to see that there *were* people on the beach, tossed it back with a smile to himself and not a smile *at* the people, and then resumed carelessly his nonchalant survey of space.

But it was time to institute a little parade, the parade of the Ideal Preedy. By devious handlings he gave any who wanted to look a chance to see the title of his book— a Spanish translation of Homer, classic thus, but not daring, cosmopolitan too—and then gathered together his beach-wrap and bag into a neat sand-resistant pile (Methodical and Sensible Preedy), rose slowly to stretch at ease his huge frame (Big-Cat Preedy), and tossed aside his sandals (Carefree Preedy, after all).

The marriage of Preedy and the sea! There were alternative rituals. The first involved the stroll that turns into a run and a dive straight into the water, thereafter smoothing into a strong splashless crawl towards the horizon. But of course not really to the horizon. Quite suddenly he would turn on to his back and thrash great white splashes with his legs, somehow thus showing that he could have swum further had he wanted to, and then would stand up a quarter out of water for all to see who it was.

The alternative course was simpler, it avoided the cold-water shock and it avoided the risk of appearing too high-spirited. The point was to appear to be so used to the sea, the Mediterranean, and this particular beach, that one might as well be in the sea as out of it. It involved a slow stroll down and into the edge of the water—not even noticing his toes were wet, land and water all the same to *him!*—with his eyes up at the sky gravely surveying portents, invisible to others, of the weather (Local Fisherman Preedy).[5]

The novelist means us to see that Preedy is improperly concerned with the extensive impressions he feels his sheer bodily action is giving off to those around him. We can malign Preedy further by assuming that he has acted merely in order to give a particular impression, that this is a false impression, and that the others present receive either no impression at all, or, worse still, the impression that Preedy is affectedly trying to cause them to receive this particular impression. But the important point for us here is that the kind of impression Preedy thinks he is making is in fact the kind of impression that others correctly and incorrectly glean from someone in their midst.

I have said that when an individual appears before others his actions will influence the definition of the situation which they come to have. Sometimes the individual will act in a thoroughly calculating manner, expressing himself in a given way solely in order to give the kind of impression to others that is likely to evoke from them a specific response he is concerned to obtain. Sometimes the individual will be calculating in his activity but be relatively unaware that this is the case. Sometimes he will intentionally and consciously express himself in a particular way, but chiefly because the tradition of his group or social

---

5   William Sansom, *A Contest of Ladies* (London: Hogarth, 1956), pp. 230–32.

status require this kind of expression and not because of any particular response (other than vague acceptance or approval) that is likely to be evoked from those impressed by the expression. Sometimes the traditions of an individual's role will lead him to give a well-designed impression of a particular kind and yet he may be neither consciously nor unconsciously disposed to create such an impression. The others, in their turn, may be suitably impressed by the individual's efforts to convey something, or may misunderstand the situation and come to conclusions that are warranted neither by the individual's intent nor by the facts. In any case, in so far as the others act *as if* the individual had conveyed a particular impression, we may take a functional or pragmatic view and say that the individual has "effectively" projected a given definition of the situation and "effectively" fostered the understanding that a given state of affairs obtains.

There is one aspect of the others' response that bears special comment here. Knowing that the individual is likely to present himself in a light that is favorable to him, the others may divide what they witness into two parts; a part that is relatively easy for the individual to manipulate at will, being chiefly his verbal assertions, and a part in regard to which he seems to have little concern or control, being chiefly derived from the expressions he gives off. The others may then use what are considered to be the ungovernable aspects of his expressive behavior as a check upon the validity of what is conveyed by the governable aspects. In this a fundamental asymmetry is demonstrated in the communication process, the individual presumably being aware of only one stream of his communication, the witnesses of this stream and one other. For example, in Shetland Isle one crofter's wife, in serving native dishes to a visitor from the mainland of Britain, would listen with a polite smile to his polite claims of liking what he was eating; at the same time she would take note of the rapidity with which the visitor lifted his fork or spoon to his mouth, the eagerness with which he passed food into his mouth, and the gusto expressed in chewing the food, using these signs as a check on the stated feelings of the eater. The same woman, in order to discover what one acquaintance (A) "actually" thought of another acquaintance (B), would wait until B was in the presence of A but engaged in conversation with still another person (C). She would then covertly examine the facial expressions of A as he regarded B in conversation with C. Not being in conversation with B, and not being directly observed by him, A would sometimes relax usual constraints and tactful deceptions, and freely express what he was "actually" feeling about B. This Shetlander, in short, would observe the unobserved observer.

Now given the fact that others are likely to check up on the more controllable aspects of behavior by means of the less controllable, one can expect that sometimes the individual will try to exploit this very possibility, guiding the impression he makes through behavior felt to be reliably informing.[6] For example, in gaining admission to a tight social circle, the

6   The widely read and rather sound writings of Stephen Potter are concerned in part with signs that can be engineered to give a shrewd observer the apparently incidental cues he needs to discover concealed

participant observer may not only wear an accepting look while listening to an informant, but may also be careful to wear the same look when observing the informant talking to others; observers of the observer will then not as easily discover where he actually stands. A specific illustration may be cited from Shetland Isle. When a neighbor dropped in to have a cup of tea, he would ordinarily wear at least a hint of an expectant warm smile as he passed through the door into the cottage. Since lack of physical obstructions outside the cottage and lack of light within it usually made it possible to observe the visitor un-observed as he approached the house, islanders sometimes took pleasure in watching the visitor drop whatever expression he was manifesting and replace it with a sociable one just before reaching the door. However, some visitors, in appreciating that this examination was occurring, would blindly adopt a social face a long distance from the house, thus ensuring the projection of a constant image.

This kind of control upon the part of the individual reinstates the symmetry of the communication process, and sets the stage for a kind of information game—a potentially infinite cycle of concealment, discovery, false revelation, and rediscovery. It should be added that since the others are likely to be relatively unsuspicious of the presumably unguided aspect of the individual's conduct, he can gain much by controlling it. The others of course may sense that the individual is manipulating the presumably spontaneous aspects of his behavior, and seek in this very act of manipulation some shading of conduct that the individual has not managed to control. This again provides a check upon the individual's behavior, this time his presumably uncalculated behavior, thus re-establishing the asym-metry of the communication process. Here I would like only to add the suggestion that the arts of piercing an individual's effort at calculated unintentionality seem better developed than our capacity to manipulate our own behavior, so that regardless of how many steps have occurred in the information game, the witness is likely to have the advantage over the actor, and the initial asymmetry of the communication process is likely to be retained.

When we allow that the individual projects a definition of the situation when he appears before others, we must also see that the others, however passive their role may seem to be, will themselves effectively project a definition of the situation by virtue of their response to the individual and by virtue of any lines of action they initiate to him. Ordinarily the definitions of the situation projected by the several different participants are sufficiently attuned to one another so that open contradiction will not occur. I do not mean that there will be the kind of consensus that arises when each individual present candidly expresses what he really feels and honestly agrees with the expressed feelings of the others present. This kind of harmony is an optimistic ideal and in any case not necessary for the smooth working of society. Rather, each participant is expected to suppress his immediate heartfelt feelings, conveying a view of the situation which he feels the others will be able to find at least temporarily acceptable. The maintenance of this surface of agreement, this veneer of

---

virtues the gamesman does not in fact possess.

consensus, is facilitated by each participant concealing his own wants behind statements which assert values to which everyone present feels obliged to give lip service. Further, there is usually a kind of division of definitional labor. Each participant is allowed to establish the tentative official ruling regarding matters which are vital to him but not immediately important to others, e.g., the rationalizations and justifications by which he accounts for his past activity. In exchange for this courtesy he remains silent or non-committal on matters important to others but not immediately important to him. We have then a kind of interactional *modus vivendi*. Together the participants contribute to a single over-all definition of the situation which involves not so much a real agreement as to what exists but rather a real agreement as to whose claims concerning what issues will be temporarily honored. Real agreement will also exist concerning the desirability of avoiding an open conflict of definitions of the situation.[7] I will refer to this level of agreement as a "working consensus." It is to be understood that the working consensus established in one interaction setting will be quite different in content from the working consensus established in a different type of setting. Thus, between two friends at lunch, a reciprocal show of affection, respect, and concern for the other is maintained. In service occupations, on the other hand, the specialist often maintains an image of disinterested involvement in the problem of the client, while the client responds with a show of respect for the competence and integrity of the specialist. Regardless of such differences in content, however, the general form of these working arrangements is the same.

In noting the tendency for a participant to accept the definitional claims made by the others present, we can appreciate the crucial importance of the information that the individual *initially* possesses or acquires concerning his fellow participants, for it is on the basis of this initial information that the individual starts to define the situation and starts to build up lines of responsive action. The individual's initial projection commits him to what he is proposing to be and requires him to drop all pretenses of being other things. As the interaction among the participants progresses, additions and modifications in this initial informational state will of course occur, but it is essential that these later developments be related without contradiction to, and even built up from, the initial positions taken by the several participants. It would seem that an individual can more easily make a choice as to what line of treatment to demand from and extend to the others present at the beginning of an encounter than he can alter the line of treatment that is being pursued once the interaction is underway.

---

7   An interaction can be purposely set up as a time and place or voicing differences in opinion, but in such cases participants must be careful to agree not to disagree on the proper tone of voice, vocabulary, and degree of seriousness in which all arguments are to be phrased, and upon the mutual respect which disagreeing participants must carefully continue to express toward one another. This debaters' or academic definition of the situation may also be invoked suddenly and judiciously as a way of translating a serious conflict of views into one that can be handled within a framework acceptable to all present.

In everyday life, of course, there is a clear understanding that first impressions are important. Thus, the work adjustment of those in service occupations will often hinge upon a capacity to seize and hold the initiative in the service relation, a capacity that will require subtle aggressiveness on the part of the server when he is of lower socio-economic status than his client W. F. Whyte suggests the waitress as an example:

> The first point that stands out is that the waitress who bears up under pressure does not simply respond to her customers. She acts with some skill to control their behavior. The first question to ask when we look at the customer relationship is, "Does the waitress get the jump on the customer, or does the customer get the jump on the waitress?" The skilled waitress realizes the crucial nature of this question. ...

> The skilled waitress tackles the customer with confidence and without hesitation. For example, she may find that a new customer has seated himself before she could clear off the dirty dishes and change the cloth. He is now leaning on the table studying the menu. She greets him, says, "May I change the cover, please?" and, without waiting for an answer, takes his menu away from him so that he moves back from the table, and she goes about her work. The relationship is handled politely but firmly, and there is never any question as to who is in charge.[8]

When the interaction that is initiated by "first impressions" is itself merely the initial interaction in an extended series of interactions involving the same participants, we speak of "getting off on the right foot" and feel that it is crucial that we do so. Thus, one learns that some teachers take the following view:

> You can't ever let them get the upper hand on you or you're through. So I start out tough. The first day I get a new class in, I let them know who's boss ... You've got to start off tough, then you can ease up as you go along. If you start out easy-going, when you try to get tough, they'll just look at you and laugh.[9]

---

8   W. F. Whyte, "When Workers and Customers Meet," Chap. VII, *Industry and Society*, ed. W. F. Whyte (New York: McGraw-Hill, 1946), pp. 132–33.

9   Teacher interview quoted by Howard S. Becker, "Social Class Variations in the Teacher-Pupil Relationship," *Journal of Educational Sociology*, XXV, p. 459.

Similarly, attendants in mental institutions may feel that if the new patient is sharply put in his place the first day on the ward and made to see who is boss, much future difficulty will be prevented.[10]

Given the fact that the individual effectively projects a definition of the situation when he enters the presence of others, we can assume that events may occur within the interaction which contradict, discredit, or otherwise throw doubt upon this projection. When these disruptive events occur, the interaction itself may come to a confused and embarrassed halt. Some of the assumptions upon which the responses of the participants had been predicated become untenable, and the participants find themselves lodged in an interaction for which the situation has been wrongly defined and is now no longer defined. At such moments the individual whose presentation has been discredited may feel ashamed while the others present may feel hostile, and all the participants may come to feel ill at ease, nonplussed, out of countenance, embarrassed, experiencing the kind of anomy that is generated when the minute social system of face-to-face interaction breaks down.

In stressing the fact that the initial definition of the situation projected by an individual tends to provide a plan for the co-operative activity that follows—in stressing this action point of view—we must not overlook the crucial fact that any projected definition of the situation also has a distinctive moral character. It is this moral character of projections that will chiefly concern us in this report. Society is organized on the principle that any individual who possesses certain social characteristics has a moral right to expect that others will value and treat him in an appropriate way. Connected with this principle is a second, namely that an individual who implicitly or explicitly signifies that he has certain social characteristics ought in fact to be what he claims he is. In consequence, when an individual projects a definition of the situation and thereby makes an implicit or explicit claim to be a person of a particular kind, he automatically exerts a moral demand upon the others, obliging them to value and treat him in the manner that persons of his kind have a right to expect. He also implicitly forgoes all claims to be things he does not appear to be[11] and hence forgoes the treatment that would be appropriate for such individuals. The others find, then, that the individual has informed them as to what is and as to what they *ought* to see as the "is."

One cannot judge the importance of definitional disruptions by the frequency with which they occur, for apparently they would occur more frequently were not constant precautions taken. We find that preventive practices are constantly employed to avoid these embarrassments and that corrective practices are constantly employed to compensate

10   Harold Taxel, "Authority Structure in a Mental Hospital Ward" (unpublished Master's thesis, Department of Sociology, University of Chicago, 1953).
11   This role of the witness in limiting what it is the individual can be has been stressed by Existentialists, who see it as a basic threat to individual freedom. See Jean-Paul Sartre, *Being and Nothingness*, trans. by Hazel E. Barnes (New York: Philosophical Library, 1956), p. 365 ff.

for discrediting occurrences that have not been successfully avoided. When the individual employs these strategies and tactics to protect his own projections, we may refer to them as "defensive practices"; when a participant employs them to save the definition of the situation projected by another, we speak of "protective practices" or "tact." Together, defensive and protective practices comprise the techniques employed to safeguard the impression fostered by an individual during his presence before others. It should be added that while we may be ready to see that no fostered impression would survive if defensive practices were not employed, we are less ready perhaps to see that few impressions could survive if those who received the impression did not exert tact in their reception of it.

In addition to the fact that precautions are taken to prevent disruption of projected definitions, we may also note that an intense interest in these disruptions comes to play a significant role in the social life of the group. Practical jokes and social games are played in which embarrassments which are to be taken unseriously are purposely engineered.[12] Fantasies are created in which devastating exposures occur. Anecdotes from the past—real, embroidered, or fictitious—are told and retold, detailing disruptions which occurred, almost occurred, or occurred and were admirably resolved. There seems to be no grouping which does not have a ready supply of these games, reveries, and cautionary tales, to be used as a source of humor, a catharsis for anxieties, and a sanction for inducing individuals to be modest in their claims and reasonable in their projected expectations. The individual may tell himself through dreams of getting into impossible positions. Families tell of the time a guest got his dates mixed and arrived when neither the house nor anyone in it was ready for him. Journalists tell of times when an all-too-meaningful misprint occurred, and the paper's assumption of objectivity or decorum was humorously discredited. Public servants tell of times a client ridiculously misunderstood form instructions, giving answers which implied an unanticipated and bizarre definition of the situation.[13] Seamen, whose home away from home is rigorously he-man, tell stories of coming back home and inadvertently asking mother to "pass the fucking butter."[14] Diplomats tell of the time a near-sighted queen asked a republican ambassador about the health of his king.[15]

To summarize, then, I assume that when an individual appears before others he will have many motives for trying to control the impression they receive of the situation. This report is concerned with some of the common techniques that persons employ to sustain such impressions and with some of the common contingencies associated with the employment of these techniques. The specific content of any activity presented by the individual participant, or the role it plays in the interdependent activities of an on-going social

---

12   Goffman, *op. cit.*, pp. 319–27.

13   Peter Blau, "Dynamics of Bureaucracy" (Ph.D. dissertation, Department of Sociology, Columbia University, forthcoming, University of Chicago Press), pp. 127–29.

14   Walter M. Beattie, Jr., "The Merchant Seaman" (unpublished M.A. Report, Department of Sociology, University of Chicago, 1950), p. 35.

15   Sir Frederick Ponsonby, *Recollections of Three Reigns* (New York: Dutton, 1952), p. 46.

system, will not be at issue; I shall be concerned only with the participant's dramaturgical problems of presenting the activity before others. The issues dealt with by stagecraft and stage management are sometimes trivial but they are quite general; they seem to occur everywhere in social life, providing a clear-cut dimension for formal sociological analysis.

It will be convenient to end this introduction with some definitions that are implied in what has gone before and required for what is to follow. For the purpose of this report, interaction (that is, face-to-face interaction) may be roughly defined as the reciprocal influence of individuals upon one another's actions when in one another's immediate physical presence. An interaction may be defined as all the interaction which occurs throughout any one occasion when a given set of individuals are in one another's continuous presence; the term "an encounter" would do as well. A "performance" may be defined as all the activity of a given participant on a given occasion which serves to influence in any way any of the other participants. Taking a particular participant and his performance as a basic point of reference, we may refer to those who contribute the other performances as the audience, observers, or co-participants. The pre-established pattern of action which is unfolded during a performance and which may be presented or played through on other occasions may be called a "part" or "routine."[16] These situational terms can easily be related to conventional structural ones. When an individual or performer plays the same part to the same audience on different occasions, a social relationship is likely to arise. Defining social role as the enactment of rights and duties attached to a given status, we can say that a social role will involve one or more parts and that each of these different parts may be presented by the performer on a series of occasions to the same kinds of audience or to an audience of the same persons.

PERFORMANCES

Belief in the Part One is Playing

When an individual plays a part he implicitly requests his observers to take seriously the impression that is fostered before them. They are asked to believe that the character they see actually possesses the attributes he appears to possess, that the task he performs will have the consequences that are implicitly claimed for it, and that, in general, matters are what they appear to be. In line with this, there is the popular view that the individual offers his performance and puts on his show "for the benefit of other people." It will be convenient to begin a consideration of performances by turning the question around

---

16   For comments on the importance of distiguishing between a routine of interaction and any particular instance when this routine is played through, see John von Neumann and Oskar Morgenstern, *The Theory of Games and Economic Behaviour* (2nd ed.; Princeton: Princeton University Press, 1947), p. 49.

and looking at the individual's own belief in the impression of reality that he attempts to engender in those among whom he finds himself.

At one extreme, one finds that the performer can be fully taken in by his own act; he can be sincerely convinced that the impression of reality which he stages is the real reality. When his audience is also convinced in this way about the show he puts on—and this seems to be the typical case—then for the moment at least, only the sociologist or the socially disgruntled will have any doubts about the "realness" of what is presented.

At the other extreme, we find that the performer may not be taken in at all by his own routine. This possibility is understandable, since no one is in quite as good an observational position to see through the act as the person who puts it on. Coupled with this, the performer may be moved to guide the conviction of his audience only as a means to other ends, having no ultimate concern in the conception that they have of him or of the situation. When the individual has no belief in his own act and no ultimate concern with the beliefs of his audience, we may call him cynical, reserving the term "sincere" for individuals who believe in the impression fostered by their own performance. It should be understood that the cynic, with all his professional disinvolvement, may obtain unprofessional pleasures from his masquerade, experiencing a kind of gleeful spiritual aggression from the fact that he can toy at will with something his audience must take seriously.[171]

It is not assumed, of course, that all cynical performers are interested in deluding their audiences for purposes of what is called "self-interest" or private gain. A cynical individual may delude his audience for what he considers to be their own good, or for the good of the community, etc. For illustrations of this we need not appeal to sadly enlightened showmen such as Marcus Aurelius or Hsun Tzŭ. We know that in service occupations practitioners who may otherwise be sincere are sometimes forced to delude their customers because their customers show such a heartfelt demand for it. Doctors who are led into giving placebos, filling station attendants who resignedly check and recheck tire pressures for anxious women motorists, shoe clerks who sell a shoe that fits but tell the customer it is the size she wants to hear—these are cynical performers whose audiences will not allow them to be sincere. Similarly, it seems that sympathetic patients in mental wards will sometimes feign bizarre symptoms so that student nurses will not be subjected to a disappointingly sane performance.[182] So also, when inferiors extend their most lavish reception for visiting

17 Perhaps the real crime of the confidence man is not that he takes money from his victims but that he robs all of us of the belief that middle-class manners and appearance can be sustained only by middle class people. A disabused professional can be cynically hostile to the service relation his clients expect him to extend to them, the confidence man is in a position to hold the whole "legit" world in this contempt.
18 See Taxel, *op. cit.*, p. 4. Harry Stack Sullivan has suggested that the tact of institutionalized performers can operate in the other direction, resulting in a kind of *noblesse-oblige* sanity. See his "Socio-Psychiatric Research," *American Journal of Psychiatry*, X, pp. 987–88.
"A study of 'social recoveries' in one of our large mental hospitals some years ago taught me that patients were often released from care because they had learned not to manifest symptoms to the environing

superiors, the selfish desire to win favor may not be the chief motive; the inferior may be tactfully attempting to put the superior at ease by simulating the kind of world the superior is thought to take for granted.

I have suggested two extremes: an individual may be taken in by his own act or be cynical about it. These extremes are something a little more than just the ends of a continuum. Each provides the individual with a position which has its own particular securities and defenses, so there will be a tendency for those who have traveled close to one of these poles to complete the voyage. Starting with lack of inward belief in one's role, the individual may follow the natural movement described by Park:

> It is probably no mere historical accident that the word person, in its first meaning, is a mask. It is rather a recognition of the fact that everyone is always and everywhere, more or less consciously, playing a role … It is in these roles that we know each other; it is in these roles that we know ourselves.[193]

> In a sense, and in so far as this mask represents the conception we have formed of ourselves—the role we are striving to live up to—this mask is our truer self, the self we would like to be. In the end, our conception of our role becomes second nature and an integral part of our personality. We come into the world as individuals, achieve character, and become persons.[204]

This may be illustrated from the community life of Shetland.[215] For the last four or five years the island's tourist hotel has been owned and operated by a married couple of crofter origins. From the beginning, the owners were forced to set aside their own conceptions as to how life ought to be led, displaying in the hotel a full round of middle-class services and amenities. Lately, however, it appears that the managers have become less cynical about the performance that they stage; they themselves are becoming middle class and more and more enamored of the selves their clients impute to them.

Another illustration may be found in the raw recruit who initially follows army etiquette in order to avoid physical punishment and eventually comes to follow the rules so that his organization will not be shamed and his officers and fellow soldiers will respect him.

As suggested, the cycle of disbelief-to-belief can be followed in the other direction, starting with conviction or insecure aspiration and ending in cynicism. Professions which

persons; in other words, had integrated enough of the personal environment to realize the prejudice opposed to their delusions. It seemed almost as if they grew wise enough to be tolerant of the imbecility surrounding them, having finally discovered that it was stupidity and not malice. They could then secure satisfaction from contact with others, while discharging a part of their cravings by psychotic means."

19   Robert Ezra Park, *Race and Culture* (Glencoe, Ill.: The Free Press, 1950), p. 249.
20   *Ibid.*, p. 250.
21   Shetland Isle study.

the public holds in religious awe often allow their recruits to follow the cycle in this direction, and often recruits follow it in this direction not because of a slow realization that they are deluding their audience—for by ordinary social standards the claims they make may be quite valid—but because they can use this cynicism as a means of insulating their inner selves from contact with the audience. And we may even expect to find typical careers of faith, with the individual starting out with one kind of involvement in the performance he is required to give, then moving back and forth several times between sincerity and cynicism before completing all the phases and turning-points of self-belief for a person of his station. Thus, students of medical schools suggest that idealistically oriented beginners in medical school typically lay aside their holy aspirations for a period of time. During the first two years the students find that their interest in medicine must be dropped that they may give all their time to the task of learning how to get through examinations. During the next two years they are too busy learning about diseases to show much concern for the persons who are diseased. It is only after their medical schooling has ended that their original ideals about medical service may be reasserted.[226]

While we can expect to find natural movement back and forth between cynicism and sincerity, still we must not rule out the kind of transitional point that can be sustained on the strength of a little self-illusion. We find that the individual may attempt to induce the audience to judge him and the situation in a particular way, and he may seek this judgment as an ultimate end in itself, and yet he may not completely believe that he deserves the valuation of self which he asks for or that the impression of reality which he fosters is valid. Another mixture of cynicism and belief is suggested in Kroeber's discussion of shamanism:

> Next, there is the old question of deception. Probably most shamans or medicine men, the world over, help along with sleight-of-hand in curing and especially in exhibitions of power. This sleight-of-hand is sometimes deliberate; in many cases awareness is perhaps not deeper than the foreconscious. The attitude, whether there has been repression or not, seems to be as toward a pious fraud. Field ethnographers seem quite generally convinced that even shamans who know that they add fraud nevertheless also believe in their powers, and especially in those of other shamans: they consult them when they themselves or their children are ill.[237]

---

22 H. S. Becker and Blanche Greer, "The Fate of Idealism in Medical School," *American Sociological Review*, 23, pp. 50–56.
23 A.L Kroeber, *The Nature of Culture* (Chicago: University of Chicago Press, 195a), p. 311.

STAGING AND THE SELF

The general notion that we make a presentation of ourselves to others is hardly novel; what ought to be stressed in conclusion is that the very structure of the self can be seen in terms of how we arrange for such performances in our Anglo-American society.

In this report, the individual was divided by implication into two basic parts: he was viewed as a *performer*, a harried fabricator of impressions involved in the all-too-human task of staging a performance; he was viewed as a *character*, a figure, typically a fine one, whose spirit, strength, and other sterling qualities the performance was designed to evoke. The attributes of a performer and the attributes of a character are of a different order, quite basically so, yet both sets have their meaning in terms of the show that must go on.

First, character. In our society the character one performs and one's self are somewhat equated, and this self-as-character is usually seen as something housed within the body of its possessor, especially the upper parts thereof, being a nodule, somehow, in the psychobiology of personality. I suggest that this view is an implied part of what we are all trying to present, but provides, just because of this, a bad analysis of the presentation. In this report the performed self was seen as some kind of image, usually creditable, which the individual on stage and in character effectively attempts to induce others to hold in regard to him. While this image is entertained *concerning* the individual, so that a self is imputed to him, this self itself does not derive from its possessor, but from the whole scene of his action, being generated by that attribute of local events which renders them interpretable by witnesses. A correctly staged and performed scene leads the audience to impute a self to a performed character, but this imputation—this self —is a *product* of a scene that comes off, and is not a *cause* of it. The self, then, as a performed character, is not an organic thing that has a specific location, whose fundamental fate is to be born, to mature, and to die; it is a dramatic effect arising diffusely from a scene that is presented, and the characteristic issue, the crucial concern, is whether it will be credited or discredited.

In analyzing the self then we are drawn from its possessor, from the person who will profit or lose most by it, for he and his body merely provide the peg on which something of collaborative manufacture will be hung for a time. And the means for producing and maintaining selves do not reside inside the peg; in fact these means are often bolted down in social establishments. There will be a back region with its tools for shaping the body, and a front region with its fixed props. There will be a team of persons whose activity on stage in conjunction with available props will constitute the scene from which the performed character's self will emerge, and another team, the audience, whose interpretive activity will be necessary for this emergence. The self is a product of all of these arrangements, and in all of its parts bears the marks of this genesis.

The whole machinery of self-production is cumbersome, of course, and sometimes breaks down, exposing its separate components: back region control; team collusion;

audience tact; and so forth. But, well oiled, impressions will flow from it fast enough to put us in the grips of one of our types of reality—the performance will come off and the firm self accorded each performed character will appear to emanate intrinsically from its performer.

Let us turn now from the individual as character performed to the individual as performer. He has a capacity to learn, this being exercised in the task of training for a part. He is given to having fantasies and dreams, some that pleasurably unfold a triumphant performance, others full of anxiety and dread that nervously deal with vital dis-creditings in a public front region. He often manifests a gregarious desire for teammates and audiences, a tactful considerateness for their concerns; and he has a capacity for deeply felt shame, leading him to minimize the chances he takes of exposure.

These attributes of the individual *qua* performer are not merely a depicted effect of particular performances; they are psychobiological in nature, and yet they seem to arise out of intimate interaction with the contingencies of staging performances.

And now a final comment In developing the conceptual framework employed in this report, some language of the stage was used. I spoke of performers and audiences; of routines and parts; of performances coming off or falling flat; of cues, stage settings and backstage; of dramaturgical needs, dramaturgical skills, and dramaturgical strategies. Now it should be admitted that this attempt to press a mere analogy so far was in part a rhetoric and a maneuver.

The claim that all the world's a stage is sufficiently commonplace for readers to be familiar with its limitations and tolerant of its presentation, knowing that at any time they will easily be able to demonstrate to themselves that it is not to be taken too seriously. An action staged in a theater is a relatively contrived illusion and an admitted one; unlike ordinary life, nothing real or actual can happen to the performed characters—although at another level of course something real and actual can happen to the reputation of performers *qua* professionals whose everyday job is to put on theatrical performances.

And so here the language and mask of the stage will be dropped. Scaffolds, after all, are to build other things with, and should be erected with an eye to taking them down. This report is not concerned with aspects of theater that creep into everyday life. It is concerned with the structure of social encounters—the structure of those entities in social life that come into being whenever persons enter one another's immediate physical presence. The key factor in this structure is the maintenance of a single definition of the situation, this definition having to be expressed, and this expression sustained in the face of a multitude of potential disruptions.

A character staged in a theater is not in some ways real, nor does it have the same kind of real consequences as does the thoroughly contrived character performed by a confidence man; but the *successful* staging of either of these types of false figures involves use of *real* techniques—the same techniques by which everyday persons sustain their real social situations. Those who conduct face to face interaction on a theater's stage must meet the key requirement of real situations; they must expressively sustain a definition of the situation: but this they do in circumstances that have facilitated their developing an apt terminology for the interactional tasks that all of us share.

Questions for discussion

1. After reading the selections in this chapter, how would you define the self?
2. How did the idea of the transcendental self serve ideological goals?
3. How does an empirical concept of the self differ from the transcendental self?
4. What does it mean to say that the self can be an object to itself?
5. Do you think a dramaturgic concept of the self suggests that we are all "phonies"?
6. Goffman writes that "the means for producing and maintaining selves" do not reside in the person. He describes the person as merely a "peg" on which a self is hung for a time. How does he support this claim? Do you agree with this portrayal of the self?
7. Cooley argued that although the idea of the self was cloaked in mystery, it should not be difficult to "get hold of" empirically. How does he suggest that we do this?
8. The distinction between the "I" and the "me" can be difficult to understand. How would you describe it? Can you give examples that help to clarify these phases of the self?

Further reading

Blumer, Herbert. 1969. *Symbolic Interactionism: Perspective and Method.* Berkeley: University of California Press.

Hewitt, John. P. 2007. *Self and Society: A Symbolic Interactionist Perspective,* 11th ed. Needham Heights, MA: Allyn and Bacon.

James, William. 1910. *Psychology: The Briefer Course.* New York: Henry Holt and Co.

Mead, George Herbert. 1934. *Mind, Self, and Society from the Standpoint of a Behaviorist* (Works of Mead, vol. 1). Chicago: University of Chicago Press.

Rosenberg, Morris. 1986. *Conceiving the Self.* New York: Basic Books.

Rousseau, Nathan. 2002. *Self, Symbols, and Society: Classic Readings in Social Psychology.* Lanham, MD: Rowman and Littlefield.

Strauss, Anselm. [1959] 2009. *Mirrors and Masks: The Search for Identity.* New Brunswick, NJ: Transaction.

Stryker, Sheldon. 1980. *Symbolic Interactionism: A Social Structural Version.* Menlo Park, CA: Benjamin/Cummings.

CHAPTER 2

Who Am I? Self and Identity as a Problem

INTRODUCTION

At some point in your life, and perhaps at several points, you will face decisions that make you wonder, "Is this really 'me'?" You might even ask yourself, "Who am I?" In these ways, the self is a problem to be solved. The problem of the self does not only arise in young adulthood, when one is first making his or her way in the world. It can arise at other times, too. The phrase "mid-life crisis" describes one such instance. The formative issues that we face in adolescence take different forms at other points in life, but they involve the same questions about one's purpose and destiny. Transitions that are now commonplace, such as divorce, job loss, and career advancement opportunities, all hold consequences for the sense of self.

Whereas the readings in Chapter 1 examined how the experience of self exists within each person, how it develops, and how we enact it, this chapter examines how we came to take for granted that there *is* a self within each person. You could say that these readings will explore the self as a cultural entity or phenomenon.

The first reading offers a historical perspective that can guide our thinking about the self as a problem. Baumeister follows the rise of individual identity in the early modern era through contemporary times. He outlines the social and cultural changes that brought people from having the courses of their lives determined by social institutions to being responsible for figuring out their own destinies—and how to fulfill them. The increased number of possibilities available to people increased their potentiality. The reading begins in the pre-modern era and explores how changes such as the Protestant Reformation and the ability to choose a mate influenced ideas about individual potentiality. The problem with having potential, of course, is that one must live up to it. Doing so requires making choices, and choosing requires having some way to know that one is making the right choice. Making a choice involves knowing what one wants. Decisions such as what career path to follow, whom to marry, or how to spend a summer vacation have different implications for one's sense of self. For example, the decision to become a doctor or a lawyer does not necessarily make one into a stereotype, but the training and socialization involved in these professions, and others, will shape the self along the way. Deciding to become a physician means devoting years to medical school, followed by a grueling internship and residency. One cannot also devote this time to becoming a master carpenter—unless one is very energetic. Choosing to follow one particular path rules out following others, at least for a time. Each set of possibilities holds different options for the self. This set of circumstances has social origins, and Baumeister can stimulate our thinking along these lines.

The reading entitled "Uncoupling and Narratives of the Self" is drawn from *Codependent Forevermore*, a book I wrote. It focuses on the problem of the self by emphasizing two points. One is the importance of intimate relationships for our sense of self. People who describe themselves as "codependent" believe they have invested their sense of self in another person. They describe their problem as having lost a sense of who they "really" are. For this reason, they offer a window into how one might discover who one "really" is. The second point this reading emphasizes has to do with seeing the self as a story, or narrative. We human beings rely heavily on language for our sense of self. When we meet someone new, we ask him or her to tell us about themselves. They give us a narrative that conveys an impression of who they are. But what happens when the story goes off course? What happens when a main character disappears, or when the future one has imagined for oneself is no longer possible? In the reading, I show how the codependents I studied solved these problems of the self by creating new stories, and new selves in the process.

The reading by Snow and Anderson summarizes extensive research the pair did on the homeless. This reading also emphasizes the importance of talk. When reading, it will help to keep in mind how they distinguish "social identity," "personal identity," and "self-concept." Social identities are assigned by others. They are based primarily on information provided by appearance and behavior. Personal identities are asserted by the person him or herself, and they can contradict social identities. This contradiction is what makes identity construction among homeless people so intriguing. Dirty, ragged clothes might lead to the social identity of a "bum." But the person so designated can construct a personal identity that incorporates or rejects that image. Snow and Anderson refer to the range of activities involved in constructing identity as "identity work." They focus on the identity work that consists of talk. They offer a fascinating glimpse into how those at the bottom rungs of society solve the problem of the self.

Medieval and Early Modern History of Identity

By Roy F. Baumeister

This chapter reviews the major developments in identity prior to 1800, focusing mainly on the culturally and politically dominant parts of Western Europe and America. Prior to 1800 identity was not generally problematic, but several trends prepared the way for it to become so.

MEDIEVAL EUROPE

The problems and crises that plague modern identity formation were largely unknown in medieval Europe. Society was much more rigidly structured and inflexible than it is today. As a result, the large institutional structures for the most part formed an individual's identity. In other words, the individual received his or her identity without much personal struggle. Society operated on the basis of lineage, gender, home, and social class—all of which were fixed by birth. This organization of life according to type I (passive assignment) self-definition processes made identity largely unproblematic. Marriage and age-related transitions introduced single-transformation processes into identity but, again, the individual's role was often passive. Marriage, for example, was often decided and arranged by one's parents. There were occasional exceptions, but the general trends and patterns were quite different from those of modern life.

To understand the medieval mentality we must set aside one pervasive modern value—the fundamental, overriding importance of the individual human being. Medieval attitudes lacked this modern emphasis on individuality. Individuality can be understood as a combination of (1) placing value on the unique characteristics and particular experiences

Roy F. Baumeister, "Medieval and Early Modern History of Identity," from *Identity: Cultural Change and the Struggle for Self*, Pp. 29-58. Copyright © 1986 by Oxford University Press. Permission to reprint granted by the publisher..

of each person, and (2) believing that each person has a special unique potentiality or destiny that may or may not be fulfilled (Weintraub, 1978).

A main reason for the relative indifference to individuality was the firm medieval faith in Christianity, which regarded life on earth as imitative or derivative of the ultimate, otherworldly realities (Auerbach, 1946; Huizinga, 1924/1954). In fact, the particulars of individual human experience were not very important. What mattered was the broad cosmic drama of faith and salvation. The life of a particular person was only a good or poor approximation of the archetypal patterns of heavenly or biblical events. The individual self was significant only as an example of the general struggle between good and evil, virtue and vice, faith and heresy, honor and disgrace. Our modern, individualistic view holds that the value of the individual life resides in what is special or unique about it; the medieval view considered the value of the person's life to reside in how well that life approximated the common ideal of correct Christian life.

One illustration of the medieval indifference to individuality is the way in which biography was practiced. (Actually, what they wrote deserves to be called hagiography, not biography.) Life histories were not written about very many persons during the Middle Ages, and those that were written were primarily the lives of saints. Even these writings exhibited nothing of what we would call "individual" or "realistic" (Altick, 1965, pp. 6–7). The authors were largely indifferent to matters of accuracy, portrayed all saints more or less according to a common stereotype, and would even embellish the life of one saint with miracle stories borrowed from the lives of others (Altick, 1965). The individuality, personality, and psychology of the individual were neglected. The person who had become a saint was just a means for the biographer to edify and inspire virtue in the reader.

If biography was rare in the Middle Ages, autobiography was almost nonexistent. The lack of autobiographical writing is a sign that people did not place much emphasis or value on the unique properties in the individual's experience and character. In the few autobiographies that were produced, the individual was always described as an approximation of the collective Christian ideal (Weintraub, 1978). Thus, even exceptional individuals such as Abelard and Petrarch tried to make their lives and their personalities conform to the general ideals and patterns.

In the late Middle Ages people increasingly learned to think in individual terms and slowly solidified concepts of the single human life as an individual totality. Learning to conceptualize an individual life and to think in terms of individuals are prerequisites for placing value and emphasis on individuality. These trends paved the way for individuality to become an important part of Western culture.

Perhaps the most profound and powerful move toward individualistic thinking was the revision of popular Christian beliefs and practices. In particular, a new view of Christian eschatology emerged around the twelfth century, which placed a greater emphasis on individual salvation and judgment. Earlier conceptions of the second coming of Christ, which entailed the end of time and the resurrection of the dead, were generally glorious and nonthreatening. Eternal salvation was pretty much guaranteed if you were a baptized Christian (Ariès, 1981, pp. 97–98). Salvation, in other words, was *collective*—it depended on your membership in the Christian community rather than on your actions as an individual.

In the twelfth century, however, this seems to have changed. Portrayals of the second coming began to stress the Last Judgment, in which souls were weighed and judged individually. The later medievals expected the archangel to evaluate your soul based on what you did during your life. Damnation to hell became a serious possibility and was seriously feared. By Petrarch's time in the fourteenth century, popular belief had further enhanced the importance of individual judgment by advancing the date. Instead of waiting until the end of time to be saved or damned, you were now judged while still on your deathbed (Ariès, 1981).

This shift shows a new sense of the continuity and totality of each single person's life; it put the all-important issue of salvation in individualistic terms. In the late medieval view, all the events of a life added up to something, namely net moral and spiritual worth, and that had drastic and eternal consequences. True, the goal or purpose of a life were shared in common in that everyone tried to conform to the same ideal patterns of piety, virtue, and duty. But success and failure were evaluated by an *individual* judgment.

The shift of Christian practices toward a more individualized basis was also reflected in the spread of the practice of individual confession of sins (Morris, 1972). After all, the confession is unlike other church rituals. One participates as an individual and presents one's own unique experiences, even though once again the overriding goals and themes invoke the general, collective model of the ideal Christian life.

The late medieval view retained its primary allegiance to general principles and universal truths, not individual experiences. But evidence suggests that individualistic thinking increasingly colored the way people understood and applied those universals. Prior to the twelfth century, sermons focused exclusively on Scripture and on the permanent and universal truths of theology, but during the twelfth century preachers began to use personal anecdotes and insights to illuminate their general points (Morris, 1972). Petrarch's writings during the fourteenth century show a major advance in the use of introspection and self-discovery as a means of understanding the universal Christian ideal of human perfection (Weintraub, 1978). The use of the personal as a means for understanding the general was also evident outside religious matters. Troubadours, for example, began to use experiences from their own lives in their love songs (Morris, 1972).

Late medieval literature also showed a rudimentary interest in personal experience. Occasional portrayals of psychological conflicts of those caught between conflicting obligations reflect this (Hanning, 1977). Such portrayals were not common, nor were they consistently maintained even by the same author, nor would the psychological characterizations be judged convincing and competent by modern standards. Still, the fact that they appeared at all suggests an incipient interest in the experience of the individual.

An intriguing literary development of the twelfth century was that dramatic plots began to use devices that depended on different characters having different points of view on the action (Hanning, 1977), as when one character was ignorant of important circumstances known to other characters. The use of such devices is a further suggestion that the late medievals were increasingly able to think in individual terms.

At the same time, literary plots explored new usages of time, emphasizing the continuity of each life (Hanning, 1977). A further sign of this growing is found in the stabilization of naming practices; a male now kept the same name for his entire life, and a female changed her name only upon marriage (Withycombe, 1947). Prior to this some surnames were acquired during adulthood, such as names based on one's adult characteristics (e.g., "Frederick Red-Beard" or "Louis the Fat"). That system was replaced by the hereditary transmission of surnames. The child received the father's surname at birth and retained it throughout life, except in the case of female marriage (Withycombe, 1947). It is necessary to add one qualification. Having the same name all one's life does suggest a solid conception of the unity of the human life, but the use of hereditary surnames frames the individual identity in terms of family lineage. The person is thus not named as a unique individual but as a current "trustee" of family status, honor, and property (cf. Stone, 1977).

TRANSITION TO THE SIXTEENTH CENTURY

The most dramatic social changes at the end of the Middle Ages were the spread of religious dissent and a great increase in social mobility. It is difficult to assess the impact on human identity of the breakup of the Catholic monopoly on religious truth, and it would be wrong to suggest that the Protestant Reformation rapidly or clearly produced a new type of personality.

The Protestant and Anglican schisms did have profound psychological effects, however. I would suggest that they affected everyone, both Catholic and Protestant, by undermining part of the universal consensus about religious truth. The religious schisms expressed and greatly increased prevailing doubts about the Christian model for living one's life. The loss of consensus foments private doubts and the individual expression of doubts (cf. Asch, 1955). In the Middle Ages one tried to conform to the collective ideal of the model Christian life; that was the purpose of life. Once the consensus about that model was undermined, one could *decide* whether to live by the traditional model or by the new Protestant model (which soon split into several models) or some combination. A single, unquestioned guide for the living of one's life no longer existed.

The religious schism, as well as the resultant plurality of life models, created a setting in which one's identity had to rely on some inner metacriteria. This pattern recurs with various identity components in the centuries that follow. In this historical pattern something that was used as a cause or basis of identity becomes its consequence. For example, in medieval Europe Catholicism was the only option. Who you were followed in large part from your Catholic Christian faith, which was "given." This faith provided the basis for defining the self in terms of *how good* a Christian you were. The Protestant Reformation, however, confronted people with a choice between Catholicism and Protestantism. Your adherence to Catholicism or Protestantism was no longer automatic; it became instead a matter of choice, and you needed a new basis for making this choice. Your basic faith now had to be based on some criterion.

Of course, not everyone faced this choice. Europe soon settled into a status quo by which many people were born Catholics and remained Catholics, while others were born Protestants and remained so. Christian plurality became an instance of type IV self-definition processes; choice was available but not required.

Actually, the problems of Christian plurality probably began during the papal schism of the fourteenth century. Out of the complex power politics of that time arose a situation in which there were two popes, each of whom excommunicated all the followers of the other. Barbara Tuchman's (1978) account of this episode suggests that considerable uncertainty and loss of faith in the Church resulted from the dual papacy. Indeed, she records a popular saying of that time that no one had entered heaven during that entire period.

The Protestant and papal schisms can be dated precisely, but the other development which brought the Middle Ages to a close— increased social mobility—was a gradual process that took place over many centuries. We can identify in this process two themes: first, social mobility transformed a relatively fixed and stable basis for identity into a changeable and problematic one. Social rank now became unstable and contingent on circumstances other than birth. Gradually even the basic criteria of social rank, namely wealth and lineage, became problematic as they came into conflict with each other. Second, social mobility made public life stressful, both by undermining traditional norms for formal social interaction and by making self-definition dependent on the uncertain course of commercial business. This may have led eventually to a retreat from public life and a corresponding emphasis on privacy, home, and family (Sennett, 1974).

EARLY MODERN PERIOD

My discussion of the early modern period focuses on six themes. Keep in mind, however, that, as in all historical accounts, periods overlap. The divisions here are used for the purposes of conceptual unity.

In the early modern period we can identify six social trends: First, there emerged a new concept of an inner or hidden self, symbolized by concern over sincerity and over discrepancies between appearances and underlying realities. Second, the idea of human individuality developed into a widespread belief and value. Third, the incipient cultivation of privacy symbolized the separation of social life and personal life. Fourth, attitudes toward death underwent a basic change, suggesting a growing concern over individual fate. Fifth, people began to have an increasing role in the selection of their own spouses, thereby putting a major component of adult identity on a basis of personal choice. And sixth, there emerged a heightened awareness of individual development and potentiality, symbolized by new attitudes toward children.

1. *The hidden self.* In the sixteenth century the concept of the person came to include having a kind of internal space and self not directly visible in social actions and roles (Trilling, 1971). People began to regard the self as a hidden entity that might or might not be reflected in outward acts. The belief in a real self that is hidden, that is not directly or clearly shown in one's public behavior, can be regarded as a first step toward making identity a problem. An abstract, hidden self is harder to know and harder to define than is a concrete, observable self.

Obviously, this idea did not appear out of a void. The contrast between the visible phenomena and underlying or hidden realities is an old one in Western thought, dating back at least to Plato. Christianity made extensive use of that distinction, and medieval Christian thought regarded events in this world as imitations of the ultimate realities of God's divine plan and of scriptural truth. This medieval "figural" view of earthly reality as deriving from theological reality began to die out in the sixteenth century (Auerbach, 1946), but the distinction between appearance and reality survived and took on a new significance. Indeed, it is fair to describe the sixteenth century as obsessed with contrasts between appearances and underlying realities. The philosophy, politics, and literature of that era—from Berkeley to Machiavelli to Shakespeare—show tireless concern and preoccupation with that issue.

Applied to human beings, the contrast between appearance and reality came in the sixteenth century to mean that persons might deliberately avoid revealing their true selves by their actions. The sixteenth century was "preoccupied to an extreme degree with dissimulation, feigning, and pretense" (Trilling, 1971, p. 13). This is evident in the advice of Machiavelli and in the disguises and mistaken identities of Shakespeare's characters. Indeed, the great rise in popularity of the theatre in England and France reflected the new interest in acting and playing roles (Trilling, 1971), although actors were not the culture heroes they are today.

The new sensitivity to human deceit made possible the emergence of a new type of dramatic character, the villain, the character whom the audience recognizes as wicked but that is not recognized as so by the other characters in the play (Trilling, 1971). The villain's character consists of an underlying evil self beneath a misleading appearance created by dissembling. This type of character flourished into the nineteenth century, after which it was generally abandoned (by serious literature, at least) as not sufficiently "true to life" (Trilling, 1971, p. 14).

A related and revealing development was the emergence of sincerity as an important virtue in sixteenth century society. The word sincerity first appeared in English early in the century, and at first it was used to describe the pure and uncontaminated condition of things (e.g., wine). Soon, however, it began to be applied to persons, with its modern meaning of honest self-presentation (Trilling, 1971). Shakespeare used the word in that sense, and the importance of sincerity is attested by various lines in his plays, the most famous being Polonius' advice to Laertes: "This above all: To thine own self be true, and … thou canst not then be false to any man" (*Hamlet*, act I, scene 3).

Sincerity is of course a kind of equivalence between the visible appearance of the person and the self underneath. Making sincerity an important virtue reflected the new concern with inferring the hidden self from its acts and appearances. Thus, in the sixteenth century the self came to be regarded as something hidden and uncertain. Of course, it was the selves of others and not one's own self that was regarded as difficult to know. Self-knowledge was not recognized as highly problematic until the influence of Puritanism. Nonetheless, it seems fair to say that sixteenth century society recognized at least one of the three functional aspects of identity as problematic—the interpersonal aspect.

2. *Individuality.* A fascination with the unique or special characteristics of the individual increased dramatically in the sixteenth century (Auerbach, 1946; Morris, 1972; Trilling, 1971; Weintraub, 1978). That development is sufficient to induce some writers to propose that individuality actually emerged in the sixteenth century (e.g., it was then that "men became individuals"—Trilling, 1971, p. 24). A more conservative definition of individuality is proposed on the basis of two criteria by Weintraub (1978). Individuality means placing value on unique characteristics *and* believing that each person has a special destiny or potentiality. Weintraub recognizes that the first criterion was abundantly met during the sixteenth century, but the second was not satisfied until the end of the eighteenth century. Still, the general conclusion is that it was during the early modern period (1500 to 1800) that individuality became a major value and a basic belief in Western society.

One important sign of individuality in the sixteenth century was the explosion of autobiographical writing. The Middle Ages produced very few autobiographies, only about one per century by one estimate (Weintraub, 1978). Late medieval writing about the self (e.g., Petrarch) showed evidence of sustained introspection, the desire for some kind of self-fulfillment, and the need for autonomous self-reliance. But the individual was not valued for what was special or unique; instead, the goal and ideal were still the general image of "the correct Christian life" (Weintraub, 1978, p. 112). In the sixteenth century writers did however begin to describe their particular characteristics and personal idiosyncracies as if intrinsically important (Auerbach, 1946; Trilling, 1971; Weintraub, 1978). Thus Cardano's autobiography, written shortly before his death in 1576, includes thorough discussions devoted to such topics as his stature and appearance, lists of his friends and enemies, personal dishonors, his dreams, his manner of dress, his gambling habits, his conversational style, his eating habits, his manner of walking, his guardian angels, odd coincidences he had experienced, his itches and body odors, and so forth (Weintraub, 1978, ch. 7). Such lengthy elaboration of personal idiosyncracies marks a substantial departure from the medieval attitude.

Like autobiography, biographical writing became more prevalent during the early modern period. Together, the two developments indicate that writing about human lives became a major focus, and that suggests a heightened interest and valuation of the individual. Whereas the medievals recorded only the legendary, even mythologized, lives of saints and heroes, the postmedieval world developed a biographical interest in the life stories of others, notably literary figures. This began during the sixteenth century and led to radical changes in biography during the seventeenth century. A new attitude emerged—biographies should be factually accurate and should portray the individual (Altick, 1965). Even in the eighteenth century, though, individuality did not mean personality. In biography, portraying the individual meant describing where he lived, whom he married, what he achieved, how he died, and the like. If a biographer did include any personal material, it was all lumped together into a miscellaneous final chapter, often with the biographer's apology for including such trivia (Altick, 1965), pp. 192–193). This changed abruptly in the nineteenth century, but not before then.

The emphasis on individuality increased partly by a change in patterns of family identification. People gradually ceased to feel that their identities and the courses of their lives were essentially or irrevocably determined by their family descent. This "loss of a sense of trusteeship to the lineage" (Stone, 1977, p. 409) helped put the definition of identity on an individual rather than a collective basis. A related development was the decline in the power and importance of kin, that is, all relatives except the immediate family. Loyalty to the state and to one's religious sect replaced loyalty to the extended family matrix (Stone, 1977). The direction of political evolution turned from the medieval organization of localities comprised of families and toward the modern organization of states comprised of individuals. A further sign of the movement toward individuality and institutionalized individualism was the decline of vendetta justice (Stone, 1977). In vendetta justice family members were interchangeable; the vendetta was satisfied by murdering the son or cousin of the offending person. Similarly, a treason or crime by one person might have led to the punishment of the entire family. By the end of the sixteenth century in England, however, vendetta justice was largely replaced with the more modern form of justice which punishes only the offender (Stone, 1977). Thus the prevailing concept and practice of justice switched from identity based on family and lineage to individual identity.

Two final comments about individuality should be made. First, the appearance of the concept of the hidden self is compatible with individualistic thinking. Seeing the individual as having an internal space implies a new view of people as self-contained units. This is associated with a new emphasis on individual awareness. Moreover, these new ideas of internal space and self-awareness are reflected in the evolution of language (Rosenthal, 1984; Whyte, 1960), for powerful thoughts require words to express them. The word "self" first was a reflexive pronoun and an adjective that meant both "own" (as in ownership) and "same." It became a noun late in the Middle Ages, but as such it had a bad connotation: "Oure own self we sal deny, And follow oure lord god al-myghty" (ca. 1400, as quoted by the *Oxford English Dictionary*). By the same token, the word "conscious" is derived from a Latin expression for "to know with," unlike its modern meaning, which refers to knowing by oneself alone. In the sixteenth and seventeenth centuries, these words took on their modern meanings. "Conscious" was first seen in English with its modern meaning in 1620, and the noun "consciousness" in 1678. The connotations of self abruptly changed from bad to good at the end of the Middle Ages, and it suddenly began to appear in numerous compound words. Thus, in 1549 the word "self-praise" appeared, and by the end of that century it had been joined by self-love, self-pride, and self-regard, among others. Self-knowledge, self-preservation, self-made, self-pity, self-interest, and self-confidence appeared in the first part of the seventeenth century. The compound "self-consciousness" appeared in 1690. In German the pattern and dates were approximately the same as in English, and in French the pattern occurred slightly later. These linguistic developments attest to the rising importance of the individual self and its inner awareness.

Second, the shift toward conceiving of persons as essentially containing inner spaces also meant a shift away from equating the person with his or her social role. In the sixteenth century the person became an individual unity with a separate existence independent of place in society (Trilling, 1971). By the eighteenth century social and institutional roles were understood as something added to the person, not part of the essence of the person (MacIntyre, 1981, p. 56). Thus the early modern period accomplished the conceptual separation of the person from his or her position(s) in the social order.

3. *Privacy.* Today we tend to regard privacy as a fundamental human right and a universal human need. But the medievals apparently got along quite well with minimal privacy; it may not even have occurred to them to want privacy. "In fact, until the end of the seventeenth century, nobody was ever left alone," asserts Ariès (1962). Only in the eighteenth century did rooms begin to have specialized functions, such as being reserved as bedrooms for the house's inhabitants, with the result that guests confined their visits to parlors and dining rooms. Prior to that a visitor could simply walk through any room in the house; at bedtime, portable beds were set up in various rooms, and overnight guests would typically pass through others' bedrooms on the way to their own bedrooms (Ariès, 1962).

In England as well as France, architectural innovations to enhance privacy first appeared in the eighteenth century. In particular, houses began to have corridors. Each room then opened onto a corridor, so that each room could be reached without one's having to pass through several other rooms. Privacy was also enhanced in eighteenth century England by the gradual replacement of "live-in" servants with servants who did not sleep in the same house with their employers (Stone, 1977).

The desire for and cultivation of privacy reflect the attitude that some part of life does not belong to public society. Privacy is conceptually related to the valuation of individuality, and it symbolizes the hidden self. Both privacy and individuality emphasize and strengthen the single self by separating it from the broader network of society. The separation of public and private domains of life (cf. Sennett, 1974) laid the foundation for a view of the self as being in conflict with society, a view which became widely influential during the nineteenth century.

4. *Death.* The importance of death as a source of authentic individuality has been emphasized in this century by existential and phenomenological thinkers (e.g., Camus, 1942; Heidegger, 1927). Heidegger described three ways in which death is a means of individuation. First, death delineates you precisely; what dies is exactly you and nothing else. Second, in an important sense, death accepts no substitutes; it is the one thing you have to do yourself. Third, death marks the end of your "becoming," or the transformation of your potentialities into actualities. The theme of Camus' novel *The Stranger* is that a passionless, apathetic man living an empty life is awakened to authenticity only by the realization of his impending death. In addition, mystical disciplines (e.g., Castaneda, 1972; Blofeld, 1970) have emphasized the usefulness of an awareness of death to lead the individual to a better understanding of self.

If awareness of death is thus intimately linked to self-awareness and individuation, then the history of death can provide evidence about the historical evolution of self-awareness and individuality. The evidence appears to confirm the argument that individuality became important during the early modern period. During this time the narrow focus on death in the final hour was abandoned. Instead, clergymen and others urged people to be aware of death throughout their lives, and it became fashionable to surround oneself with pictures and objects that reminded one of the brevity of human life (Ariès, 1981). As an awareness of death was diffused throughout the life span, the individuating power of this awareness presumably became more effective. This reinforces what we have already observed as an increasing awareness of individuality.

Attitudes toward death during the early modern period also curiously parallel the emphasis on the contrast between appearances and reality. In early modern Europe there was for a century and a half widespread hysterical fear of being buried alive (Ariès, 1981). People were afraid of seeming to die but actually being alive. This fear was reflected not only in proliferation of stories about premature burials but also in the wills and testaments people left. Many people left detailed instructions for ensuring that they were completely dead before burial was to be permitted! These included leaving the putative corpse lying for several days with bells attached to it so that any movement would create a sound, and even cutting the foot with a razor to ascertain whether the body would cry out (Ariès, 1981).

Thus early modern attitudes about death symbolize both the increased concern with individual fate, as a theme to be reflected on throughout life, and the tension between appearances and their underling reality.

5. *Choice of mate.* According to the historian Lawrence Stone (1977), a basic change in family formation and organization occurred during the second half of the early modern period. The absolute power of the father declined and was replaced by the view that there

should be positive emotional ties within the family. Possibly as a corollary, it became increasingly necessary to arrange marriages that held the promise of good companionate relationships, which entailed consulting the preferences of the person who was to be married.

The traditional system had decided marriages without necessarily paying any attention to personal preferences. Parents chose spouses for their children on the basis of "economic or social or political consolidation or aggrandizement of the family" (Stone, 1977, p. 182). In other words, one's marriage was determined by and for the family. This system was replaced during the early modern period by a system under which an individual chose his or her own spouse and parents had only veto power. The spread of the new system coincided with an increasing reliance on individual motives in mate selection. People chose spouses who seemed likely to be compatible companions and with whom they shared a friendly affection. (This is still quite different from the modern reliance on passionate "romantic" love as the primary basis for selecting mates. Stone asserts that even into the eighteenth century parents and children agreed that passionate and physical attractions were bad bases for marriage because they were unreliable and temporary mental disturbances.)

Marriage is a major component of identity. Indeed, in view of the limited rights and opportunities available to women in past centuries, the choice of husband was probably the most momentous decision in the formation of many a woman's adult identity. Thus a basic change in the way marriage was decided signifies a major shift in the construction of identity. In seventeenth and eighteenth century England such a change occurred (Stone, 1977) in the shift from an institutional to an individual criterion as decisive in mate selection. Spouses were chosen by personal preferences and expectations for happiness; they were not based on the financial and social interests of the extended family. That shift is symptomatic of a general trend—identity had been determined by the institutions into which one was born, but increasingly it became determined instead by personal acts of choice based on criteria that were supposed to exist inside the person.

6. *Childhood and growth.* If the late Middle Ages had an increased sense of the *continuity* of the single human life, the early modern period contributed an increased awareness of human growth and development. A new view of childhood emerged, and it was put into practice with a vengeance.

The "discovery of childhood" began in the thirteenth century but became widespread only in the sixteenth century according to Ariès (1962). Prior to that, he says, children were not considered a different kind of creature from adults. Ariès is not talking about infancy; an infant cannot be mistaken for an adult. But late childhood, which runs from age six or seven to puberty, is an age at which people can walk and talk and take care of themselves sufficiently. Given that medieval life required relatively little responsible or mature *choice* from people, there was no need to consider the eight-year-old as qualitatively different from the thirty-year-old. Beginning around the sixteenth century, however, that qualitative difference *was* accepted, and of course that distinction continues to be accepted today.

For example, one feature that supposedly distinguishes children from adults is the alleged "innocence" of children, their supposed lack of knowledge about or interest in sexual matters. Ariès (1962) observes that today we consider it wrong and even perhaps harmful to discuss sex or display erotica in front of children, but the medieval mentality had no such concerns. Ariès' arguments have been influential, although some other scholars have disputed his evidence (e.g., Hunt, 1970).

Actually, *two* concepts about late childhood emerged during the sixteenth century (Ariès, 1962). The first regarded children as amusing and beautiful creatures upon whose antics parents (and others) doted fondly. This was soon supplanted by a second attitude, which regarded children as unformed persons who needed guidance, protection, and education in order to become good adults. This second attitude attributed to the child the potentiality to become either good or bad. It followed that adult efforts were necessary to ensure that the child would grow up to be good. In practice this meant that family and school discipline became strict to the point of harshness. Ariès' observations are based in France, but Stone cites similar developments in England. "There can be no doubt … that more children were being beaten in the sixteenth and early seventeenth centuries, over a longer age span, than ever before" (Stone, 1977, p. 117).

The important implication of these new attitudes toward childhood is the enhanced awareness of human development, change, and potentiality. That awareness opens the way for some identity problems; the more you think of yourself as changing during life, the harder it is to find aspects of self that remain constant and thus unify the self into an identity. I have listed continuity across time as one of the two defining criteria of identity. That criterion is hard to satisfy if the continuity is that of a process of change rather than that of a stable component.

Moreover, the recognition that a person has various potentialities for future development raises the issue of choice. Once the firm moral and religious bases for making choices are abandoned, identity problems can be concerned with issues of choice. Indeed, the whole functional aspect of individual potentiality became a gigantic problem of choice by the nineteenth century.

But that is getting ahead of the story, because the early modern period did not yet confront such identity problems. The developments of the sixteenth to eighteenth centuries simply fulfilled the necessary conditions for making such problems possible. All six themes I have used in discussing the early modern period contribute to the identity problems faced by individuals in the centuries that followed. Conceiving of an inner or hidden self paved the way for making self-knowledge problematic. The increased concern with human individuality made the issue of individual identity important; it focused attention on it, as did the increased concern with individual death and fate. The separation of social and personal spheres of life required a new complexity in the self, as did requiring the self to contain criteria for making choices (as in selecting a spouse) that defined adult identity.

The end of the early modern period did not yet experience identity per se as a problem, but identity was much closer to becoming a problem than it had been three centuries earlier.

PURITANISM

Puritanism was an important cultural development of the early modern period, and it had its effect on identity and self-definition. The Puritans were a Protestant sect who based their practices on the teachings of John Calvin. They came to national power in England for two decades in the middle of the seventeenth century. After that they were defeated, and many left the country. Most of those who left came to "New England" (America) where they established Puritan communities which flourished into the nineteenth century. Thus their dominance lasted longer in America than it had in England, and it is reasonable to assume that their effects on the national psyche were stronger and longer lasting in America.

Most historians seem to agree that one main legacy of Puritanism was a vast increase in self-consciousness, and Puritan beliefs provide a good basis for that increase. Calvin emphasized that some people ("the Elect") were predestined to enter heaven, but most would spend eternity in hell. (Puritans believed in hell quite literally.) Because God knows everything, God knows what will happen to you; your eternal fate is already sealed when you are born. Calvin added a corollary that he regarded as minor but that had major consequences—there were ways in which you could tell whether you were among the Elect. But Calvin also said not to spend time wondering whether you were one of the Elect. It is doubtful, however, that the average Puritan could resist wondering whether he or she was to receive eternal salvation or eternal damnation! As a result, Puritans kept a close watch over their thoughts and acts in order to detect any possible signs of impiety or faithlessness that might reveal their eternal fate (Weintraub, 1978).

A second reason for the Puritan enhancement of individual self-consciousness was the highly private nature of their religion. Catholics did not have to face their God alone; they had an elaborate system of priests, nuns, rituals, and saints to mediate with God. The Protestants generally downplayed that structure, and the Puritans especially sought to do away with it. The Puritan thus did face God alone, in the privacy of the individual mind. Thus religious life was greatly *individualized* by Protestant and especially Puritan theology. It is worth adding that these trends favoring privacy and individuality were consistent with major themes of the early modern period.

The Puritan self, then, can be described as having an important hidden part; the acts and thoughts of the self are merely clues about the permanent and unchanging nature of the hidden self. Moreover, the eternal condition of this hidden self was either very good or very bad. A lifetime of human behavior, however, rarely reveals an uninterrupted and coherent pattern of either impeccable virtue or unmitigated depravity. As the average Puritan tried to infer the absolute and eternal condition of his soul from the inconsistent, ambiguous data of his daily life, something became obvious—the temptation to leap to an unwarranted conclusion that one was among the Elect. Puritans thus began to recognize the pervasive possibility of self-deception.

Puritans felt a strong aversion to hypocrisy (Weintraub, 1978). To some extent, this can be seen as an extension of the general concern over insincerity and deceptive self-presentation (e.g., Trilling, 1971) that characterized the early modern period. With the Puritans, however, the concern was not over the deliberate, calculated deception of others but rather focused on the temptation to deceive oneself. You *wanted* to believe yourself predestined to heaven, but were your virtuous acts signs of inner goodness or merely attempts to bolster your pride by creating the appearance of virtue? Did you take pride (a sin) in your good deeds, which would imply hypocrisy rather than true virtue? Yet how could someone deny any feeling of satisfaction from doing good deeds, or any pleasure at the possible implication that he might be one of God's chosen few? And so forth. The endless inner struggles of the Puritans are preserved for us in the unprecedented number of diaries they wrote; these reveal the Puritans' confrontation with the possibility of self-deception.

Concern over self-deception is very different from a concern over the insincerity or deception of others. Once the possibility of self-deception is accepted, self-knowledge can never be certain. For example, when the sixteenth century writer Montaigne described himself at length, he justified the project partly on the basis of its epistemological superiority over other forms of knowledge. For Montaigne, self-knowledge was regarded as precise, comprehensive, and (given some effort) perfect, but no cultural heir of Puritanism could ever again regard self-knowledge so highly. Indeed, the problem of self-deception implied that self-knowledge was *less* reliable than some other forms of knowledge precisely because there was so much incentive to distort and deceive in drawing conclusions about oneself.

Thus far I have discussed an increase in self-consciousness and an increased recognition of self-deception as two Puritan legacies. Two additional features of Puritanism pertaining to child development are relevant to identity—the practice of "breaking the child's will" and the adolescent rebellion or "sins of youth." Both patterns existed before Puritanism, but they were especially prevalent among the Puritans. I shall describe them together because they are related.

Puritan child-rearing techniques were linked to their belief that most (or all) children were innately depraved and in need of stern discipline to be steered toward righteousness (Greven, 1977; I rely on his discussion of "evangelical" Protestants in America). Privately obsessed with their own sinfulness, the Puritans considered the natural self an enemy of virtue. Child-rearing therefore took the form of a program designed to break the child's will. Complete subjugation and obedience of children to parents was stressed. Because of this, Puritans favored an isolated nuclear family over a family having numerous relatives, guests, servants, and so forth. They feared that grandparents or others might indulge the children or otherwise interfere with parental discipline. Children grew up with stern consciences and a well-cultivated readiness to submit to authority (Greven, 1977).

During adolescence many of these young Puritans, especially perhaps the males, went through something of an adolescent rebellion. In this rebellious phase the young person would indulge various lusts and sinful appetites. Presumably this occurred in part because the adolescent gave up on himself as a hopeless sinner once the sexual desires of puberty compounded his already strong sense of badness. The "sins of youth" phase often ended with an abrupt religious experience in which the young person's religious and authoritarian personality reasserted itself. A central part of these religious conversion experiences was that of submission to society's authoritarian patterns and ideals. The young Puritan dutifully returned to the fold and the mold (Greven, 1977).

The significance of these two trends deserves comment. The first, the emphasis on breaking the child's will, goes along with the early modern pattern of strict and sometimes cruel child-rearing. As stated earlier, that broader pattern is indicative of increased sensitivity to human development and potentiality. The second trend, the sins of youth, is an important forerunner of the modern identity crises experienced by adolescents.

One last feature of the psychological legacy of Puritanism, or in this case, of Protestantism in general, deserves mention—the emphasis on work. Ever since Max Weber's classic turn-of-the-century work (*The Protestant Ethic and the Spirit of Capitalism*) it has been common to describe the "Protestant ethic" as a set of values that stresses the importance of hard work as a means (and indication) of spiritual improvement. Work was valued for its own sake and not for extrinsic rewards such as money. If there was an extrinsic motivation in work, it was Calvin's suggestion that success in one's work was another sign that one was among the Elect because God would tend to bless the efforts of his chosen few. Thus a little extra hard work might tip the balance and produce the results which would imply that God was on your side.

The early American concept of success may well have been primarily one of inner success—the triumph of self-discipline, reason, and diligence over one's carefree, lazy, or pleasure-seeking impulses (Lasch, 1978). Ben Franklin's pithy maxims (e.g., "God helps them that help themselves") are often quoted as indicative of the Puritan emphasis on the spiritual significance of work (e.g., Lasch, 1978; Weintraub, 1978). One important consequence of this newly spiritual attitude toward work was a heightened identification with one's career, or one's "calling" as it was then known. The notion that one had a "personal calling" to a particular kind of work meant that one's destiny was intimately connected to one's occupation. The particular job thus gained in importance as an identity component.

EIGHTEENTH CENTURY AS TRANSITION

In the next chapter I discuss the Romantic period, which contained sweeping changes in identity and ushered in the new view of the human self that dominated nineteenth century thought. Of course, the Romantic developments did not arise spontaneously. In this brief section I cover the eighteenth century developments that prepared the way for the nineteenth century's concept of human identity.

At the root of the eighteenth century trends was the decline of Christianity, a difficult topic to write about because it is so easily misunderstood. I do not mean that everyone stopped believing in Christianity; there are still many devout Christians today. Nor do I mean that the most influential group or the majority rejected Christian beliefs, because outright repudiation of faith was rare. The institutional Church came under criticism, but that had happened earlier. Perhaps the best way to express the decline of Christianity during the eighteenth century is to say that it lost its grip on the collective mentality and was demoted from a major to a minor role in the daily lives of most people.

It is easy to see that Christianity's position in the collective mind of Western culture has declined. One need only consider how many modern works of literature, music, or art are inspired by a positive attitude toward Christianity and then compare the number with the Renaissance. The decline of Christianity has been a long process, and critical steps in this decline were taken in the eighteenth century.

Certainly there was outspoken criticism of Christianity during the eighteenth century. The best-known critics were perhaps Voltaire in Europe and Paine in America. The intellectual community in general considered itself in "the age of reason" and felt free to use logic to question Christian creed and practices. The typical result was not a wholesale rejection of religion. Rather, as in Deism, the result was a belief that a Supreme Being had set up the universe to run according to natural laws and had then more or less ceased to meddle in it. Psychologically, this attitude meant that God existed but didn't matter very much. For the pursuit of knowledge, scientific observation and philosophical analysis were preferred to biblical exegesis. For practical affairs, hard work and shrewdness were more effective than prayer.

Thus although the core doctrines of Christianity survived the eighteenth century, many consequences and applications of the Christian world view did not. The demise of two Christian ideas during the eighteenth century was related to important trends finances. This was greatly complicated, however, by the fact that much of the wealth was drifting into the hands of the bourgeoisie.

The bourgeoisie knew that, money or no, they ranked below the aristocrats. If they could marry into the aristocracy, however, they felt they would be joining "the quality." So they began to expend considerable effort on learning to pass for "gentlemen" and "ladies." One's only hope of marrying into the aristocracy depended on effective concealment of one's humble origins. Toward the end of the eighteenth century, England had an increasing number of boarding schools that trained young, middle-class girls to pass for upper-class young ladies (Stone, 1977, p. 231).

Thus, during the eighteenth century social rank, which had long been a major component of identity, began to break down. Two main criteria of social rank, wealth and lineage, began to conflict because of a new middle class, and intermarriage between the humbly born rich and the highly born poor created further ambiguity. The legitimacy of the system of social rank was also undermined as people abandoned the medieval Christian view that God intentionally ensured that aristocrats were better people. The newer Calvinist belief that divine favor would be helped by financial success also helped to undermine the older view that a noble birth was a sign of God's favor. This was especially true in America, where the influence of Puritanism helped to prevent the establishment of a monarchy after the Revolution. Thus both in practice and in principle, the age-old system of assigning identity based on social rank deteriorated to the point of crisis.

So far I have considered the first of the two developments related to the decline of Christianity—namely, the abandonment of the medieval Christian political philosophy. The second development concerns the Christian moral scheme. The deterioration of this is linked to two important themes in the history of identity. The first is individuality; the second is the concept of human potentiality.

Morality and potentiality. In the medieval conception of mankind, the individual's goal in life was the achievement of Christian salvation. This meant going to heaven after death. The means for achieving it were twofold: participation in religious ritual, and daily practice of faith and virtue. Over the course of time, prevailing views placed more and more weight on the latter. Individuals were thus provided with a concept of human potential that gave meaning and purpose to life; they were also provided with a reasonably clear-cut set of procedures for fulfilling that potential. When Christianity lost its grip on society, however, this aspect of human identity fell into conceptual chaos.

According to MacIntyre, the traditional view of morality had three elements. The first was "untutored human nature" (1981, p. 52), often understood as being no better (and sometimes much worse) than the natural state of lower animals. The second was the concept of human potential or perfection, "man-as-he-could-be-if-he realized-his-telos." The third was the rules and precepts of morality, which enabled the individual to pass from the first state to the second.

The decline of Christianity removed the second element from the system. This removal left morality with only the concept of ordinary, perhaps depraved, human nature plus a set of rules to follow. But why should anyone follow such rules? They had lost their functional purpose. MacIntyre analyzes the philosophical exertions of eighteenth century moral philosophers as attempts to answer the unanswerable question of why anyone should behave in a morally good fashion. Even Kant, widely recognized as the greatest moral philosopher of that century, eventually conceded that a moral system falls apart conceptually without a teleological context. But this was not just a problem for philosophical debate. By the late nineteenth century, society in general was concerned with the issue of whether morality could survive without religious context.

For identity, the important point was that the person ceased to be regarded in functional terms. The concept of what a person was ceased to be a *functional* concept. Instead, "man is thought of as an individual prior to and apart from all roles" (MacIntyre, 1981, p. 56). To understand this it is necessary to recall that the earlier medieval concept of virtue included fulfilling the tasks and duties of one's station in society. The way the medievals understood it, the person was equated with the social roles. According to the medieval view, *in order to fulfill one's potential, one had to do the tasks assigned by society to him or her.*

When that system broke down, however, the person ceased to be equated with the social role. The Christian concept of human potentiality lost its appeal and powerful influence. In the new (eighteenth century) view, persons could be permitted to choose their own forms of potential to try to fulfill, instead of just accepting, what society assigned to them. A person's potentiality thus became an unknown instead of a fixed and known quantity.

In the medieval view, a blacksmith's oldest son had a moral obligation to become a loyal, diligent, and pious blacksmith himself. To reject that duty would jeopardize his chances of going to heaven. In the eighteenth century view, the blacksmith's son did not have a moral obligation to become a blacksmith himself. If he felt such an obligation, it was probably due to family pressure and was not based on the will of God. If he did yield to it and become a blacksmith, that was still not a means toward salvation. Moreover, he remained perhaps a person first and a blacksmith second.

The basic understanding of the individual's relation to society thus changed. People gradually ceased to equate the individual with the individual's place in society, and they ceased to feel that the person was morally obligated to fulfill the role assigned by society. In addition, fulfilling the assigned role was no longer the main means of achieving one's potential.

The decline of Christianity thus removed the Christian context and basis for morality. Morality survived as a set of rules about right and wrong, but morality was no longer the means used for fulfilling one's potentiality. As the concept of human potentiality became problematic with the decline of Christianity, the potentiality aspect of identity became a problem both in terms of technique and goals. This problem is essential to an understanding of the developments of the early nineteenth century—the Romantic concerns with love, passion, and creativity. Moreover, the decline of Christian moral and political views erased the requirement that the individual be content with his lot in society. This strengthened the general movement toward greater individuality because the concept of the person was separated from the concept of his or her place in the social structure.

SUMMARY

In medieval Europe the important components of identity were largely defined for the individual by social structure and institutions. The medieval mentality did not place much emphasis on the uniqueness and worth of each individual. Still, several trends prepared the way for the valuing of individuality. One set of trends included a revision of Christian attitudes and practices to emphasize individual judgment, individual participation in

Church ritual, and the use of individual viewpoints to understand the Church's collective themes and truths. Alongside these trends, we can observe a growing literary interest in themes pertaining to the individual perspective and intrapersonal conflict.

The transition from the medieval to the early modern period included two developments important for identity. First, the Protestant Reformation split the ideological consensus among the dominant classes about the correct version of fundamental Christian truth. Instead of being a firm basis for identity, Christian belief became itself somewhat problematic—and became a problem of identity. Second, social mobility made it quite possible to change one's rank in society, at least to some extent. Thus, one major component of identity (social rank) came to depend on individual achievement rather than on passive assignment.

In many areas the early modern period (1500 to 1800) witnessed a dramatic rise in individualistic attitudes and values, preparing the way for the modern problem of identity. New concepts of the hidden or inner self revealed the difficulty of knowing the true selves of others, and this was a step toward understanding that self-knowledge could be problematic. An increased desire for privacy symbolized both the emphasis on individuality and the split between public and private life. Concern over individual fate was reflected in early modern attitudes toward death, in the revision of marriage customs that left choice of spouse up to the potential mates themselves, and in new biographical practices. Finally, a new understanding of human growth and development emerged and was reflected in new attitudes about childhood.

To these larger trends the Puritans contributed an enhanced self-consciousness and an enhanced awareness of individual self-deception. In addition, they gave work a spiritual significance.

Uncoupling and Narratives
of the Self

By LESLIE IRVINE

People are not pulled into CoDA by a corrupt recovery juggernaut. They are pushed
there by the disruption that comes with "uncoupling," or ending a relationship. If
codependency is "about" anything, it is about resolving the disruption that uncoupling does to the self. With very few exceptions, people seek out CoDA after the breakup
of a serious, committed relationship or in a relationship's terminal stages. Every one of
the thirty-six people I interviewed had done so. Breaking up was a constant theme in
the meetings I attended. In some cases, the breakups had to do with children. A divorce
separates a father from his children and he must adjust to seeing them only on weekends.
Or, a sporadically employed, alcoholic, thirty-something son wants to move back home
for the third time, and his mother, tired of having money stolen from her purse, wants to
bring herself to say "no." This kind of uncoupling certainly differs from separation and
divorce. Nevertheless, it can bring similar social and emotional disruption. Consequently,
some people in this situation also seek support in CoDA. More often, however, the breakups involved divorce. Since people who divorce typically remarry within a few years, and
since one divorce increases the likelihood of a second, some of the people I encountered
had experienced the end of two or more marriages. The same logic applies to cohabiting
relationships. People who cohabit usually split up or marry within about a year and a
half (see Cherlin 1992; see also Blumstein and Schwartz 1983). If cohabiting couples
marry, the somewhat "liberated" attitude that allowed them to cohabit also increases
the likelihood that they will eventually divorce. This first divorce, in turn, increases the
likelihood that they will remarry and divorce again. By the time a person reaches forty or
forty-five—roughly the most common age range of the CoDA members I observed—he
or she may have a history of several failed relationships.[1] Melody Beattie noted this

\n

characteristic—although she attributed it differently—when she observed that "multiple marriages are common in people recovering from codependency" (1990, 209). (I argue that multiple relationship failures may lead certain people to consider the codependency discourse as a means of making sense of what went wrong; I do not believe that there is an underlying codependency that leads them into unhappy relationships, which is how Beattie would put it.) Actual marital status is largely irrelevant, however. As Weiss explains, "It is separation, not divorce, that disrupts the structure of the individual's social and emotional life" (1975, 4). That disruption, and the hope of resolving it, draws people to CoDA.

Of all the disruption that uncoupling causes, the disruption of the experience of selfhood is no doubt the greatest. Peter Marris (1974), who has done one of the few extant studies on responses to loss, concurs that "the fundamental crisis of bereavement [and here he includes divorce] arises, not from the loss of others, but the loss of self" (33). When two people begin a commitment, their identities gradually merge so that the two form the single social unit known as a "couple." They make common friends, usually other couples. They lead a joint social life; a host or hostess does not consider extending an invitation to one partner, but not the other. They establish a common household. They open a joint bank account. The phone listing appears under both names. They may pay joint income taxes. They plan a common future. They coordinate schedules; individual departures from the routine require explanation, if not a form of permission. In short, two separate individuals become *a couple*.

Doing so involves far more than settling these practical and "administrative" details, however. Love songs often contain the phrase "I've built my whole world around you," and for good reason. The other person increasingly becomes part of the stories you tell about yourself and, consequently, that person becomes a part of you. Initially, the other person is an audience for the storytelling that begins during courtship, with the revealing of histories, likes, and dislikes. The audience role continues with the daily recounting of events that occurred at home or work, but the other person gradually joins those events, and a shared history emerges. Storytelling of this sort has a purpose beyond merely conveying information. Stories enclose narratives of the self within them. In the telling, people reassure themselves that they exist. As their stories unfold, they reaffirm the existence of the self as audience to themselves (see Schafer 1981, 1992). The stories people tell about themselves include significant other people—as audiences, co-authors, participants, and critics. The level of disclosure that characterizes intimacy means that this is all the more so for couples.

Studies of uncoupling describe breaking up as reversing the merger that took place during the relationship's formation. The process involves "confirm[ing] an identity independent of the coupled identity created with the other person" (Vaughan 1986, 28; see also Weiss 1975; Riessman 1990). Two people who had publicly and privately merged their identities have to establish themselves once more as separate individuals. Again, this manifests itself in tangible or practical acts, such as finding separate places to live, separate bank accounts, and new telephone listings. For women, it can mean a change of name, which in turn involves innumerable bureaucratic inconveniences. It can entail serious economic loss, especially for women with children.[2] Moreover, it can require rethinking the structure of your day. Simple acts of eating and sleeping lose their taken-for-granted quality. When do you eat, without the "cues" from a partner who has prepared or shared your meals? When do you sleep, without signals from the other that the day has ended? Uncoupling also requires filling a "skill gap" by doing things, such as cooking or keeping track of bills, that the other had done while the relationship was intact.

But just as becoming a couple involves more than sharing a phone number and checking account, uncoupling, too, involves more than establishing physical separation.[3] Some of the members of CoDA described the experience to me in these words:

> It was completely draining. I lost my whole life. *(woman, thirty-six)*

> Absolutely a nightmare. *(woman, thirty-nine)*

> What does it feel like? It feels empty. That you can't figure a freaking thing out. That you feel so ... so helpless, *(man, forty-two)*

> I was devastated. My life stopped for about four months, *(woman, forty five)*

> Everything all of a sudden just ... everything fell apart, *(man, fifty)*

The language is telling: "I lost my whole life." "It feels empty." "My life stopped ..." What they are describing, although no one put it in these particular words, is the loss of selfhood. They had lost the ability to tell stories of themselves that made sense. Marriage and committed relationships provide formulas and contexts for your stories. They are not free-floating, as others have argued (see Baudrillard 1983). People do not simply make up stories about themselves on a whim. Rather, they draw plots, scripts, casts, and audiences from institutions. Although I will refine my use of the term somewhat in the following chapter, I mean "institution" to refer to patterns of activities organized around a similar goal. Marriage and relationships, as institutions, provide opportunities for people to "be" or "become" themselves because they anchor the stories told by those within them. When a relationship ends, that institutional anchor is dislodged. This is at the heart of the "narrative wreckage" that the members of CoDA described.[4] Uncoupling disrupted the continuity in their existing stock of stories. It derailed the plots. It removed key characters. It made future chapters or episodes unimaginable. It meant that two people whose language had evolved from "I" to "we" must now think of themselves as "I" again. Doing so does not come easily:

During the time that we were splitting up, when Gina hadn't left yet, I ran into an acquaintance of hers. She said, "Aren't you Gina's boyfriend?" I didn't know what to say. I think I said, "Well, I'm her future ex-boyfriend," or something. But I hadn't thought about what to call myself, and it felt really strange. *(man, age forty-two)*

You know, society seems to have this rule about talking about ex-s. You're not supposed to bash them, but you're not supposed to go around saying good things about them either. I mean, if your ex- was so great, why aren't you still together, right? So you can't really say anything about them. So here's this person, who's been an important part of your life for years, maybe, and you can't even talk about them. What do you do with those memories? It's like you have to deny them, and it's so screwed up. *(woman, age thirty-nine)*

Implicit in becoming an "I" again is the question of *"Who will I be now, without this other person?"* In this sense, uncoupling does have a positive side to it, in that it offers opportunities to pursue avenues not possible within the relationship. But there are often obstacles to taking hold of those opportunities and answering the question of "Who will I be?" For with the loss comes the specter of self-doubt: *Can I trust my judgment, in light of having failed?*

The implication of failure may seem implausible in times when divorce and separation have become commonplace. Yet, even today, "relationships are almost universally viewed in success/failure terms," writes McCall (1982). The ability to maintain a relationship is "a major test of adulthood" (Vaughan 1986, 160). Therefore, "any party to a terminated or even a spoiled relationship is tarred by failure" (219). Even if you do not take your *own* divorce as a sign of failure, others often see it in that light.[5] Research suggests that, while divorce *itself* has become more accepted, divorced *people* have not (Gerstel 1987). The process is still widely held as indicative of some personal flaw. For example, socializing with couples becomes difficult after uncoupling, and not only because of the inevitable "splitting of friends" (see Gerstel 1987; see also Spanier and Thompson 1984; Weiss 1975). Divorced people report feeling that married friends exclude them from social interaction because they seem to find them threatening in some way (see Gerstel 1987). Married couples may fear that the experience will "rub off" on them, or that a now-single friend will move in on a husband or wife. As a woman in CoDA explained, even the act of telling others elicits their judgment:

There's no booklet that comes with your divorce papers, you know, telling you how to be a divorced person. Marriage comes with a set of rules, more or less. Even if there are no rules, everything is pretty optimistic. It's cute and giggly when you have to decide things like what name to take. People smile at you. Divorce doesn't work like that. You have to figure it out on your own. You tell people you're using a different name now and they don't smile. They look down and go, "Ohhh." *(age thirty-eight)*

The stories that people tell after uncoupling must redeem this experience of failure. On the way to answering the question of "Who will I be now," they must also answer the question of *What happened?* Lurking beneath this are questions such as *Why me? What's wrong with me?* And *what am I really like?* (McCall 1982; La Gaipa 1982).[6] To provide satisfying answers, uncoupling stories must take the form of "accounts" (Scott and Lyman 1968). Accounts are "linguistic devices [that] explain unanticipated or untoward behavior" (46). They either mitigate responsibility for your conduct or accept responsibility but neutralize the consequences of doing so. Accounts that accomplish the former are known as "excuses"; those that accomplish the latter are called "justifications," By either relieving or neutralizing personal responsibility, accounts help to diminish blame and, therefore, reduce the effects of stigma. Moreover, accounts not only convey information to *others;* they also explain your own conduct *to yourself.* In so doing, they restore your own sense of self-approval.[7]

For accounts to be honored, they have to use vocabulary that is "anchored in the background expectations of the situation" (Scott and Lyman 1968, 53). Self-consciously or not, audiences have standards for what they will find credible. Anyone who has been late for an important engagement or stopped for speeding knows this well. Accounts must be consistent with what "everybody knows" about what they purport to explain, or at least with what "everybody" in a particular setting "knows." In the case of uncoupling, accounts have to convey legitimate reasons for breaking up. In middle-class, American culture, it is generally legitimate to emphasize the importance of the individual over the relationship. Although few people would give fulfillment as the sole reason for breaking up, the sense of obligation to oneself constitutes an appropriate explanation for doing so. Studies suggest that even those who do not have this view initially come to acquire it eventually as a means of making positive sense of the loss (Weiss 1975; Vaughan 1986; Riessman 1990). People repair the "narrative wreckage" of uncoupling, and, consequently, redeem damaged selves, using accounts that follow standards set by their audiences—including themselves. These standards—and new audiences—-then become important in the revision of the story of who they are.

There are, then, crucial ways that selfhood, as a narrative accomplishment, depends on institutions. Marriages and relationships, as institutions, provide anchors for the stories of the self. When these anchors are lost, others must replace them. Until then, life "feels empty," and "everything falls apart."

This is not how the contemporary self is supposed to work. For some time, and from a variety of perspectives, scholars have charted the declining importance of institutions for the experience of selfhood.[8] In a classic essay on the experience of "The Real Self," Turner (1976) documented "a long-term shift" away from locating the self socially, in institutions, roles, and values.[9] Alongside this pre-therapeutic ethos, "institutional" self, an "impulsive" orientation had gained strength. The "impulsive" locates the experience of "real" selfhood in "deep, unsocialized, inner impulses" (992).[10] The image evokes the romanticism of the nineteenth-century concept of the self, and some would characterize the "impulsive" type as neo-Romantic (see Anderson 1997).[11] I would add that it is a pillar of the therapeutic ethos.

In both the "institutional" and "impulsive" types, belief in a "real" self still exists. The distinction lies in where people locate it. Recently, however, some have claimed that even the belief in a "real" self, as a permanent, continuous entity, has "cease[d] to be intelligible" (Gergen 1991, 170). The idea of a "real" self has allegedly evolved into an awareness that we are all "populated *with fragments of the other*" (172, emphasis original). This fragmentation is ostensibly well-suited to life in these "postmodern" times. "The cumulative result," writes Kenneth Gergen, "is that we are readied for participation in a world of incoherence, a world of anything-goes" (173).

Perhaps. But judging from the evidence in CoDA, the idea of a "real" self remains inviolable. While the idea of empty, postmodern incoherence may appeal to some academics, a sizeable number of people outside academia are working frantically to create enduring meaning and coherence. Consider what two members of CoDA had to say:

> I recognize that, within me, there's a self—I prefer the term "inner child." And this child knows what's right for me to do, and this child has always been with me, but my codependency has boxed it in. In recovery, I'm trying to set that child free so that my life makes sense. I'll keep working the Program, and I'll see who I was supposed to be, and I'll be that person. *(woman, age forty)*

> All this time, because of codependency, I haven't been able to be myself. I didn't know it, though, until CoDA. Now I can see that there's been a purpose to that, so that I could find out who I am now. You know what they say at the meetings about becoming who you were meant to be, "precious and free"? Well, through working the Program and through sharing and listening to other people, I've learned who I really am, for the first time in my life. *(man, age thirty-nine)*

At CoDA meetings, one concern dominates all others. This is the idea of a "real" self that is solely and completely your own possession. On the surface of things, this seems "impulsively" oriented. The members talk, for example, of finding out who they are "supposed" to be by freeing the "inner child." However, while the "impulsive" self may be what CoDA members *say* they "have," their means of "having" it is wholly "institutional." At the meetings, they learn to piece together events of their lives using an institutionalized formula. Each meeting brings a new installment to the story. The narrator and the listeners situate the new information within the context of existing themes. With each telling, the narrators integrate new experiences and insights into an evolving "socio-biography" (Plummer 1983; Wuthnow 1994), which is a story about one's life and one's formative experiences that is created in a public setting. At each CoDA meeting, the narrators pick up the story where it left off, taking it in a new direction, and taking the story of the self in a new direction, as well. Over the long term, the narrator and the group remember these themes and, consequently, legitimate them as the narrator's identity. As Wuthnow explains, "What a person chooses to share in a group becomes ever more important to that person's identity. The group's affirmation of this identity reinforces and legitimates it" (302).

> I have a self now because, in CoDA, I've learned about why my life has taken its particular path. It's like I know who I am. These people here know me, the real me. *(man, forty-five)*

This is not to say that everyone in CoDA tells exactly the same story. To the contrary, they tell quite *different* stories—using the same formula. Much of the discourse's appeal no doubt stems from its ability to do both, to work at the somewhat universal level of a legitimate account of uncoupling and at the idiosyncratic level of a unique, personal history. At the universal level, codependency's core tenets echo popular beliefs about relationships and uncoupling. "Everybody knows," for example, that no one should have to sacrifice a sense of who he or she "is" for a relationship. Self-sacrifice fell out of favor with the arrival of the therapeutic ethos and the women's movement (see Cancian 1987). As a discourse, codependency legitimates the belief that relationships fail to work, in a universal sense, when people "give away" their "true" selves. Yet, it is not enough to say only that your relationship failed because you gave up the sense of who you "are." This may suffice for the most casual of acquaintances, but you must also have a more detailed explanation of the breakup that will satisfy yourself. Accounts of uncoupling must, therefore, be specific and idiosyncratic as well as universal. If a universal level of explanation would suffice, then people could attribute divorce to simple probability. But when the experience strikes home, statistical probability makes for a poor explanation. Most people never imagine that it will happen to them. Divorce rates may be predictable, but your *own* divorce is unique. Accounts of uncoupling must, therefore, follow cultural standards, but they must simultaneously accommodate individual lives. The codependency discourse's open quality allows people to use it to create accounts that do both. "Becoming" codependent involves an interaction between structure and culture, or between the circumstances of your life and the resources that you can draw upon to make sense of them. As codependency comes to include the variety of experiences that individuals see as problematic, its meaning expands and changes. This evolution represents the individual shaping of culture.

It also represents the institutional shaping of the self. This is best demonstrated in the segment of the meetings devoted to sharing.[12]

Sharing exemplifies a class of events and situations that Robert Zussman calls "autobiographical occasions" (1996). Autobiographical occasions require people to tell stories about themselves. Audiences for these occasions generate different standards for what constitutes a "good" story. The medical history given to a specialist would not satisfy a family member who simply wants to know how you feel (see Frank 1995). The story told during a job interview would not be the same one conveyed to a love interest. Likewise, the audience at CoDA meetings holds specific expectations about what constitutes a "good" story of codependency and recovery. By listening to hundreds of people share, I began to understand their expectations. I began to see the characteristic sequence through which believers in codependency order the events of their lives. This sequence, or "narrative formula," as I call it, follows a five-part chronology that produces a special type of life history.

Each speaker begins by describing the childhood circumstances that fostered his or her codependency. Next comes a recounting of the "dysfunction" that followed from that childhood. In the third part of the formula, the speaker gives a depiction of what is known in Twelve Step groups as "hitting bottom," the low point at which he or she recognized that something was wrong. In the fourth part, the speaker portrays how he or she is "working a Program," or what he or she is doing to "recover" from codependency. Fifth, and finally, the speaker redeems the past by describing the positive changes that have transpired since being in recovery. These five elements appeared in all the group sharing I observed and in every interview. Together, they create a "good" story of codependency, The *content* of each narrative differs among individuals, but the *order* is formulaic and provided by the codependency discourse.

The group attempts to ensure that speakers will share according to the formula, thereby giving members the "good" codependency stories that they expect to hear. The text read at every meeting suggests that only those who have spent "enough time in the Program to generally qualify" as "recovering" share in front of the entire group. By restricting the open sharing to more seasoned members, the group transmits a set of ideas about how recovery works. Moreover, because the more seasoned members tend to tell stories of success, newcomers learn not only *how* recovery works, but *that* it works.

At The House of Life, I learned just how important this is. A woman who seemed to be developmentally disabled began coming to meetings. "Beth" shared after attending only twice. She talked about a string of unrelated events, none of which kept to the chronological formula. She did not have enough time in recovery to inspire the others with tales of improvement. In addition, she volunteered to share two weeks in a row, pleading the need to talk about current crises that lacked any resemblance to a "good" story of codependency. After doing this a few times, the "glue" that normally held the meeting together would dissolve as soon as Beth started speaking. The others began quiet side conversations.

They rolled their eyes. They glanced impatiently at their watches. Through their behavior, the others told her that the meeting had effectively ended, and some even left. On one particularly pathetic day, all the small groups had formed and individual sharing had begun, and Beth was left standing in the middle of the room, holding onto a chair and looking around helplessly. She eventually stopped coming to meetings, although I cannot say for sure why she did so. Beth nevertheless made something clear to me in the few times I saw her: While there are few explicit rules for sharing, there is a "correct" way of doing so.[13] Let me illustrate this systematically.

"ABUSIVE" CHILDHOODS AND THE ORIGINS OF CODEPENDENCY

Codependency, as the text read at each meeting explains, "is born out of our sometimes moderately, sometimes extremely dysfunctional family systems." Since all families are dysfunctional—either "moderately" or "extremely"—all manner of experiences become refrained to this end. In this view, families, by definition, "abuse" their children. As a result, any and everyone's family history becomes reconceptualized as "abusive." Those who do not come from families of addicts or alcoholics—and this includes most CoDA members—find other sorts of problems. I was struck by the ways that seemingly unexceptional childhoods became "dysfunctional." Even in the absence of any obvious family troubles, members went to great lengths to find or invent them. For example, I found that childhood "abuse" included general inadequacy, overwork, and Catholicism.

> There's no drug addiction or alcoholism in my immediate family … Just a super codependent, shame-based family. I just never felt good enough. *(woman, age thirty-six)*

> There was so much abuse in my family. Abuse and neglect. There was always food on the table, always a roof over our heads. But my parents were both working all the time and never there for us. It was so abusive emotionally. Really dysfunctional. *(man, age forty-one)*

> Nobody in my family was alcoholic or into drugs. We were just guilt-ridden Catholics. *(woman, age thirty-eight)*

> My father came from the old country, you know, where a man doesn't hug his kids. I never got a hug from my father. That's so abusive to a kid. *(man, age forty-two)*

Granted, some members of CoDA *did* give accounts of authentic-seeming physical and emotional mistreatment they endured as children. For the most part, however, I found that the term "abuse" was used indiscriminately. When a person cannot recall an instance of "abuse," it does not imply its absence, but its severity. The inability to recall "abuse" allegedly means that the "victim" has "denied" the experience in order to survive it. The "abuse" must have been so intense that the mind blocked it out as a survival mechanism. For example:

> My upbringing was so dysfunctional that it's hard to remember. I shut down so much. *(woman, age forty-two)*

> I can't remember anything before the age of 21, so I know it must have been pretty bad. My parents must have abused me so bad that I just shut down in order to survive it. *(man, age forty-five)*

As Rice (1992) puts it, "The canon CoDA members tap for their life stories systematically, however inadvertently, alters their lived experiences to fit neatly within its boundaries" (355). Thus, every childhood becomes an "abusive" childhood. Conversely, of course, this means that, "to 'explain' their lives using [codependency's rhetoric], members must sacrifice those aspects that lie beyond the outline of a 'good' theory of 'co-dependency'" (356). The possibility of "denial" makes this sacrifice less final.

It also raises the issue of the "truth" of the stories. Narratives of codependency—and narratives in general—do not correspond with any objective reality. That is not their point. Their point is to show how a particular "past came to be, and how, ultimately, it gave birth to the present" (McAdams 1993, 102). Audiences have standards for what constitutes a "good" story, and the person who shares in CoDA must adhere to them. The question is not whether any given item is true, but whether it makes for a "good" story. What is interesting about forgotten instances of childhood "abuse" is not their veracity. It is how they make particular kinds of stories possible, and so remake the lives of those who tell them. As Frank has written, "The stories we tell about our lives are not necessarily the lives as they were lived, but these stories become our experiences of those lives" (1995, 22). The person who begins a commitment to CoDA and its discourse enters a world in which all families are considered "abusive." Within the group, you can only legitimately tell stories that begin with "abuse." Were it not for the "abuse," your life would have turned out differently. Since you have ended up in CoDA, the "abuse" *must* have happened. Consequently, members develop stories about "abusive" childhoods, and those stories become their experience. Their histories gradually resemble what the formula for a "good" story of codependency prescribes. That this history may have only a weak resemblance to actual events is irrelevant, for the purpose is to "correct fortune by *remaking* history" (Berger 1963, 61, emphasis added).

EXCUSING "DYSFUNCTION"

The narrative continues with a description of how the "abusive" childhood set you up for "dysfunction." The chronology makes the present seem like the logical, and even inevitable, outcome of the past (Slavney and McHugh 1984). It attributes your recent past or present situation to undiagnosed codependency, which originated in childhood circumstances. By blaming relationship troubles on your unrecognized codependency in this way, the account reduces individual blame and its accompanying stigma.

As was the case with "abuse," what constitutes "dysfunction" varies widely. Within the discourse, any relationship or situation that has a less-than-satisfactory outcome qualifies as "dysfunctional." To be sure, someone occasionally described an appalling emotional or physical situation. But, often as not, the term described far less dramatic elements of dissatisfaction. Consider these examples from one small group:

A man described a vague but troubling need to be "in control" of his relationship with his girlfriend. I say "vague" because he never got around to explaining what he actually did to be controlling, but kept repeating phrases such as, "I've got to surrender my need to be in control. It's so 'dysfunctional,'" and "Having to be in control leads to a lot of 'dysfunction' in my life."

A woman described a falling-out with a friend who disapproved of the way she spent money. The woman speaking had planted a lot of flowers around her yard, and the friend questioned the expense. "We've got it [the money], and seeing the flowers makes me happy," she said. "I like to have my house looking a certain way and she shouldn't have anything to say about it," She "needed" to put in these flowers, she said, to have the kind of environment she wants. Her friend's disapproval is evidence of the friendship's "dysfunction"; she does not want to be around that kind of "unhealthiness."

A woman voiced concern about feeling resentment over her daughter-in-law's absence from a family gathering. She saw this as an attempt by the younger woman to ruin her day. "She shouldn't be able to control my feelings," the woman said. "This has taught me that I've got to detach. I won't be part of that 'dysfunction.'"

A woman expressed pride in her new ability to "take care of" herself by refusing to baby-sit for a family member who had asked her to do so on the spur of the moment. To do otherwise would have encouraged "dysfunction."

A man talked about a recent meal at a restaurant. The waitress had made an error in his order, and he did not bring it to her attention. He wondered what makes him "relate to people in such 'dysfunctional' ways."

A man described his general feelings of resentment and anger stemming from his "dysfunctional" relationship with his mother. She had recently recommended that he go to see the movie *Nell*, and he struggled to figure out why.

I offer these illustrations not to question their putative "dysfunction," but to highlight its role in the narrative. These were clearly instances that had not gone the way the speakers had hoped. By calling them "dysfunctional," the speakers could excuse their own role in the outcome. They could blame it on an intrinsic flaw, or "dysfunction," in the relationship, thereby relieving themselves of their share of the interactional responsibility. They could acknowledge that they acted badly, but disavow responsibility by claiming that, in light of such "dysfunction," things could not have gone otherwise. Things may have gone wrong, but through no fault of their own. In this way, "dysfunction" can excuse entire relationships, as well as discrete interactional instances:

I married my father. I grew up thinking that he was what a husband should be like. So I went out and married a man just like him. What else did I know? My relationship with my husband brought out all the issues I had with my father. All I knew was dysfunction. *(woman, age thirty-six)*

I realize now that I picked her because she repeated all that chaos from when I was growing up. It was hell—both the marriage and my childhood. I did some really rotten things, I know, but it's because of the total dysfunction I saw as a kid. What I thought was love was really something else, some toxic stuff that went on at home. I acted the same way I saw my parents act. *(man, age thirty-nine)*

"HITTING BOTTOM"

The term is self-explanatory. Although the "bottom" differs among speakers, it is always an emotional low point.

I hit my bottom around Christmas. I couldn't stop crying, and, being a man, you know, I wondered what was wrong with me! [he chuckles] But I just couldn't do anything else. It was miserable. Miserable. *(man, forty-nine)*

> When I was at my bottom, I went and bought a piece of hose, you know, to use in my exhaust pipe. I just wanted to have it around, to keep that option open. I was walking around feeling this dread, this constant feeling of dread. And in my more lucid moments I would say, "Geez, I've really got to do something or I'm going to end up dead." *(woman, age thirty seven)*

The account of the "bottom" is an important aspect of the narrative. It foregrounds a self that has not only endured hardship and conflict, but one that has found an intriguing solution. The "bottom" brings richness and complexity to the self that will emerge from the story. As the narrative progresses, having survived the "bottom" will suggest a competence and maturity that help redeem the self from failure. More immediately, it introduces an optimistic tone to the narrative. Psychologists suggest that this better allows people to cope with adversity (see McAdams 1993). Sociologically speaking, optimism reveals the narrator's underlying faith in the belief that life can be good and that one is, to some extent, able to direct oneself toward that good life.

> You really do, you hit bottom and you say, "Look, I'm happy for the air that I'm breathing," and you start from there and everything else is a plus. *(man, age forty-five)*

> [The relationship] didn't serve me anymore. It was really devastating to realize that it didn't serve my growth. It brought me to a big dead end. And then I found CoDA, and it opened up a whole new avenue for me. *(woman, age thirty-six)*

WORKING A PROGRAM

This refers to how each speaker describes what he or she is doing to encourage recovery from codependency. Sometimes, particular meetings use particular Steps as points of discussion, and, in such cases, the leader asks the speaker to focus his or her sharing accordingly. One group I visited devoted the first meeting of each month to sharing about one of the Steps. Over the course of a year, the group addressed all Twelve Steps.

This is where, to use a Twelve Step phrase, you show that you can not only "talk the talk," but also "walk the walk." You demonstrate to yourself and to the group that you are serious about recovery. It is not simply something that you talk about once a week, but it is something that you "work on" the remaining six days, as well. Typically, speakers describe working through particular Steps or what they are doing to "get in touch with" themselves. The Steps, incidentally, involve a continuous process of self-assessment. You never "complete" the Twelve Steps. The "personal inventory" of Steps Four and Ten must be taken regularly. Consequently, the amends of Step Eight must be periodically made to those you have wronged. For example, in one depiction of working through Step Six, a striking, platinum blonde woman in her early forties described how she had become "entirely ready to have God remove all [her] defects of character." This Sixth Step assumes that you have already worked through the Fifth, which requires admitting "to God, to ourselves, and to another human being the exact nature of our wrongs." On this particular evening, the woman spoke of defensively clinging to one of her "defects of character," which was a hatred for her mother. She had finally become ready to give up that hatred, with the help of her Higher Power. She believed that she had been born to a mother who "abused" her, she said, in order to learn how to "take care" of herself emotionally. She had hated her mother for not loving her, but now saw that she had learned from the "abuse." For a long time, she had not known how to "take care" of herself, and although the details remained cloudy in her account, she said she had learned enough to begin to do so, and so, was ready to have her Higher Power eliminate her hatred for her mother.

What constitutes "working a Program" can vary widely, since each person alone knows best what he or she should do to foster recovery. It is difficult to fake—or at least it would have been for me. For this reason, I never spoke in front of the entire group. Because I was not "working a Program," I could not have given the group what they were expecting to hear, and if I had, I would have felt deceptive for doing so. In small group sharing, I could talk about other things. When I had to talk about "working a Program," I said things like "trying to figure out what's best for me."

My experience illustrates an important point: it is not enough to simply tell a story about yourself; you must also believe in your own story. Although I understood the formula for a narrative of codependency, I did not "become" codependent because I did not believe in that story as who I "am." I seem to have managed impressions successfully enough to have others attribute a codependent identity to me; no one ever called it into question, and, on several occasions, "my" codependency was even the subject of friendly teasing. But the impressions others had of me did not translate into my identifying myself in that way. Since a self "involves something internally felt as well as socially enacted, it cannot be constructed out of material the actor himself or herself believes to be untrue" (Vinitzky-Seroussi and Zussman 1996, 233). Although I could tell a story that convinced others that I belonged in the group, I never convinced myself, or even tried to.

Sometimes, convincing others is an important aspect of convincing yourself. I interviewed a woman who had come to CoDA because her grown son had alcohol and drug problems. She had nursed him through numerous rehabs, and her dedication had caused considerable friction with her husband. She eventually decided to "detach" from her son to preserve her marriage. Through reading numerous therapeutic books, she had begun to see her problem as one of codependency. But she had never said as much aloud, largely because she never had a sympathetic audience for her claim. She had withdrawn from friendships because she felt that her friends would not understand why she had banned her son from the house. "I felt like a failure," she said. What she claimed to appreciate about

CoDA was having an arena in which she could say, "I am codependent. My son has drug and alcohol problems," without fear of a negative reaction from others. "For a long time," she told me, "I couldn't even bring myself to say it at a meeting. But there's no judgment here." Gradually, through practice in front of an audience that had heard it all before, she integrated "My son has drug and alcohol problems" into her narrative of the self. She can now speak of it without embarrassment; indeed, her embarrassment has been replaced by pride at what she has "overcome." It was not enough to be convinced of her codependency in private; saying it aloud among others who believed her was a turning point.

REDEEMING THE PAST

Here, the speaker talks about life in recovery. He or she recounts how codependency, though painful, was ultimately beneficial for personal "growth." The hardship it brought is portrayed as all for the best, thereby showing that he or she has indeed learned something through the misfortune. Consider the woman who said:

> I finally have come to the other side of the anger, the blaming, the bitterness, and finally have been truly able to see the benefits of it, that the characteristics that developed out of the abuse and dysfunction—I'm realizing that maybe if these things hadn't happened, I might not have the characteristics that I have today. *(age forty-five)*

Another had this to say:

> I think the pain was all worth it when I see what's happened for my growth. *(age forty-six)*

The redemptive quality of the accounts fits a pattern already observed among people attempting to make sense of loss. For example, Marris (1974) maintains that people demonstrate what he calls a "conservative impulse" in response to significant loss and change. In order to make new experiences manageable, people apply information from one situation to another and consolidate experiences into familiar categories. They depend on a "continuity of conceptions and experiences" to make sense of their lives. When an event disrupts your ability to find meaning in experience, as when an important relationship comes to an end, coming to terms with that experience "depends on restoring a sense that the lost attachment can still give meaning to the present" (149).

The experience of loss arouses contradictory reactions: return to the past, if possible; or forget it completely. Either of these would ultimately prove detrimental, since the former denies the reality of the present, and the latter denies "the experience on which the sense of self rests" (Marris 1974, 151). The resolution most people eventually reach reconciles both alternatives. People master grief, Marris claims, "by abstracting what was fundamentally important in the relationship and rehabilitating it" (34). Thus, bereaved family members often try to do what the deceased "would have wanted." This abstracts the intimacy once shared with the deceased and rehabilitates it in the lives of those who go on living. The process of abstraction and rehabilitation demonstrates the "conservative impulse." New, confusing information (the absence of the spouse) is integrated into an established framework (the spouse's preferences). In this way, the bereaved effectively restore the continuity of purpose that the death of a spouse disrupts. Likewise, codependents manifest a similar "conservative impulse" in their accounts. They abstract what had once been provided by their relationships—a coherent, reasonably optimistic story about their lives—and rehabilitate it in revised self-stories. Even the bad becomes part of a story about how your life is progressing in a manner in an order that is all for the best.

Good stories need satisfying endings. Since the lives of those telling the stories are still in progress, the endings must tolerate ambiguity. They must keep a number of alternatives open for the future, and they must have the flexibility to change as the tellers change. Yet, they must not have so much openness that they suggest immaturity and a lack of resolve. In sharing, ambiguity is accomplished through recovery clichés such as "Taking care of" or "Believing in myself" and "Getting in touch with my feelings." These and similarly vague phrases indicate a positive course of thought and action for the future without pinning you down to specifics. For example:

> The biggest help to me has been being honest with myself. CoDA has given me the courage to believe in myself and not believe all the lies from the past, from the way I was raised. (woman, forty-five)

> I'm more in touch with the power in the universe now. I pray and meditate every day. I read meditation books in the morning. I read spiritual books. I've been journaling. I've really been focusing on myself. I have more of a sense of self now, and I have Program* to thank for that. (man, age forty)

Even if life had not yet taken a turn for the better, narrators seemed certain that things would improve in due time. They played up a sense of mastery over their lives—if tentative—as in "I'm not sure how this will end up, but I'll be fine as long as I keep doing what I've learned to do." For example:

> I've been in a real crummy spot, and it's been hard to try to do recovery and keep it all together. CoDA has made me realize that I have no control over what my wife decides to do. I can just take care of myself and know that, whatever happens, I'll get through it. (man, age thirty-seven)

With such endings—"Whatever happens, I'll get through it"—narrators affirm the "growth" of the self. They suggest the ability to reconcile the tough issues of adult life with their own capabilities and goals. This new skill at reconciliation is recognized as what was lacking in their lives before recovery.

The idea of a life in recovery raises a question. If people go to CoDA when a relationship ends, but continue to attend long after the sting of uncoupling has subsided, what, then, do they see themselves "recovering" *from?* I met people who had spent three, four, and even five years in the group. They came to CoDA on the heels of disruption and stayed. What were they *doing* there? Quite simply, they were "recovering" from codependency, but they never got a clean bill of health.

The discourse builds in large part on a medical metaphor: it portrays codependency as a *condition,* not an *injury.* You do not recover from a condition. It causes varying degrees of discomfort and inconvenience. It requires varying levels of intervention. But it forever affects the way you go about your life, and it never completely heals. Once people identify themselves as codependents, they can never fully "recover."[14] Even though the pain of a particular relationship may pass, the underlying condition that fostered the troublesome "dysfunction" does not. Your codependency may go into a remission of sorts as you begin to make "healthier" choices, but it will never go away. As a condition, it requires continuous monitoring, hence continued participation in CoDA. This subtly but effectively transforms your purpose for attending. People come to the group for support during uncoupling. In the course of repairing that damage, they discover (or create) so many fundamental problems that they end up with a lifelong project. The loss starts the introspection, but it often continues long afterwards.[15]

Meanwhile, however, a more social phenomenon has also taken place, through the development of a socio-biography. By the time the crisis period ends, people feel little need to move on. They have "become" codependent—or at least they have in the sense that they see *themselves* that way. It is true that, as Wuthnow puts it, "people in groups do not simply tell stories—they become their stories" (1994, 301). But they must also find their own stories convincing. The existence of an established narrative formula of codependency does not reduce the experience of having a self to mastering a story. I am not proposing that narrators have established coherent identities if they have simply managed to use CoDA's rhetorical resources to their own advantage. If this were so, anyone who understood the conventions of a coherent narrative of self could speak one and, by doing so, could make it happen. Individual lives "could be improved with exercises in rhetoric" (Rosenwald 1992, 269), and I would have spent more time reading *Think and Grow Rich* than I did reading Sartre.

Because the narrative of the self is, as Gagnon (1992) put it, an "internal conversation," the experience of selfhood hinges as much or more on believing in your *own* stories than on getting *others* to believe them. The narrative accomplishment of selfhood is decidedly not analogous to the impression management that constitutes selfhood for Preedy at the

Beach (see Goffman 1959, 4–6). Preedy carries a Spanish translation of Homer, others think him intelligent, and so he effectively is. Goffman claims that, "in so far as the others act as if the individual had conveyed a particular impression" (6), he or she has effectively done so. What I am describing is much more internal; it is impression management *directed at yourself* (see Vinitzky-Seroussi and Zussman 1996). As Hewitt explains, "much of the conversation in which we construct and reconstruct [our biographies] occurs within ourselves and not in interaction with others" (1989, 183). In short, we must not only "talk the talk," we must also "walk the walk."

The desire for integrity—whether phrased as an "internal conversation" or simply a feeling that we are "in some peculiarly subtle sense the same" (James 1910), seems in no danger of disappearing. Despite various claims that selfhood, in a permanent sense, has been irretrievably lost (and some would say, "Good riddance"), this seems not to be the case outside the ivory tower. If CoDA members are indicative of anything, they are indicative of the strength and ubiquity of the belief in the essential self, experienced as continuous and coherent. This continuity and coherence takes the form of a running story that people tell to themselves, as well as to other people. While the story has integrity, it also leaves room for a great deal of ambiguity, for it is not yet finished. This does not mean that stories of the self are capriciously cobbled together; rather, they are grounded in institutions, which give life to the internal conversations. Neither does it mean that institutions simply provide set and setting for your narrative performances, only to fade away after the show. Rather, they remain long after the curtain falls. We cannot "do" selfhood alone, but it must work when we are alone if it is to work in front of others.

NOTES

1. The extent to which an observer sees this as remarkable seems to come with age. During the course of my research, I took a friend, then in her mid-twenties, to a meeting with me. Having had only two significant relationships herself, she saw the members of CoDA as "losers." I took another friend who was closer to 40. Although the discourse of codependency did not appeal to him, he saw that the members had had experiences very similar to his own.

2. For several years, the figure most commonly used to document this loss came from Weitzman (1985). She reported a 73 percent decline in women's status of living after divorce, and a 42 percent improvement in the status of living enjoyed by men. Re-analysis of her data proves these figures erroneous (see Duncan and Hoffman 1985; Hoffman and Duncan 1988). The most recent correction suggests a 27 percent decline for women, and a 10 percent improvement for men (Peterson 1996).

3. For a discussion of the variables that contribute to one's response to separation, see Spanier and Thompson 1983.

4. The term comes from Dworkin (1993), who describes the experience of immobilizing illness as leaving one's life a "narrative wreck, with no structure or sense."

5. Gerstel (1987) found that stigmatization is contingent on the specific conditions of the divorce and on gender. Among men, those who had affairs while married and continued them during separation reported experiencing the most disapproval. Among women, those with children did so, especially if the children were young.

6. Several studies have examined more generally the importance of talking about uncoupling. For example, Vaughan (1986) points out the importance of talking to confidants and "transitional people" (chapter 2). Riessman (1990), who works in the narrative analysis tradition, documents a prevailing theme of the failure of the marriage to measure up to a companionate ideal (chapter 2). Weiss (1975, chapter 2) and Davis (1973, chapter 8) both note a consistent effort to allocate blame.

7. Similar strategies have been addressed by Mills (1940), Hewitt and Stokes (1975), and Stokes and Hewitt (1976).

8. This group includes Turner (1976); Zurcher (1977); Lifton (1968); and Hewitt (1994) (although Hewitt disputes and reconceptualizes the shift from an institutionally grounded self to an impulsively grounded one).

9. Turner himself makes no claims about the existence of a "real self." He writes that "there is no objectively, but only a subjectively, true self" (1012); his essay examines the *experience* of self, not the existence of it. He points out that "each person develops at least a vague conception by which he recognizes some of his feelings and actions as more truly indicative of his real self than other feelings and actions" (1011).

10. The trend towards impulsively anchored images of self has the support of two national studies. *The Inner American,* by Veroff, Douvan, and Kulka (1981a) reports that between 1957 and 1976, Americans had moved from a "social" to a "personal" paradigm for structuring well-being. According to data from a 1957 survey, people of that era took "comfort in culture," as did Turner's institutionals. The 1976 population had become more impulsive, "gathering much more strength in its own personal adaptations to the world" (529). The research team noted three types of changes consistent with Turner's trend towards impulsivity: (1) the diminution of role standards as the basis for defining adjust-ment; (2) increased focus on self-expressiveness and self-direction in social life; and (3) a shift in concern from social-organizational integration to interpersonal intimacy (529). In the seventies, people thought more in psychological terms, instead of the moral or material terms of the fifties. In 1957, people would have asked themselves "Should I do this?" or "What will this get me?" when weighing alternatives. In 1976, they asked "How does this make me feel?" (see Wilkinson 1988, 44).

The same year that *The Inner American* appeared, opinion pollster Daniel Yankelovich's *New Rules: Searching for Self-Fulfillment in a World Turned Upside Down* noted many of the same trends. Using data from surveys and interviews, he documented varying degrees of preoccupation with self-fulfillment, with a trend suggesting an overall increase in such concerns. He claimed that post–World War II generations had rejected the "giving/getting covenant" that had motivated earlier generations to work, as well as to enjoy the fruits of their labors. Instead, the Baby Boomers wanted fulfillment without much sacrifice, and psychological fulfillment, in particular, had moved to center stage.

In many ways, the argument in *New Rides* takes up where *The Lonely Crowd* had left off (Riesman, Glazer, and Denney 1950). Yankelovich attributed this "psycho-culture" largely to the growth of the consumer economy. He speculated that the emphasis on fulfillment, especially in its extreme version expressed by what he called the "strong formers," would eventually have devastating economic consequences. He also saw a positive side to the changes, in the form of a new tolerance that could prove productive in times of austerity. He also documented that the mid-to-late 1970s saw an upsurge in membership in voluntary associations, belief in the value of commitment to others, and civic involvement, all trends remarked upon by Riesman (1980) in his reappraisal of the American social character.

Over the same period of time, in social-psychological research involving instruments such as the Twenty Statements Test, which asks for twenty answers to the question "Who am I?" fewer people defined themselves by their roles, and more used individualistic, attitudinal traits. In the language of the Test, the answers began to shift from B mode roles ("I am a father," or "I am a teacher") to C mode attitudes ("I am a happy person," or "I like music") (see especially Zurcher 1977).

11. For a discussion of how the culture of Romanticism rested on the innovative belief in the self, see Gagnon 1984 (see also Gagnon 1992).

12. Sharing, or, more generally, storytelling, is commonplace in small groups of all lands. For more on this, see Wuthnow 1994, especially chapter 10. There are many other "narrative auspices," or "people processing institutions that increasingly elicit, screen, fashion, and variously highlight personal narratives" (Gubrium and Holstein 1998, 164). These include schools, clinics, hospitals, jails, and counseling centers, just to name a few.

13. Gubrium and Holstein (1998) use the phrase "formal narrative control" to address the ways that stories are "geared to institutional agendas, with preferred plot structures, 'points,' or morals" (173). Rice also makes note of "how thoroughly faithful [CoDA] speakers are to the norms governing their role" (1996, 149).

14. Arthur Frank refers to people in this position as belonging to "the remission society" (1995, 8). He puts in this group people who have had cancer or heart conditions, diabetes, allergies, people with prostheses of various sorts, and former drug addicts and alcoholics.

15. This reliance on the group has often been misunderstood as replacing one "addiction" with another (see Katz and Liu 1991).

*CoDA members typically speak of "Program," omitting the definite article.

Identity Work among the Homeless: The Verbal Construction and Avowal of Personal Identities[1]

By David A. Snow and Leon Anderson
University of Texas at Austin

This paper elaborates processes of identity construction and avowal among homeless street people, with two underlying and interconnected objectives in mind: to advance understanding of the manner in which individuals at the bottom of status systems attempt to generate identities that provide them with a measure of self-worth and dignity and to shed additional empirical and theoretical light on the relationships among role, identity, and self-concept. The data are from an ethnographic field study of homeless street people. "Identity talk" constitutes the primary form of "identity work" by means of which homeless street people construct and negotiate personal identities. Three generic patterns of identity talk are elaborated and illustrated: distancing, embracement, and fictive storytelling.[1] Each form contains several subtypes that vary in usage according to the length of time one has spent on the streets. The paper concludes by discussing the theoretical implications of the findings and suggesting a number

---

1   This is a revised and updated version of an earlier paper presented at the annual meeting of the Society for the Study of Symbolic Interaction, Washington, D.C., August 1985. Preparation of the paper was facilitated by a grant to study homelessness provided by the Hogg Foundation for Mental Health. We would also like to thank the three anonymous reviewers for AJS whose comments were most constructive and insightful. Requests for reprints should be sent to David A. Snow, Department of Sociology, University of Texas, Austin, Texas 78712.

of grounded propositions regarding the relationships among role, identity, and self.

Congregated at the bottom of nearly every social order is an aggregation of demeaned and stigmatized individuals variously referred to historically as the *ribauz* (Hohnes 1966), the *lumpenproletariat* (Marx and Engels 1967), untouchables (Srinivas and Beteille 1965), the underclass (Myrdal 1962), or superfluous people (Harrington 1984). However they come to be situated at the lowest reaches of a status system, whether through political design, structural push, inadvertent slippage, or birth, they tend to be viewed and discussed primarily in terms of the characterological problems they are thought to have (e.g., cultural deprivation, genetic inferiority, and mental depravity), the problems they are thought to pose for the larger community (e.g., crime, contamination, demoralization, and welfare), or the problems associated with their material survival (e.g., food, shelter, and clothing). Their inner life, and particularly the problem of generating and maintaining a sense of meaning and self-worth, is rarely a matter of concern. There are exceptions to this tendency, of course, exemplified by Goffman's (1961a) elaboration of the secondary adjustments of mental patients in an asylum, the observations of Bettelheim (1943), Frankl (1963), and Dimsdale (1980) on the psychological coping strategies of concentration camp inmates, and the research of Liebow (1967) and Anderson (1976) among black street-corner men. But, in general, questions pertaining to the inner life of those at or near the bottom have been of secondary concern.

This lacuna is also evident in research on America's current wave of homelessness. To date, research has focused almost solely on the demographic characteristics of the homeless, their physiological survival needs, and the problems they have or pose (e.g., alcoholism, mental illness, criminality, and urban blight). That an understanding of life on the streets and variation in patterns of adaptation may be contingent in part on the webs of meaning the homeless spin and the personal identities they construct has rarely been considered empirically or theoretically.[2] Our primary aim in this paper is to fill this void in part and thereby further understanding of the manner in which a sense of personal significance and meaning is generated and sustained among individuals who have fallen through the cracks of society and linger at the very bottom of the status system. We pursue this objective by ethnographically examining processes of identity construction and avowal among homeless street people.[3] This method of inquiry is consistent with the Blumerian version of symbolic interactionism (Blumer 1969) and the Geertzian strand of interpretive anthropology (Geertz 1973). Both hold, among other things, that an understanding of the social worlds people inhabit requires consideration of the meanings imputed to the objects that constitute those worlds and that these meanings can be apprehended best by intimate familiarity with the routines and situations that are part and parcel of those social worlds.

In examining identity construction processes among the homeless, we also seek to further empirical and theoretical understanding of the concept of identity and its relationship to role and self. Pursuit of this objective is consistent with longstanding sociological concern with the relationship between the individual and society (Dawe 1978) and with the theoretical function of identity as a kind of interface or conceptual bridge linking the two. The concept of identity is a problematic one laden with considerable ambiguity, however. A recent review essay on the identity concept notes that, although it has become

---

2 Absence of concern with such issues in recent research is clearly apparent in the U. S. House Committee on Government Operations' (1985) compilation of numerous studies throughout the country and in a General Accounting Office (1985) report on research on homelessness. Much of the previous research on earlier generations of homeless individuals also sidestepped such cognitive considerations by focusing on the demographic characteristics of the homeless and the problems (particularly alcoholism) they had or posed for their communities, as reflected most prominently in the large-scale survey studies by Bogue (1963) and Bahr and Caplow (1973) and the ethnographic research of Spradley (1970) and Wiseman (1970). Conspicuous exceptions to this problem-oriented focus are provided by the classic studies of Nels Anderson (1923, 1931) and Harper's (1982) recent travelogue about his adventures with an avowed tramp. In both cases, concern is primarily with portraying the nature of life on the streets or road from the standpoint of the participants but without attending systematically or theoretically to the manner in which personal identities are constructed and sustained. Liebow's (1967) and Anderson's (1976) research among black street-corner men clearly exhibits concern with the identity issue, but comparisons with the homeless have to be made cautiously since the structural situations and ways of life of the two groups are not identical. Black street-corner men, although on the margins of the larger order, can still descend a notch or two in the status hierarchy; homeless street people, as we conceptualize them here, can fall no further.

3 Although we use the terms "homeless" and "street people" interchangeably throughout this paper, it is important to keep in mind that the former includes but is not limited to the latter. Homelessness is a generic concept, with street people constituting a variant. Our focus in this paper is on homeless street people, conceptualized as individuals living in urban areas whose lives are characterized by the absence of permanent housing, supportive familial bonds, and consensually defined roles of social utility and moral worth.

a "stock technical term in sociology and social psychology" and even a "widespread cultural buzzword" the past 40 years, its widespread diffusion does "not imply agreement on or even a clear understanding of its various meanings" (Wiegert 1983, pp. 183, 202). The presence of this ambiguity, which is due in part to the preeminence of the self-esteem dimension of the self-concept as an object of research and in part to the absence of theoretical agreement on the nature and wellsprings of identity (Gecas 1982, p. 10), clearly indicates that work needs to be done "to unpack, codify, apply, and speculatively expand" the identity concept (Weigert 1983, p. 203).

The intent of this paper, then, is to elaborate processes of identity construction and avowal among homeless street people, with two underlying and interconnected objectives in mind: to advance understanding of the manner in which individuals at the lowest reaches of status systems attempt to generate identities that provide them with a measure of self-worth and dignity and to shed additional empirical light on the relationships among role, identity, and self-concept. We begin by framing more precisely the problem of identity construction among the homeless. We then discuss our data sources and procedures. Next, we conceptualize identity and related terms and then elaborate the processes of identity construction and avowal we have observed. And last, we discuss the theoretical implications of these observations, concluding with a number of grounded propositions regarding the relationships among role, identity, and self.

THE PROBLEM OF IDENTITY CONSTRUCTION AMONG THE HOMELESS

In *The Birth and Death of Meaning*, Ernest Becker (1962), drawing on the ideas of Alfred Adler (Ansbacher and Ansbacher 1946), argues that our most basic drive is for a sense of self-worth or personal significance and that its accessibility depends in part on the roles available to us. If so, then it is sociologically axiomatic that, because of their differential distribution throughout the social structure, not all individuals have equal access to a measure of self-worth. Homeless street people are a case in point. Unlike nearly all other inhabitants of a society, the homeless are seldom incumbents of social roles that are consensually defined in terms of positive social utility and moral worth. As does any highly stigmatized class, the homeless serve various societal functions, such as providing casual labor for underground economies, but these are not the sorts of functions from which personal significance and self-worth can be easily derived. As a consequence, the homeless constitute a kind of superfluous population, in the sense that they fall outside the hierarchy of structurally available societal roles and thus beyond the conventional, role-based sources of moral worth and dignity that most citizens take for granted. The intriguing question thus arises of how the homeless attend to what Adler and Becker, among others, regard as the basic need for a sense of self-worth. More specifically, To what extent and how do the homeless generate personal identities that yield a measure of self-respect and dignity?

In his classic essay on stigma, Goffman (1963) notes a variety of strategies frequently used by the stigmatized to minimize the deleterious social and psychic consequences of their discrediting attributes. One such strategy is to to "pass" by concealing or withholding information about the stigma so that it is not easily perceived by others. This strategy is not a feasible alternative for dealing with all varieties of stigma, however. As Goffman noted, its utility varies inversely with the obtrusiveness of the stigma. For those whose stigma is not readily visible, such as members of some deviant religious orders, passing can be relatively easy. For the more visibly stigmatized, however, passing is largely impossible. Most homeless street people fall into this latter category. Their tattered and soiled clothes function as an ever-present and readily perceivable "role sign" (Banton 1965) or "stigma symbol" (Goffman 1963) that immediately draws attention to them and sets them apart from others. Actual or threatened proximity to them not only engenders fear and enmity in other citizens but also frequently invites the most visceral kinds of responses, ranging from shouts of invective to organized neighborhood opposition to proposed shelter locations to "troll-busting" campaigns aimed at terrori-zation.[4] Moreover, these sorts of reactions seldom go unnoticed. As one homeless young man who had been on the streets for only two weeks lamented, "The hardest thing has been getting used to the way people look down on street people. It's real hard to feel good about yourself when almost everyone you see is looking down on you."[5]

Physical isolation might offer an escape from this dilemma, but the homeless seldom possess the requisite survival resources. Consequently, the vast majority find themselves "hanging out" on city streets and migrating from one agency to another that provides for such basic survival needs as food and shelter. Their daily routines thus bring them in contact with many other citizens on a regular basis. Because of this and the fact that they are always "in uniform," strategies other than passing and total withdrawal have to be devised in order to develop and maintain a measure of self-worth. Homeless street people are thus confronted continuously with the problem of constructing personal identities that are not a mere reflection of the stereotypical and stigmatized manner in which they are regarded as a social category.

To what extent and how do they manage this identity problem? How do they carve out a modicum of self-respect given their pariah-like status? And, What are the implications of

---

4   Such responses have occurred rather frequently in Austin, as well as elsewhere throughout the country, as the number of homeless people has mounted (see *Austin American-Statesman* 1985a, 19856, 1985c, 1985d; *Los Angeles Times* 1984a, 19846; *Newsweek* 1984; *New York Times* 1985).

5   All such spoken material throughout the paper represents verbatim quotes of some of the homeless whom we encountered. They are used for illustrative purposes and are representative of what we heard or were told. The process by which these materials were discerned and recorded will be discussed in detail in the Procedures and Context section following.

the answers to these questions for understanding more generally the relationships among social roles, identity, and the self? What, in short, can we learn from the homeless about identity and identity-construction processes?

PROCEDURES AND CONTEXT

We address these questions with data from a field study of homeless street people in Austin, Texas.

We pursue the identification of these processes with data gathered during a year-long ethnographic field study conducted among homeless individuals living in or passing through Austin from September 1, 1984, to August 31, 1985. The major research strategy was to "hang out" with as many of these individuals as possible on a daily basis, spending time with them in varied settings (e.g., meal and shelter lines, under bridges, in parks, at day-labor pickup sites), over the course of the 12-month period. The basic task was to acquire an appreciation for the nature of life on the streets and the ways in which the homeless managed street life both experientially and cognitively. We thus followed the homeless we encountered through their daily routines and listened not only to what they told us but also to what they told one another. In this way, we were able to secure "perspectives in action" as well as "perspectives of action."[6] We asked questions and probed from time to time and also "interviewed by comment,"[7] but the major task was that of listening to conversations among the homeless to enhance the prospect of securing perspectives that

---

6   Perspectives *in* action refer to accounts or patterns of talk formulated for the purpose of realizing a particular end or accomplishing a particular task in a naturally occurring situation that is part of some ongoing system of action, as when homeless street people engage in identity talk among themselves while queuing up in front of a shelter, drinking beer under a bridge, or eating in a soup kitchen. Perspectives *of* action are constructed and articulated in response to the queries of researchers or other outsiders, as when two transients explain to the police what they were doing in an alley or when a street person tells a researcher about how he or she regards himself or herself. Perspectives of action are thus produced "not to act meaningfully in the system being described, but rather to make the system meaningful to an outsider" (Gould et al. 1974, p. xxv). Both perspectives yield useful information, but they are of different orders. Perspectives of action are post-factum, idealized accounts that place the action in question within a larger normative framework, whereas perspectives in action refer to the cognitions that emerge with and are inseparable from the sequence of action that perspectives of action may be invoked to explain. For further discussion of these two perspectives, see Gould et al. (1974, pp. xxiv-xxvi).

7   Interviewing by comment refers to an attempt to elicit spoken information from a respondent or informant by making an intentional statement rather than by asking a direct question. Comments can vary, just as questions do, in the degree to which they are focused or unfocused and in their level of specificity or generality, ranging, e.g., from general and commonplace statements of puzzlement, such as "I don't get it" or "I don't understand," to more focused statements that cast others into a specific identity or role, such as "He sure looks like a greenhorn" or "I didn't think you were a regular Sally [Salvation Army] user." For a discussion of interviewing by comment as a supplementary data-gathering technique, the rationale and logic underlying its use, and the variety of forms comments can take, see Snow, Zurcher, and Sjoberg (1982).

seemed to arise naturally rather than only in response to the researcher's coaxing or intervention. This relatively unobtrusive listening took two basic forms: eavesdropping, which involved listening to others within a bounded interactional encounter without being a part of that encounter, as when waiting in meal lines or in day-labor offices; and a kind of nondirective, conversational listening that occurred when we engaged in encounters with two or more homeless individuals.[88]

VARIETIES OF IDENTITY TALK AMONG THE HOMELESS: FINDINGS AND OBSERVATIONS

Up to this point, we have used the term "identity" in a general and undefined fashion. It is necessary to clarify what we mean by the term "identity" and related concepts before proceeding further. Although there is no agreement on whether identity should be conceptualized as a unitary entity or disaggregated into several types, we find it preferable to pursue the latter tack. Accordingly, we distinguish among social identities, personal identities, and self-concept.[9] By social identities, we refer to the identities attributed or imputed to others in an attempt to place or situate them as social objects. They are not self-designations or avowals but imputations based primarily on information gleaned on the basis of appearance, behavior, and the location and time of action.[10] In contrast,

---

8   While it might be argued that the information secured during such encounters represents more a reaction to the researcher's presence than a naturally occurring phenomenon among the homeless, our field experiences suggest that this is not so. Although some of the homeless were apprised of the field researcher's true status, they typically seemed to lose sight of it quickly as he continued to spend time on the street with them, dressed in old clothes, and more or less walked in their shoes. This forgetfulness was forcefully illustrated one night when the field researcher gave an ill, homeless woman a ride to a health clinic. On the way back from the clinic to the abandoned warehouse where she was going to spend the night, she asked, "Are you sleeping in your car these days or down at the Sally?" The researcher had explained his position to this woman many times during the previous two-and-half months and had even asked her one time to fill out a short survey, but she had forgotten or not fully believed what he had told her.

9   While the distinction between identity and self-concept is commonplace in the literature, the disaggregation of identity into two or more dimensions or aspects is lessfrequent. In his essay on the relationships among appearance, self, and identity, Stone (1962) highlights the negotiated character of identities by conceptualizing them in terms of the "coincidence of placements and announcements," but he does not differentiate and articulate what we see as the distinct social and personal dimensions implied therein. The role-based conceptualization of identity provided by Stryker (1980, pp. 51–85) and Burke (see Stryker 1980, pp. 129–34) also highlights the coalescence or coincidence of both social and personal considerations, but it does not fully disaggregate these dimensions and allow for their disjunction as well as congruence, a point to which we will return later in the paper. Goffman (1963) and McCall and Simmons (1978) do make clear-cut conceptual distinctions between social and per sonal identities but not in ways that we find fully satisfactory or congruent with our observations.

10   This conceptualization of social identity is consistent with both Goffman (1963, pp. 2–3) and McCall and Simmons (1978, p. 62), as well as with Turner's (1978, p. 6) "appearance principle," which

personal identities refer to the meanings attributed to the self by the actor. They are self-designations and self-attributions brought into play or asserted during the course of interaction.[11] Since personal identities may be inconsistent with imputed social identities, the two need to be kept analytically distinct. Standing in contrast to these two variants of identity is the self-concept, by which we refer to one's overarching view or image of her- or himself "as a physical, social, spiritual, or moral being" (Gecas 1982, p. 3). Following Turner (1968), we view the self-concept as a kind of working compromise between idealized images and imputed social identities. Presented personal identities provide a glimpse of the consistency or inconsistency between social identities and self-concept, as well as indications of the latter.

Our empirical concern here is primarily with personal identities and particularly with the ways in which the homeless construct and utilize such identities. We conceptualize identity construction and assertion as variants of the generic process we call *identity work*, by which we refer to the range of activities individuals engage in to create, present, and sustain personal identities that are congruent with and supportive of the self-concept. So defined, identity work may involve a number of complementary activities: (*a*) procurement or arrangement of physical settings and props; (*b*) cosmetic face work or the arrangement of personal appearance; (*c*) selective association with other individuals and groups; and (*d*) verbal construction and assertion of personal identities. In this paper, we concentrate on the last variety of identity work, which we refer to as *identity talk*. Since the homeless seldom have the financial or social resources to pursue the other varieties of identity work, talk is perhaps the primary avenue through which they can attempt to construct, assert, and maintain desired personal identities, especially when these personal identities are at variance with the general social identity of a street person. Because the structure of their daily routines ensures that they spend a great deal of time waiting here and there, many homeless also have ample opportunity to converse with one another about a range of topics.

Inspection of these conversational data yielded three generic patterns of identity talk: (1) distancing, (2) embracement, and (3) fictive storytelling. Each was found to contain several varieties that tended to vary in use according to the duration of one's street career. We discuss and elaborate in turn each of the generic patterns and their subtypes,

---

holds that "people tend to conceive another person (and thus impute social identities) on the basis of the role behavior they observe unless there are cues that alert them to the possibility of a discrepancy between person and role."

11 This conceptualization differs from Goffman's (1963, p. 57) and McCall and Sim-mons's (1978, pp. 62–63) in that they define personal identity in terms of unique, biographical facts and items that function as pegs on which social identities can be hung. It is our contention, which we will illustrate and elaborate, that biographical facts and experiences, just as the roles one plays or is cast into, influence but do not fully determine the construction and assertion of what we call personal identities. Thus, rather than taking for granted the relationship between biography and personal identity, we see it as problematic and variable.

summarizing statistically (in tables 3, 4, and 5) at the end of each section the relationship between the various types and time on the streets.

Distancing

When individuals have to enact roles, associate with others, or utilize institutions that imply social identities inconsistent with their actual or desired self-conceptions, they may attempt to distance themselves from those roles, associations, and institutions (Goffman 1961a, 1961b; Levitin 1964; Stebbins 1975; Sayles 1984). Our findings reveal that a substantial proportion of the identity talk of the homeless we studied was consciously focused on distancing themselves from other homeless individuals, from street and occupational roles, and from the institutions serving them. Nearly a third of the 202 identity statements were of this variety.

Associational distancing.—Since one's claim to a particular self is partly contingent on the imputed social identities of one's associates, one way to substantiate that claim, in the event that one's associates are negatively evaluated, *is* to distance oneself from them. As Anderson (1976, p. 214) noted, based on his research among black street-corner men, claims to a particular identity depend in part "on one's ability to manage his image by drawing distinctions between himself and others he does not want to be associated with." This distancing technique manifested itself in two ways in our research: dissociation from the homeless as a general social category and dissociation from specific groups of homeless individuals.

Categorical associational distancing was particularly evident among homeless individuals who had been on the streets for a comparatively short time. Illustrative of this technique is the following comment by a 24-year-old white male who had been on the streets for less than two weeks: "I'm not like the other guys who hang out down at the 'Sally' [Salvation Army]. If you want to know about street people, I can tell you about them; but you can't really learn about street people from studying me, because I'm different."

Such categorical distancing also occurred among those individuals who saw themselves as on the verge of getting off the street. One 22-year-old white male who had been on the streets for several years but who had just secured two jobs in hopes of raising enough money to rent an apartment indicated, for example, that he was different from other street people: "They have gotten used to living on the streets and are satisfied with it. But not me! Next to my salvation, getting off the street is the most important thing in my life." This variety of categorical distancing was particularly pronounced among homeless individuals who had taken jobs at the local Salvation Army shelter and thus had one foot off the street. These individuals were frequently criticized by other street people for their condescending and holier-than-thou attitude. As one regular shelter user put it: "As soon as these guys get inside, they're better than the rest of us. They've been out on the street for years, and as soon as they're inside they forget it."

Among the homeless who had been on the street for some time and who appeared firmly rooted in that life-style, there were few examples of categorical distancing. Instead, these individuals frequently distinguished themselves from other groups of the homeless. This form of associational distancing was most conspicuous among the homeless who were not regular social service or shelter users and who thus saw themselves as being more independent and resourceful. These individuals not only wasted little time in pointing out that they were "not like those Sally users," but they were also given to derogating the more institutionally dependent. Indeed, while they were among those furthest removed from the middle class in their way of life, they sounded at times much like middle-class citizens berating welfare recipients. Illustrative is the comment of an alcoholic, 49-year-old woman who had been on the streets for two-and-a-half years: "A lot of these people staying at the Sally, they're reruns. Every day they're wanting something, wanting something. People get tired of giving. All you hear is 'give me, give me.' And we transients are getting tired of it." In sum, we have seen that, although associational distancing provides one means by which some of the homeless set themselves apart from one another and thus develop a somewhat different and more self-respecting personal identity, such distancing varies in scope according to the duration of time on the streets.

Role distancing.—Role distancing was the second form of distancing employed by the homeless in order to buffer the self. Following Goffman (1961*b*, pp. 107–8), role distancing involves an active and self-conscious attempt to foster the impression of a lack of commitment or attachment to a particular role in order to deny the virtual self implied. Thus, when an individual finds himself cast into or enacting a role in which the social identity implied is inconsistent with the desired or actual self-conception, role distancing is likely to occur. Since the homeless routinely find themselves cast into or enacting low-status, negatively evaluated roles (e.g., panhandler, day laborer, vagrant), it should not be surprising that many of them would attempt to dissociate themselves from those very roles.

As with associational distancing, role distancing manifested itself in two ways: distancing from the basic or general role of street person and distancing from specific occupational roles. The former, which we construe as a variant of categorical distancing, was particularly evident among individuals who had been on the street for less than six months. It was not uncommon for these individuals to make explicitly clear that they should "not be mistaken as a typical street person." Role distancing of the less categorical and more situationally specific type, however, was most evident in day-labor occupational roles, such as painters' helpers, hod carriers, warehouse and van unloaders, and unskilled service occupations, such as dishwashing and janitorial work. Although the majority of the homeless we encountered would avail themselves of such job opportunities, they seldom did so enthusiastically because of the jobs' low status and low wages. This was especially true of the homeless who had been on the streets between two and four years,[12] who frequently reminded others of their disdain for such jobs and of their belief that they deserved better, as exemplified by the remarks of a drunk young man who had worked the previous day as a painter's helper: "I made $36.00 off the labor corner, but it was just 'nigger' work. I'm 24 years old, man. I deserve better than that." Similar distancing laments were frequently voiced over the disparity between job demands and wages. While we were conversing with a small gathering of homeless men on a Saturday afternoon, one of them revealed, for example, that he had turned down a job earlier in the day to carry shingles up a ladder for $4.00 an hour because he found it demeaning to "do that hard of work for that low of pay." Since day-labor jobs seldom last for more than six to eight hours, perhaps not much is lost monetarily in forgoing such jobs in comparison with what can be gained in pride. But even when the ratio of dollars to pride would appear to make rejection costly, as with permanent jobs, dissatisfaction with the low status of the menial job roles may prod some homeless individuals to engage in the ultimate form of role distancing by quitting current jobs. As one informant recounted the day after he quit in the middle of his shift as a dishwasher at a local restaurant: "My boss told me, 'You can't walk out on me.' And I told her, 'Fuck you, just watch me. I'm going to walk out of here right now.' And I did. 'You can't walk out on me,' she said. I said, 'Fuck you, I'm gone.'"

The foregoing illustrations suggest that the social identities lodged in available work roles are frequently inconsistent with the desired or idealized self-conceptions of some of the homeless. Consequently, "bitching about," "turning down," and even "blowing off" such work may function as a means of social identity disavowal, on the one hand, and personal identity assertion, on the other. Such techniques provide a way of saying, "Hey, I have some pride. I'm in control. I'm my own man." This is especially true among those individuals for whom such work is no longer just a stopgap measure but rather a permanent feature of their lives.

Institutional distancing.—An equally prevalent distancing technique involved the derogation of the very institutions that attended to the needs of the homeless in one way or another. The one agency that was the most frequent object of these harangues was the local Salvation Army. It was frequently typified by many of the homeless who used it as a greedy corporation run by inhumane personnel more interested in lining their own

---

12 Pursuit of day-labor jobs rarely occurred among the homeless who had been on the streets for more than four years. Instead, they tended to survive by other means, such as panhandling, collecting aluminum cans, and scavenging. Retreat from the day-labor market among these individuals might be interpreted as a form of behavioral distancing that ideally reduces the prospect of interaction with other citizens and thereby lessens the need for constructing alternative identities. The problem with this proposition, however, is that many of the longtime homeless intentionally engage the public with their panhandling activities. In addition, it is frequently the more chronic homeless who are the most visible to the public—e.g., shopping-cart people and bag ladies. It is perhaps because of such considerations that embracement, which will be discussed in the next section, is a more common mode of identity construction among the homeless who have been on the streets for two or more years.

pockets than in serving the needy. The flavor of this negative characterization is captured by such comments as the following, which were heard most often among individuals waiting in the Salvation Army dinner line: "The Major is money-hungry and feeds people the cheapest way he can. He never talks to people except to gripe at them. The Salvation Army is supposed to be a Christian organization, but it doesn't have a Christian spirit. It looks down on people. ... The Salvation Army is a national business that is more worried about making money than helping people"; "The Sally here doesn't nearly do as much as it could for people. The people who work here take bags of groceries and put them in their cars. People donate to the Sally, and then the workers there cream off the best"; and "If you spend a week here, you'll see how come people lose hope. You're treated just like an animal."

Given that the Salvation Army is the only local facility that provides free shelter, breakfast, and dinner, it is understandable why attention would be riveted on it more than on any other local agency. But that the Salvation Army would be continuously derogated by the very people whose survival it facilitates may appear puzzling at first glance, especially given its caretaker orientation. The answer lies in part in the organization and dissemination of its services. Clients are processed in an impersonal, highly structured, assembly-line fashion. The result is a leveling of individual differences and a decline in personal autonomy. Bitching and complaining about such settings thus allow one to gain psychic distance from the self implied and to secure a modicum of personal autonomy.[13] Criticizing the Salvation Army, then, provided some regular users with a means of dealing with the implications of their dependence on it. It was, in short, a way of presenting and sustaining a somewhat contrary personal identity.

While this variety of distancing was observable among all the homeless, it was most prevalent among those regular service users who had been on the streets for more than two years. Since these individuals had used street institutions over a longer period of time, their self-concepts were more deeply implicated in them, thus necessitating distancing from those very institutions and the self implied.

---

13 Wiseman (1970, pp. 187–88,194–98) similarly notes the "harsh sentiments" of Skid-Row alcoholics toward their benefactors. Similar patterns of bitching and griping have also been observed in relation to more all-encompassing institutions, such as prisons and mental hospitals. In commenting on such verbal insubordination, Goffman (1961a, p. 319) offers an interpretation that dovetails with ours: "This recalcitrance is not an incidental mechanism of defense but rather an essential constituent of the self" that allows the individual "to keep some distance, some elbow room, between himself and that with which others assume he should be identified."

TABLE 3: Types of Distancing tby Time on the Streets (in percentages)

| | Type of Distancing | | |
| | Categoric* | Specific[b] | Institutional[c] |
Time on the Streets	(N = 16)	(N = 23)	(N = 22)
	75.0	4.3	9.1
Six months to two years	6.3	26.1	13.6
Two years to four years	6.3	56.5	40.9
More than four years	12.5	13.0	36.4

Note.—χ^2 = 35.06, df = 6, P < .001.

* Comments or statements coded as categoric included those indicating dissociation or distancing from such general, street role identities as transient, bum, tramp, drifter or from street people in general, regardless of variation among them.

[b] Comments or statements reflective of specific or situational distancing included those indicating dissociation from specific groupings of homeless individuals or from specific survival or occupational roles.

[c] Comments or statements suggestive of institutional distancing included those indicating dissociation from or disdain for street institutions, such as the Salvation Army, soup kitchens, and the like.

Thus far, we have elaborated how some of the homeless distance themselves from other homeless individuals, from general and specific roles, and from the institutions that deal with them. Such distancing behavior and talk represent attempts to salvage a measure of self-worth. In the process, of course, the homeless are asserting more favorable personal identities. Not all homeless individuals engage in similar distancing behavior and talk, however. As indicated in table 3, which summarizes the foregoing observations, categorical distancing tends to be concentrated among those who have been on the street for a comparatively short time, typically less than six months. The only instances of such distancing we heard from those who had been on the streets for more than four years were made by individuals categorized as "mentally ill," as in the case of one 32-year-old white male who expressed disdain for the homeless in general even though he had been on and off the street for 10 years between stays in Texas state mental hospitals.[14] For those who are more firmly entrenched in street life, then, distancing tends to be confined to distinguishing themselves from specific groups of the homeless, such as novices and the institutionally

---

14   The homeless who were categorized as mentally ill composed only 10% (17) of our field sample of 168 individuals. For a discussion of the criteria used for categorizing individuals as mentally ill and for a detailed discussion of mental illness among the homeless in general, see Snow et al. (1986).

dependent, from specific occupational roles, or from the institutions with which they have occasional contact.

Embracement

By "embracement," we refer to the verbal and expressive confirmation of one's acceptance of and attachment to the social identity associated with a general or specific role, a set of social relationships, or a particular ideology.[15] So defined, embracement implies consistency between self-concept and imputed or structurally based social identities. Social and personal identities are congruent, such that the individual accepts the identities associated with his status. Thus, embracement involves the avowal of implied social identities rather than their disavowal, as is true of distancing. Thirty-six percent of the identity statements were of this variety.

Role embracement.—The most conspicuous kind of embracement we encountered was role embracement of the categorical variety, which typically manifested itself in the avowal and acceptance of street role identities such as the "tramp" and "bum."[16] Occasionally, we would encounter an individual who would immediately announce that he was a tramp or a bum.[16] A case in point is provided by our initial encounter with a 49-year-old man who had been on the road for 14 years. When we engaged him in conversation on a street corner, he proudly told us that he was "the tramp who was on the front page of yesterday's newspaper." In that and subsequent conversations, his talk was peppered with references to himself as a tramp. He indicated, for example, that he had appeared on a television show

---

15   15   This conception of embracement is derived from Goffman's (19616, pp. 106–7) treatment of role embracement but with two differences. First, we conceive of embracement as a generic process through which attachment to and involvement in a particular entity or activity is expressed, with role embracement constituting only one form. And, second, we think embracement can be expressed without the kind of active, behavioral engrossment or spontaneous involvement that suggests disappearance into the activity at hand and corresponding inattention to the flow of other proximate activities. Such engagement should be viewed as a variable feature of embracement, not as a defining characteristic.

16   These two identities, along with that of the hobo, constituted the triadic folk typology that was particularly prominent in the vernacular of the road during the first third of the century, especially among the hoboes (migratory workers) who regarded themselves as the cream of the road and who looked down scornfully on the tramps (migratory nonworkers) and the bums (nonmigratory nonworkers) (Anderson 1923, 1931). By the 1950s, this threefold distinction had apparently lost its conceptual utility. The terms "tramp" and "bum" were still bandied about, but the hobo concept no longer seemed to be a useful, generalized descriptor. Whether its decline in usage on the street was due to the disappearance of the hoboes' supportive subculture, as some romanticists have lamented (Bruns 1980), or to a blurring of the previous distinctions between hoboes and the tramps and bums is unclear. What does seem to be certain, though, is that by the last third of the century homeless men were no longer imputing or avowing the hobo identity. The tramp and bum constructs were, and still are, part of the lexicon of the streets, however, as indicated by Spradley's (1970) and Harper's (1982) research, as well as by ours.

in St. Louis as a tramp and that he "tramped" his way across the country, and he revealed several "cons" that "tramps use to survive on the road."

This tramp, as well as others like him, identified himself as being of the more traditional "brethren of the road" variety. In contrast, we also encountered individuals who identified themselves as "hippie tramps." Interaction with a number of these individuals who hung out together near the local university similarly revealed attachment to and temporal continuity of this particular street identity. When confronted by a passing group of young "punkers," for instance, several of the hippie tramps voiced agreement with one's remark that "these kids will change but we'll stay the same." As if to buttress this claim, they went on to talk about "Rainbow," an annual gathering of old hippies, which functions in part as a kind of identity reaffirmation ritual. For these street people, there was little doubt about who they were; they not only saw themselves as hippie-like tramps, but they embraced that identity both verbally and expressively.

This sort of enthusiastic embracement also surfaced on occasion with Skid Row-like "bums," as evidenced by a hunchbacked alcoholic's repeated reference to himself as a "bum." As a corollary of such categorical role embracement, we found that most individuals who identified themselves as tramps or bums had also adopted nicknames congruent with these general street roles. Not only did we find that they routinely referred to themselves in terms of these new names, but others also referred to them similarly. Street names such as Shotgun, Muskrat, Boxcar Billy, Panama Red, Gypsy Bill, and the like can thus be construed as symbolizing a break with the past and suggesting a fairly thoroughgoing embracement of life on the streets.

Role-specific embracement was also encountered occasionally, as when a street person of several years referred to himself as an "expert dumpster diver." In street argot, "dumpster diving" refers to scavenging through garbage bins in search of clothes, food, and salable items. Many street people often engage in this survival activity, but relatively few pridefully identify themselves in terms of this activity. Other role-specific survival activities that functioned in a similar manner included panhandling, small-time drug dealing, and street performing, such as playing a musical instrument or singing on a street corner for money. Illustrative of this type of embracement was a 33-year-old white male known on the streets as Rhymin' Mike, who called himself a street poet and made his money by composing short poems for spare change from passersby. For some homeless individuals, then, the roles they enact function as a source of positive identity and self-worth.

Associational embracement.—A second variety of embracement used to denote or embellish a personal identity entailed reference to oneself as a friend or as an individual who acknowledges the norm of reciprocity and who thus takes his social relationships seriously.[17]

---

17 Anderson (1976) found that this form of embracement figured prominently in the identity work of the black street-corner men he studied. Indeed, the identity work of these men consisted mainly of associational distancing and embracement.

A case in point is provided by the individual alluded to who pridefully acknowledged that he was a bum. On one occasion, he told us that he had several friends who either refused or quit jobs at the Salvation Army because they "weren't allowed to associate with other guys on the streets who were their friends." Such a policy struck him as immoral: "They expect you to forget who your friends are and where you came from when you go to work there. They asked me to work there, and I told them, 'No way.' I'm a bum and I know who my friends are."

Avowal of such social ties and responsibilities manifested itself in other claims and behavior as well. Identification of oneself as a person who willingly shares limited resources, such as cigarettes and alcohol, occurred frequently, particularly among avowed tramps and bums. One evening after dinner at the Salvation Army, for example, a 29-year-old white male who had been on the street for several years quickly responded to the researcher's offer of a cigarette with an offer of his own to take a drink from his Coke, commenting, "See, man, I'm all right. I share, man. I don't just take things."

Associational embracement was also expressed in self-identification as protector or defender of one's buddies. Two older drinking partners whom we came to know claimed repeatedly to "look out for each other." When one was telling about having been assaulted and robbed while walking through an alley, the other said, almost apologetically, "It wouldn't have happened if I was with you. I wouldn't have let them get away with that." Similar claims were made to the field researcher, as when two street acquaintances indicated one evening after an ambiguous encounter with a clique of a half-dozen other street people that, "If it wasn't for us, they'd have had your ass."

Although protective behaviors that entailed a risk were seldom observed, protective claims, particularly of a promissory character, were frequently heard. Whatever the relationship between such claims and action, they functioned not only to cement tenuous ties but also to express something concrete about the claimant's desired identity as a dependable and trustworthy friend.

Ideological embracement.—A third variety of embracement that can provide an individual with a special niche in which to lodge the self and thereby distinguish himself from others entails the acceptance of a set of beliefs or ideas and the avowal of a cognitively congruent personal identity. We refer to this as ideological embracement.

Among the homeless we studied, ideological embracement manifested itself primarily as an avowed commitment to a particular religion or set of religious beliefs. One middle-aged tramp called Banjo provides an example. He routinely identified himself as a Christian, he had painted on his banjo case "Wealth means nothing without God," and his talk was sprinkled with references to his Christian beliefs. When asked whether he was afraid to sleep at the Salvation Army following a murder that had occurred the night before, he replied: "I don't have anything to worry about since I'm a Christian, and it says in the 23d Psalm: 'Yea though I walk through the valley of death, I shall fear no evil, for Thou art with me.'" Moreover, he frequently pointed out that his religious beliefs transcended his situation on the streets. As he indicated on one occasion, he would like to get off the street but not for money: "It would have to be a bigger purpose than just money to get me off the streets, like a religious mission."

An equally powerful but less common functional equivalent of religion as a source of identity is the occult and related supernatural beliefs. Since traditional occupational roles are not readily available as a basis for identity and since few street people have the material resources that can be used for construction of positive personal identities, it is little wonder that some of them turn elsewhere—to mystical inner forces, to the stars, to the occult—in search of a locus for a positive identity. Illustrative of this was a 29-year-old male who read books on the occult regularly, identified himself as a "spirit guide," and informed us that he had received "a spiritual gift" at the age of 13 and that he now had special prophetic insights into the future that allowed him to foresee the day when "humans will be transformed into another life form."

In addition to mainstream religious and occult beliefs, conversionist, restorative ideologies, such as that associated with Alcoholics Anonymous, provide some of the homeless with a readily available locus for identity, providing they are willing to accept AA's doctrine and adhere to its program. The interesting dynamic here, however, is that AA's successes seldom remain on the street. Consequently, those street people who have previously associated with AA seldom use it as a basis for identity assertion. Nonetheless, it does constitute a potentially salient identity peg, as well as a way off the street.

TABLE 4: Types of Embracement by Time on the Streets (in percentages)

Time on the Streets	Type of Embracement		
	Categoric[a] (N = 39)	Specific[b] (N = 20)	Ideological[c] (N = 13)
		25.0	15.4
	5.1	20.0	7.7
	59.0	35.0	46.1
	35.9	20.0	30.8

Note.—$\chi^2 = 14.88$, $df = 6$, $P < .05$.

[a] Comments or statements coded as categoric included those indicating acceptance of or attachment to street people as a social category or to such general, street role identities as bum, tramp, drifter, and transient.

[b] Comments or statements coded as specific embracement included those indicating identification with a situationally specific survival role, such as dumpster diver and street performer, or with a specific social relational role, such as friend, lover, or protector.

[c] Comments or statements coded as ideological embracement included those indicating self-identification with a set of beliefs or ideas, such as those associated with a particular religion.

We have seen how the personal identities of the homeless may be derived from the embracement of the social identities associated with certain stereotypical street roles, such as the tramp and the bum; with role-specific survival activities, such as dumpster diving; with certain social relationships, such as friend and protector; and with certain religious and occult ideologies or belief systems. While embracement and distancing are not necessarily mutually exclusive means for constructing personal identities among the homeless, we have noted how their usage tends to vary according to the stage or point in one's street career. More specifically, we have found, as summarized in table 4, that the longer one has been on the street and the more adapted one is to street life, the greater the prevalence of categorical embracement in particular. That relationship is emphasized even further when it is noted that the only cases of such embracement among those who had been on the streets for less than two years occurred among those categorized as mentally ill, as in the case of a 33-year-old black female who avowed the nonstreet identity of The Interracial Princess, which she said had been bestowed on her by "a famous astrologer from New York."

Fictive Storytelling

A third form of identity talk engaged in by the homeless is what we refer to as fictive storytelling. It involves the narration of stories about one's past, present, or future experiences and accomplishments that have a fictive character to them. To suggest that these stories about the self are fictional to some degree is not to imply intentional deception, although it may and frequently does occur. Rather, we characterize these stories as fictive because they tend to range from minor exaggerations of experience to fanciful claims and fabrications. We thus distinguish between two types of fictive storytelling: embellishment of the past and present and fantasizing about the future.[18] Slightly more than a third of the identity statements we recorded fell into one of these two categories.

Embellishment.—By "embellishment," we refer to the exaggeration of past and present experiences with fanciful and fictitious particulars so as to assert a positive personal identity. It involves an overstatement, an enlargement of the truth, a "lamination," in Goffman's terms (1974), of what has actually happened or is unfolding in the present. Embellished stories, then, are only partly fictional.

Examples of such embellishment for identity construction purposes abound among the homeless. While an array of events and experiences— ranging from tales about the accomplishments of one's offspring to sexual and drinking exploits and predatory activities—were found to be the object of embellishment, the most common form of embellished storytelling tended to be associated with past and current occupational and financial themes. In the case of financial embellishment, the typical story entailed an exaggerated claim regarding past or current wages. An example is provided by a 40-year-old homeless male who spent much of his time hanging around a transient bar boasting about having been offered a job as a Harley-Davidson mechanic for $18.50 per hour, while constantly begging for cigarettes and spare change for beer.

Equally illustrative of such embellishment is an encounter we overheard between an inebriated 49-year-old homeless woman passing out discarded burritos and a young homeless man in his early 20s. When he took several burritos and chided the woman for

---

18   Given the categorization of this line of talk as "fictive," it is important to make explicit the criteria used to determine whether a particular narration was indeed fictive. As we previously noted, we not only talked with and listened to each of the 70 individuals within our identity subsample, but we encountered nearly all of them in a range of situations at different points in time, with an average of 4.5 encounters per individual. We were thus able to monitor many of these individuals across time and space. This enabled us to discern the fictive character of stories by noting one or more of three kinds of narrative contradictions: (1) those among multiple stories told by the same individual, as when one street person claims to be 36-years-old on one occasion and 46 on another; (2) those between stories and observed behaviors in various situations, as when someone claims to be working regularly but is seen panhandling or intoxicated during the course of the day; and (3) those between current situations and future projections and claims, as when a disheveled, penniless street person claims to have a managerial job awaiting him at a local business. In each of these situations, credulity is strained because of objective discrepancies or because of the vast gap between current and projected realities.

being drunk, she yelled stridently at him: "I'm a floating taper and I make 14 bucks an hour. What the fuck do you make?" Aside from putting the young man in his place, the statement functioned to announce to him, as well as to others overhearing the encounter, the woman's desired identity as a person who earns a respectable wage and must therefore be treated respectfully. Subsequent interaction with this woman revealed that she worked only sporadically and then most often for a temporary day agency at $4.00 per hour. There was, then, a considerable gap between claims and reality.

Disjunctures between identity assertions and reality appear to be quite common and were readily discernible on occasion, as in the case of a 45-year-old transient from Pittsburgh who had been on the streets for a year and who was given to excessive embellishment of his former military experiences. On several occasions, he was overheard telling tales about his experiences "patrolling the Alaskan-Russian border in Alaskan Siberia" and of encounters with Russian guards, who traded vodka for coffee with him. Since there is no border between Alaska and Siberia, it is obvious that this tale is outlandish. Nonetheless, such identity constructions, however embellished, can be construed as attempts to say something concrete about oneself and how one would like to be regarded in a particular situation.

Fantasizing.—The second type of fictive storytelling that frequently manifested itself during the course of conversations with and among the homeless is verbal fantasizing. In contrast to embellishment, which involves exaggerated laminations of past and present activities and experiences, fantasizing involves future-oriented fabrications about oneself. By "future-oriented fabrications," we refer to fanciful constructions that place the narrator in positively framed situations that seem distantly removed from, if at all connected to, his past or present. These fabrications were almost always benign, usually had a Walter Mitty, pipe-dream quality, and varied from fanciful reveries involving little self-deception to fantastic stories in which the narrator appeared to be taken in by his constructions.[19]

Regardless of the degree of self-deception, the spoken fantasies we were privy to were generally organized around four themes: self-employment, money, material possessions, and the opposite sex, particularly for men.[20] Fanciful constructions concerning self-employment were usually expressed in terms of business schemes. A black 30-year-old male

---

19 Fanciful identities are constructed by other people as well, but it is our sense that, with movement up the class structure, they tend to be more private and temporally or spatially ritualized rather than publicly articulated, ongoing features of everyday life, as was true for many of the homeless we studied and the black street-corner men observed by Liebow (1967) and Anderson (1976). Regarding the latter, Liebow (1967, p. 213) noted that the construction of fictive identities allows them to "be men once again providing they do not look too closely at one another's credentials." While many of the personal identities they construct, such as "going for brothers," are different in content from those constructed by the homeless, they are functionally similar. We will return to several of these points.

20 That these four factors function as springboards for fanciful identities constructed by homeless men in particular is hardly surprising, given that success as an adult male in America is defined in large part in terms of job, money, possessions, and women. This thematic connection also suggests that, while home-

from Chicago told us and others on several occasions, for example, about his plans "to set up a little shop near the university" to sell leather hats and silverwork imported from New York. In a similar but even more expansive vein, two white men in their early 20s who had become friends on the street seemed to be scheming constantly about how they were going to start one lucrative business after another. On one occasion, they were overheard talking about "going into business for ourselves, either roofing houses or rebuilding classic cars and selling them." And a few days later, they were observed trying to find a third party to bankroll one of these business ventures.

An equally prominent source of fanciful identity construction was the fantasy of becoming rich. Some of the homeless daydreamed openly about what they would do if they had a million dollars, as did one 32-year-old white male, who assured us that, if he "won a million dollars in a lottery," he was mature enough so that he "wouldn't blow it." Others would make bold claims about becoming rich, without offering any details. The following is illustrative: "You might laugh and think I'm crazy, but I'm going to be rich. I know it. I just have this feeling. I can't explain it, but I am." And still others would confidently spin fairly detailed stories about being extravagant familial providers in the future. Illustrative of this was an emaciated 25-year-old unemployed roofer who had just returned to Austin after a futile effort to establish himself in a city closer to his "girlfriend." Despite his continuing financial setbacks, he assured us: "I'm going to get my fiancée a new pet monkey, even if it costs me $1,000. And I'm going to get her two parrots too, just to show her how much I love her."

As we previously noted, fanciful identity assertions were also constructed around material possessions and encounters with the opposite sex. These two identity pegs were clearly illustrated one evening while we were hanging out with several homeless men along the city's major nightlife strip. During the course of making numerous overtures to passing women, two of the fellows jointly fantasized about how they would attract these women in the future: "Man, these chicks are going to be all over us when we come back into town with our new suits and Corvettes. We'll have to get some cocaine too. Cocaine will get you women every time."

We have seen how respectable work, financial wealth, material possessions, and the opposite sex figure prominently in the fanciful, future-oriented talk of some of the homeless. While all these themes may be interconnected in actuality, only one or two of them were typically highlighted in the stories we heard. Occasionally, however, we encountered a particularly accomplished storyteller who wove together all four themes in a grand scenario, as illustrated by the following fanciful construction told by the transient from Pittsburgh over a meal of bean stew and stale bread at the Salvation Army and repeated again later that night prior to going to sleep on a concrete floor in a warehouse converted

---

less males tend to stand outside the normative order in their way of life, some of them are, nonetheless, very much of that order in their dreams and fantasies.

into a winter shelter for 300 men: "Tomorrow morning I'm going to get my money and say, 'Fuck this shit.' I'm going to catch a plane to Pittsburgh and tomorrow night I'll take a hot bath, have a dinner of linguini and red wine in my own restaurant ... and have a woman hanging on my arm." When encountered on the street the next evening, entangled in his own fabrication, he attempted to explain his continued presence on the streets of Austin by saying he "had been informed that all my money is tied up in a legal battle back in Pittsburgh," an apparently fanciful lamination of the original fabrication.[21]

Although both the embellished and fanciful variants of fictive storytelling surfaced rather frequently during the course of the conversations we overhead, they were not uniformly widespread or randomly distributed among the homeless. As indicated in table 5, embellishment occurred among all the homeless but was particularly pronounced among those who had been on the street for two to four years. Fantasizing, on the other hand, occurred most frequently among those who still had one foot anchored in the world they came from and who could still envision a future; it occurred least often among those individuals who appeared acclimated to street life and tended to embrace one or more street identities. For these individuals, especially those who have been on the street for four or more years, the future is apparently too remote to provide a solid anchoring for fictive, identity-oriented spinoffs that are of this world. Again, the only exceptions to this pattern among the long-term homeless were the mentally ill who had been on the street for four or more years.

TABLE 5: TYPES OF FICTIVE STORYTELLING BY TIME ON THE STREETS (in percentages)

Type of Fictive Storytelling		
Embellishment[a] TIME ON THE STREETS (N = 38)		Fantasizing[b] (N = 31)
Less than six months	13.2	S1.6 32.3 9.7 6.4

Note.—χ^2 = 17.SS, df = 3, P < .001.

[a] Comments or statements were coded as embellishment if they entailed the elaboration and exaggeration of past and present experiences with fictitious particulars. See fn. 22 for criteria used for determining the fictive character of comments and stories.

[b] Comments or statements were coded as fantasizing if they entailed future-oriented fabrications that placed the narrator in positively framed situations. See fn. *22* for criteria used for determining the fictive, fabricative character of comments and stories.

---

21 It is important to note that this account was elicited by the field researcher rather than by another homeless individual. In fact, we rarely overheard the homeless call into question one another's stories and asserted identities. Interestingly, this contrasts strikingly with Anderson's finding in peer groups of black street-corner men that "people 'shoot down' and 'blow away' each other's accounts frequently" (1976, p. 18). Reasons for this difference will be suggested in Conclusions and Implications below.

CONCLUSIONS AND IMPLICATIONS

We have identified and elaborated three generic patterns of identity talk through which the homeless we studied construct and avow personal identities that yield a measure of self-respect and dignity. We have noted that each pattern of talk—distancing, embracement, and fictive storytelling—contains several varieties and that their frequency of use tends to vary with the duration of one's street career. Categorical role and associational distancing and the construction of fanciful identities were found to occur most frequently among those who had been on the streets a comparatively short time. Categorical embracement and embellishment, however, tended to manifest themselves most frequently among those who had been on the streets for two or more years.

Glossed in our presentation of these findings are three related considerations that warrant brief discussion. First, in focusing attention on the construction and assertion of more positive personal identities, we do not intend to suggest that the homeless we encountered did not sometimes view themselves in terms of the more negative, stereotypical identities that are frequently imputed to them. On one occasion, for example, a long-time street person lamented in a demoralized tone that he was "nothing but a bum." But such self-deprecating comments were relatively rare in comparison with the avowal of more positive identities. We suspect that this is partly because the homeless have little to fall back on in their attempts to salvage the self other than their own identity construction efforts.

The second caveat concerns the kinds of causal inferences that might be derived from the various patterns of identity talk we have elaborated. Given that slightly more than a third of the identity statements are of the embracement variety, it might be tempting to conclude that a sizable proportion of the homeless are on the street because they have chosen that life-style. From this vantage point, homelessness is seen as a matter of choice rather than as a function of structural forces beyond one's control. Such a voluntaristic interpretation strikes us as empirically unwarranted and theoretically misguided, however. In the first place, it is nearly impossible to infer causal dynamics from voluntaristic-sounding assertions apart from an understanding of the range of options available to a person. Homelessness may indeed be a matter of choice for some people, but perhaps only when there is a scant number of alternatives that are no more palatable than life on the street. To the extent that this is true, the choice is of the lesser of evils and takes on a rather different meaning than if it were made in the face of more attractive options. Thus, to attribute homelessness to choice without an understanding of the context in which that choice is made adds little to our understanding of the precipitants of homelessness.

Our finding that patterns of identity talk vary with length of time on the street provides an even more compelling reason for cautiously refraining from making inferences about the causes of homelessness, at the individual level, based on those patterns. In fact, our findings tell us relatively little about the reasons for homelessness. What they do seem to make clear, however, is that the personal identities homeless people construct and avow are not static but, instead, change with the passage of time on the streets. The typical progression is from categorical distancing and the assertion of fanciful, future-oriented identities to categorical embracement, distancing from specific types of homeless individuals and street institutions, and the embellishment of past experiences and encounters. Accordingly, our findings suggest that identity statements implying choice can best be regarded as manifestations of life on the street rather than as indicators of initial precipitants, especially since such statements tend to be more common among those who have been on the streets for more than two years.

Finally, it is important to emphasize that our research, unlike most research on identity, was based on in situ observations of and encounters with individuals engaged in natural ongoing interaction. The identities discerned and recorded were thus "in use" in an ongoing system of action rather than responses to prestructured questions in purely research contrived situations. Whatever the limitations of this research tack, we think they are outweighed by the fact that it provides a relatively rare glimpse of the actual construction and use of personal identities in the course of everyday life among individuals at the very bottom of society.

REFERENCES

Allardt, Erik. 1973. *About Dimensions of Welfare: An Exploratory Analysis of a Comparative Scandinavian Survey.* Helsinki: Research Group for Comparative Sociology.

Anderson, Elijah. 1976. *A Place on the Corner.* Chicago: University of Chicago Press.

Anderson, Nels. 1923. *The Hobo: The Sociology of the Homeless Man.* Chicago: University of Chicago Press.

-----. 1931. *The Milk and Honey Route: A Handbook for Hobos.* New York: Vanguard.

Ansbacher, Heinz, and Rowena Ansbacher. 1946. *The Individual Psychology of Alfred Adler.* New York: Basic.

Austin American Statesman. 1985 a. "Community Effort Needed to Find a Home for 'Sally.'" January 31.

------ . 1985*b.* "Homeless Called Content as Shelter Plans Opposed." February 7.

------ . 1985c. "It's Time for the City Council to Get Tough on Sally Site." July 3.

------- . 1985d. "Twisted Pathway of 'Sally' Paved by Many Designs." September 22.

Bahr, Howard M., and Theodore Caplow. 1973. *Old Men Drunk and Sober.* New York: New York University Press.

Banton, Michael. 1965. *Roles: An Introduction to the Study of Social Relations.* New York: Basic.

Becker, Ernest. 1965. *The Birth and Death of Meaning.* New York: Free Press.

Bettelheim, Bruno. 1943. "Individual and Mass Behavior in Extreme Situations." *Journal of Abnormal Social Psychology* 38:417–52.

Blumer, Herbert. 1969. *Symbolic InteracHonism: Perspective and Method.* Englewood Cliffs, N.J.: Prentice-Hall.

Blumstein, Phillip W. 1973. "Audience, Machiavellianism, and Tactics of Identity Bargaining." *Sociometry* 36:346–65.

Bogue, Donald J. 1963. *Skid Row in American Cities.* Chicago: Community and Family Study Center, University of Chicago.

Brown, Carl, S. McFarlane, Ron Paredes, and Louisa Stark. 1983. *Homeless of Phoenix: Who Are They? What Should Be Done?* Phoenix: Phoenix South Community Mental Health Center.

Bruns, Roger A. 1980. *Knights of the Road: A Hobo History.* New York: Methuen.

Burke, Peter J. 1980. "The Self: Measurement Requirements from an Interactionist Perspective." *Social Psychology Quarterly* 43:18–29.

Burke, Peter J., and Judy Tully. 1977. "The Measurement of Role Identity." *Social Forces* 4:881–97.

City of Chicago. 1983. *Homelessness in Chicago.* Chicago: Social Services Task Force.

Crystal, S., and M. Goldstein. 1984. *The Homeless in New York City Shelters.* New York: Human Resources Administration, City of New York.

Dawe, Alan. 1978. "Theories of Social Action." Pp. 362–417 in *A History of Sociological Analysis,* edited by Tom Bottomore and Robert Nisbet. New York: Basic.

Dimsdale, Joel E. 1980. "The Coping Behavior of Nazi Concentration Camp Survivors." Pp. 163–74 in *Survivors, Victims and Perpetrators: Essays on the Nazi Holocaust,* edited by Joel E. Dimsdale. Washington: Hemisphere.

Douglas, Jack D. 1976. *Investigative Social Research: Individual and Team Field Research.* Beverly Hills, Calif.: Sage.

Frankl, Viktor. 1963. *Man's Search for Meaning.* New York: Washington Square.

Gecas, Viktor. 1982. "The Self-Concept." *Annual Review of Sociology* 8:1–33.

Geertz, Clifford. 1973. *The Interpretation of Cultures.* New York: Basic.

General Accounting Office. 1985. *Homelessness: A Complex Problem and the Federal Response.* Washington, D.C.: U.S. General Accounting Office.

Gergen, Kenneth J. 1982. *Toward Transformation in Social Knowledge.* New York: Springer.

Goffman, Erving. 1961 a. *Asylums: Essays on the Social Situations of Mental Patients and Other Inmates.* New York: Doubleday Anchor.

-----. 1961b. "Role Distance." Pp. 84–152 in *Encounters: Two Studies in the Sociology of Interaction.* Indianapolis: Bobbs-Merrill.

-----. 1963. *Stigma: Notes on the Management of Spoiled Identity.* Englewood Cliffs, N.J.: Prentice-Hall.

-----. 1974. *Frame Analysis: An Essay on the Organization of Experience.* New York: Harper & Row.

Gould, Leroy C, Andrew L. Walker, Lansing E. Crane, and Charles W. Lidz. 1974. *Connections: Notes from the Heroin World.* New Haven, Conn.: Yale University Press.

Harper, Douglas A. 1982. *Good Company.* Chicago: University of Chicago Press.

Harrington, Michael. 1984. *The New American Poverty.* New York: Holt, Rinehart & Winston.

Holmes, Urban Tigner. 1966. *Daily Living in the Twelfth Century: Based on the Observations of Alexander Neckham in London and Paris.* Madison: University of Wisconsin Press.

Hombs, Mary Ellen, and Mitch Snyder. 1982. *Homelessness in America: A Forced March to Nowhere.* Washington, D.C.: The Community for Creative Non-violence.

Inglehart, Ronald. 1977. *The Silent Revolution.* Princeton, N.J.: Princeton University Press.

Knutson, Jeanne M. 1972. *The Human Basis of the Polity: A Psychological Study of Political Men.* Chicago: Aldine.

Levitin, T. E. 1964. "Role Performances and Role Distance in a Low Status Occupation: The Puller." *Sociological Quarterly* 5:251–60.

Liebow, Elliot. 1967. *Tally's Corner: A Study of Negro Streetcorner Men.* Boston: Little, Brown.

Lofland, John, and Lynn H. Lofland. 1984. *Analyzing Social Settings: A Guide to Qualitative Observation and Analysis.* Belmont, Calif.: Wadsworth.

Los Angeles Times. 1984a. "Santa Barbara—A Lid on Hobos' Food?" December 13.

------. 1984b. "'Troll Busters' in Santa Cruz Prey on the Homeless." October 26.

McCall, George J., and J. L. Simmons. 1978. *Identities and Interactions.* New York: Free Press.

MacIntyre, Alasdair. 1981. *After Virtue: A Study in Moral Theory.* Notre Dame, Ind.: University of Notre Dame Press.

Marx, Karl, and Friederich Engels. (1848) 1967. *The Communist Manifesto.* New York: Penguin.

Maslow, Abraham H. 1962. *Toward a Psychology of Being.* New York: Van Nostrand.

Myrdal, Gunnar. 1962. *Challenge to Affluence.* New York: Pantheon.

Newsweek. 1984. "Homeless in America." January 2, pp. 20–29.

New York Times. 1985. "Plan to Shelter the Homeless Arouses Concern in Maspeth." June 7.

Pollner, Melvin, and Robert M. Emerson. 1983. "The Dynamics of Inclusion and Distance in Fieldwork Relations." Pp. 235–52 in *Contemporary Field Research: A Collection of Readings,* edited by Robert M. Emerson. Boston: Little, Brown.

Robertson, Marjorie J., Richard H. Ropers, and Richard Boyer. 1985. *The Homeless of Los Angeles County: An Empirical Evaluation.* Document no. 4. Los Angeles: Basic Shelter Research Project, School of Public Health, University of California, Los Angeles.

Roth, Dee, Jerry Bean, Nancy Lust, and Traian Saveanu. 1985. *Homelessness in Ohio: A Study of People in Need.* Columbus, Ohio Department of Mental Health.

San Antonio Urban Council. 1984. *Robert Wood Johnson Grant Application: Health Care for the Homeless.* San Antonio, Tex.: San Antonio Urban Council.

Sarbin, Theodore R., and Karl E. Scheibe, eds. 1983. *Studies in Social Identity.* New York: Praeger.

Sayles, Marnie L. 1984. "Role Distancing: Differentiating the Role of the Elderly from the Person." *Qualitative Sociology* 7:236–52.

Shibutani, Tamotsu. 1961. *Society and Personality.* Englewood Cliffs, N.J.: Prentice-Hall.

Snow, David A., Susan G. Baker, Leon Anderson, and Michael Martin. 1986. "The Myth of Pervasive Mental Illness Among the Homeless." *Social Problems* 33:407–423.

Snow, David A., Robert D. Benford, and Leon Anderson. 1986. "Fieldwork Roles and Informational Yield: A Comparison of Alternative Settings and Roles." *Urban Life* 15:377–408.

Snow, David A., Louis Zurcher, and Gideon Sjoberg. 1982. "Interviewing by Comment: An Adjunct to the Direct Question." *Qualitative Sociology* 5:285–311.

Spradley, James P. 1970. *You Owe Yourself a Drunk: An Ethnography of Urban Nomads.* Boston: Little, Brown.

———. 1980. *Participant Observation.* New York: Holt, Rinehart & Winston.

Srinivas, M. N, and Andre Beteille. 1965. "The Untouchables of India." *Scientific American* 216:13–17.

Stebbins, Robert A. 1975. "Role Distance, Role Distance Behavior and Jazz Musicians." Pp. 133–41 in *Life as Theater: A Dramaturgical Sourcebook,* edited by D. Brissett and C. Edgely. Chicago: Aldine.

Stone, Gregory P. 1962. "Appearance and the Self." Pp. 86–118 in *Human Behavior and Social Processes,* edited by Arnold M. Rose. Boston: Houghton Mifflin.

Strauss, Anselm L. 1959. *Mirrors and Masks: The Search for Identity.* Glencoe, III: Free Press.

Stryker, Sheldon. 1968. "Identity Salience and Role Performance." *Journal of Marriage and the Family* 30:558–64.

———. 1980. *Symbolic Interactionism: A Social Structural Version.* Menlo Park, Calif.: Benjamin-Cummings.

Turner, Ralph H. 1968. "The Self-Conception in Social Interaction." Pp. 93–106 in *The Self in Social Interaction,* edited by C. Gordon and K. J. Gergen. New York: Wiley.

———. 1978. "The Role and the Person." *American Journal of Sociology* 84:1–23.

U.S. Conference of Mayors. 1985. *Health Care for the Homeless: A 40-City Review.* Washington, D.C.: United States Conference of Mayors.

U.S. Department of Housing and Urban Development. 1984. *A Report to the Secretary on the Homeless and Emergency Shelters.* Washington, D.C.: U.S. Department of Housing and Urban Development.

U.S. House Committee on Government Operations. 1985. *The Federal Response to the Homeless Crisis:* Hearings before a Subcommittee of the Committee on Government Operations. House of Representatives, 98th Congress, 2nd Session. Washington, D.C.: Government Printing Office.

Weigert, Andrew J. 1983. "Identity: Its Emergence within Sociological Psychology." *Symbolic Interaction* 6:183–206.

Whyte, William F. 1943. *Street Corner Society: The Social Structure of an Italian Slum.* Chicago: University of Chicago Press.

Wiseman, Jacqueline. 1970. *Stations of the Lost: The Treatment of Skid Row Alcoholics.* Chicago: University of Chicago Press.

Znaniecki, Florian. 1934. *The Method of Sociology.* New York: Farrar & Rinehart.

Questions for discussion

1. How do you think the experience of self has varied across history?
2. How does increased potentiality make the self a problem?
3. What does it mean to refer to the self as a "problem" to be solved? Do you agree with this formulation?
4. How do the changes described by Baumeister vary across populations? In other words, did potentiality and individuality increase for everyone at the same time? Why or why not?
5. After reading the selection from *Codependent Forevermore*, can you think of other instances and settings that offer a narrative formula for stories of the self? What are the elements of the formula? What constitutes a "good" story in that situation?
6. Think of all the self-help books and programs currently available. Do you think these work? Is it possible to change the self?
7. How might one embark on a journey to find out who one "really" is?
8. Consider the "identity talk" engaged in by the homeless people in the selection by Snow and Anderson. Can you use this as a tool for analysis in other situations? For example, can you examine the ways your friends talk about themselves and sort them into different strategies for building or maintain self-worth?

Further reading

Bellah, Robert N., Richard Madsen, William M. Sullivan, Ann Swidler, and Steven M. Tipton. 1985. *Habits of the Heart*. New York: Harper and Row.

Gagnon, John. 1992. "The Self, Its Voices, and Their Discord." Pp. 221–243 in *Investigating Subjectivity*. Edited by Carolyn Ellis and Michael Flaherty. Newbury Park, CA: Sage.

Gergen, Kenneth. 1991. *The Saturated Self: Dilemmas of Identity in Contemporary Life*. New York: Basic Books.

Giddens, Anthony. 1991. *Modernity and Identity: Self and Society in the Late Modern Age*. Stanford: Stanford University Press.

Hewitt, John P. 1989. *Dilemmas of the American Self*. Philadelphia: Temple University Press.

Riesman, David, with Nathan Glazer and Reuel Denney. 1950. *The Lonely Crowd: A Study of the Changing American Character*. New Haven: Yale University Press.

Taylor, Charles. 1989. *Sources of the Self: The Making of the Modern Identity*. Cambridge: Harvard University Press.

CHAPTER 3

✶

New Directions in the Study of the Self

INTRODUCTION

The selections in this chapter suggest new possibilities for the study of the self. The first two readings examine the impact of inequality, prejudice, and discrimination on the self. The classic scholarship on the self was conducted by white men. The readings in Chapter 1, from Cooley, Mead, Blumer, and Goffman, explain how the self works, as if it were a universal experience. Perhaps it is. But some scholars argue that we are missing something if we assume that the white, male account of the self is definitive.

The reading by O'Brien highlights the contradictions faced by lesbian and gay Christians, and it provides unique insight into how people can reconcile identities that are in opposition. Most Christian doctrines condemn homosexuality. Consequently, many gays and lesbians find themselves defined and treated as sinners, condemned and cast off by the groups that potentially provide meaning and purpose in life. In response, gays and lesbians have often rejected Christianity, sometimes with fervor. Some, however, manage to define themselves as queer and Christian. O'Brien not only reveals how they come to "live a contradiction," but she illustrates how the research led her to question her own original assumptions about the experience of living as a queer Christian.

Nagel's article focuses on phenomena called "ethnic switching" and "ethnic renewal," and their impact on collective and individual identity. Nagel presents us with a puzzle. During the 1970s and 1980s, the number of U.S. residents identifying themselves on the U.S. census as "American Indian" more than tripled. There was not, however, an increase in birth rates or a decrease in death rates. Nagel attributes the increase to ethnic switching, in which people who had previously identified themselves as white switched their identification to Indian in later censuses. She traces the process of ethnic renewal among the American Indian population, whereby individuals and communities reasserted their pride. Her analysis offers a vivid account of the power people have to reinvent themselves.

The next two readings highlight a pitfall in Mead's thinking. For Mead, spoken language formed a barrier between humans and non-humans. To be sure, language allows humans to understand and communicate the symbols for self, such as our names and the names of other objects. But Mead made language the pinnacle of being. He acknowledged that animals have their own social arrangements, but he gave their interaction the lower status of a "conversation of gestures." These are instinctual acts, such as when a dog growls at another who threatens to steal his bone or a cat hisses at a rival. Mead considered the "conversation of gestures" insignificant because it allegedly had only one set of meanings, as opposed to language, which he referred to as significant symbols. Lacking the capacity to use significant symbols, Mead considered animals incapable of meaningful social behavior. He wrote, "The animal has no mind, no thought, and hence there is no meaning [in animal behavior] in the significant or self-conscious sense" (Strauss 1964, 168).

The selections by Sanders and Irvine challenge Mead's claim and open up ways to extend selfhood to animals. In "Understanding Dogs," Sanders focuses on interactions between people and their canine companions. He draws on research on interactions between people with severe mental disabilities and their family members. In daily interactions, the non-disabled attribute the status of "human" to people who possess few of the characteristics we usually associate with that status. It sounds harsh to refer to the disabled as "not human," so allow me to clarify. As Sanders explains, "the designation of another as 'human' is an eminently social activity" (210). Throughout history, various groups have found reasons to exclude certain others from this status. African Americans, members of indigenous groups, and prison inmates are just a few examples of those who have been designated as less than human. The mentally disabled, too, have been denied fully human status—except within their families. Research reveals four ways that family members assign human status to the disabled. Sanders identifies these in people's interactions with their dogs. In doing so, he opens up the boundary that excludes animals, or in this case, dogs, from the human world. He shows how people see their dogs as minded social actors and sheds light on how we construct the status of "person."

The selection I wrote extends Sanders's work to offer a model of selfhood that can incorporate animals. When I began the research, I found, as Sanders did, that people talked about their dogs and cats as if they, too, were people. I wanted to consider the possibility that people who thought this were not just foolishly sentimental, as Mead suggests in his work, *Mind, Self, and Society*. Instead, I thought, What if they're not foolish? How can we think about the selves of animals? Because of Mead's insistence on language, his work was a dead end. I brainstormed about what other beings had selves but lacked the use of spoken language. Ultimately, I drew on early work by William James, which has been applied to studies of subjective experience among infants. Babies, who cannot speak, nevertheless have goals and experiences that indicate a self. Because we share the same basic physiology and neurology with animals, it is likely that the same capacities for self exist, too. Humans acquire spoken language as they develop the skills necessary for survival as a human being, and animals acquire the skills to survive in their social environments. By examining selfhood among those who cannot speak, Sanders and I hope to enrich our knowledge of what it means to "be" a social being—regardless of species.

The final selection comes from neuroscience. This area holds tremendous potential for clarifying and refining our understanding of the self. The reading offered here draws on current research that emphasizes memory. Scholars of the self consider memory indispensable for the self. We remember who we are from day to day. We juggle various roles, and we must remember what we do in all of them. Memory is essential in our ability to do this.

Neuroscience has revealed much about how memory works. LeDoux, a brain expert, emphasizes the role of synapses, the minute spaces between the sending end of one neuron and the receiving end of another. Neurons make our brain functioning possible. Whenever we do anything, whether we have an experience, a thought, or a feeling, information is transmitted through neurons in the brain. These transmissions across neurons create patterns, and different experiences create different patterns. The synapses are changed. Our brains are thus encoded with memories that make us who we are. In important ways, the self *is* synaptic.

There are many other possibilities for expanding research on the self. The areas of focus chosen here merely illustrate two directions. There remains much to know, and many ways to find out.

Strauss, Anselm (ed.). 1964. *George Herbert Mead on Social Psychology*. Chicago: University of Chicago Press.

WRESTLING THE ANGEL OF CONTRADICTION: QUEER CHRISTIAN IDENTITIES

By Jodi O'Brien

This ethnographically based article is about the ways in which individuals who choose to remain in mainstream Christian denominations while being out about their sexuality make sense of and manage the presumed discontinuity of homosexuality and Christianity. In this article I focus specifically on the processes whereby lesbian and gay Christians forge an integration of Christian doctrine, spirituality and sexuality. My central interpretive claim is that this integrative struggle is experienced by lesbian and gay Christians as a raison d'être. Wrestling this contradiction has given rise to a particular expression of queer Christian identity. Among the many implications of these expressions of queer Christian identity is their impact on mainstream Christian congregations and Christian ideologies and practices.

KEYWORDS Christianity; homosexuality; self and identity

I wanted gays to be in the vanguard, battling against racial and economic injustice and religious and political oppression. I never thought I would see the day when gays would be begging to be let back into the Christian Church, which is clearly our enemy. (Edmund White, author)

Jodi O'Brien, "Wrestling the Angel of Contradiction: Queer Christian Identities," from *Culture and Religion*, Vol. 5 No. 2, Pp. 179-202. Copyright © 2004 by Taylor & Francis Ltd. Permission to reprint granted by the publisher.

Seven reasons why you should absolutely, positively stay away from church … [reason number four]. The way some churches can get God to fit into those little boxes. (Posted flyer, Spirit of the Sound: Gay and Lesbian Followers of Jesus)

I had to go to a non-Christian church for four years before I understood what it means to be a good Christian. A good Christian has a very big god. (Larry, Gay male and practicing Catholic)

INTRODUCTION

Several years ago I attended Pride Parades in three different cities during the same month. The San Francisco Parade is becoming an increasingly somber affair, I thought to myself as I noted the serious faces on the police who monitored the barriers holding back protesters. An air of gaiety prevailed. But the atmosphere also carried indications of what some observers have called the 'homogenisation' or commercialisation of gay culture.[1] The San Francisco parade, more so than any other perhaps, marks the contradictions of an expanding lesbian and gay presence in public spheres, including the protest movements. In Seattle, a bastion of politically correct postures, locals pride themselves on their tolerance. Here the parade is just another occasion to bring the family and have a good time—whoever you are. In this city the contradictions exist behind the scenes. Each year, during the planning of the parade, questions of inclusion and exclusion arise as the planning board debates whether to include groups such as North American Man-Boy Love Association[2] or 'too obvious drag queens'— anyone who may evoke discomfort in this crowd that is trying so hard to be accepting of difference. Chicago seems the most relaxed. Perhaps it is the heat, but the cops seem indifferent to the public drinking and appear almost jovial, occasionally flirtatious. It feels like a neighborhood block party among causal, easy-going friends.

Each parade feels distinct to me. The differences do not surprise me. In many ways, they reflect the mosaic of responses to the proliferation of lesbian and gay presence and politics in recent decades. Perhaps this is why I am so surprised at one notable similarity that occurs at all three parades. Among the marchers in each parade are groups representing friends and supporters of lesbians and gays: PFLAG, AT&T Queer Allies, US Bank LGBT Employee Support, and so forth. In each case, the crowd responds enthusiastically at this display of support and acceptance. People clap and cheer and whistle in appreciation. The marchers glow in acknowledgement. This is not what surprises me. Rather, it is the contrast in the crowd's response to another group of marchers: lesbian and gay Christians and, specifically, Mormons (who march under the banner of Affirmation) and Catholics (who call their association Dignity). In these three very distinct US cities I wandered up and down the streets during each parade, watching as merry crowds fell silent at the appearance of these marchers. Everywhere the response was the same: silence, broken only by an occasional boo. I was stunned.

These otherwise very 'normal' looking but openly queer men and women (some of whom really did look like the stereotypical Mormon missionary) were being booed at their own Pride Parades.

On reflection, this response—at best indifferent, at worst disdainful— makes sense if viewed within the framework of the cultural secularism that pervades 'progressive' US politics. Religion in general, and Christianity in particular, are often perceived as an anathema to liberal progressive politics. It is likely that many parade bystanders were genuinely confused at what must have seemed an obvious contradiction: openly queer, openly religious. For some parade-goers, the presence of these lesbian and gay Christians might even have been a form of betrayal given the active anti-homosexual preaching of both the Vatican and Mormon leaders. In any case, my curiosity was aroused. What compelled someone to want to parade both statuses? My initial impression was that lesbian and gay Christians must experience a form of 'double stigma'. Christian denominations routinely denounce homosexuality. For many lesbians and gays, a flight from religious intolerance is a central aspect of personal 'coming out' stories. Religion is clearly the enemy. Further, there is a pronounced secularism in the rhetoric of the small but prolific elite whose words and images have propelled lesbian and gay literature and culture into the mainstream. Good queers are not religious.

Obviously there are many closeted gays and lesbians. Similarly, although I really had not thought much about it until the occasion of the parades, there are probably many open lesbians and gays who harbor secret religious inclinations. What seemed to confuse and unsettle the crowd was the open expression of such an apparent contradiction. Why would any self-respecting queer want also to embrace Christianity with its seemingly inevitable denouncement and exclusion? And why, especially, would they want to announce this involvement to fellow queers, knowing the disdain and rejection that this was likely to incur?

Compelled by these questions I began to research what I called 'double stigma.' Specifically, I was interested in lesbians and gays who are openly queer and openly Christian. How did they make sense of and manage this 'double stigma' I wondered? The concept of 'double stigma' was sociologically rigorous enough to garner me research support for the project. Armed with this idea, the financial blessing of the American Sociological Association, and a solid track record of ethnographic experience, I set off in search of answers. Five open-ended interviews into the project, I knew the concept of 'double-stigma' was completely off the mark. I was missing the main point. When I raised the idea of 'double-stigma'—How do you deal with it? Why do you deal with it?—the first round of interviewees all looked at me with similar confusion. Yes, they understood the question. Yes, they could understand how others would see it that way. But it did not resonate for them. Each of these five people, none of whom knew one another, said the same thing. This was not about stigma. It was about 'living a contradiction that defines who I am.'

Forty-two interviews and many hours of congregational participation later I was still hearing the same thing: the contradiction of being Christian and being queer is who I am. When I gave talks describing the research project I noticed the vigorous head-nodding among self-described queer Christians at the mention of the phrase, 'living the contradiction.' My orienting perspective at the launch of this project reflected my penchant for sociological abstraction and personal experiences that disincline me toward participation in mainstream religions (I am a former Mormon with a typical 'flight from religion' experience through the process of becoming a lesbian). Through sustained contact and participatory experience with self-described 'queer Christians' and the congregations that welcome them, I developed an understanding of the deeply complex process of living the contradiction of being queer and Christian. In fact, over time, I have come to have considerable appreciation for this process.

RESEARCH SETTING AND METHODOLOGY

This article is based on a more comprehensive project in which I develop the thesis that the contradictions between Christianity and homosexuality are the driving tensions in the formulation of a historically specific expression of queer religiosity. These expressions are manifested in individual identities and practices, in community practices (i.e. Christian congregations), and in ideological discourses (i.e. theological and doctrinal discourses). The transformative processes occurring at each of these levels are mutually constitutive. In this article I focus specifically on the processes whereby lesbian and gay Christians[3] forge an integration of Christian doctrine, spirituality and sexuality.[4] My central interpretive claim in this paper is that this integrative struggle is experienced by lesbian and gay Christians as a raison d'etre. Wrestling this contradiction has given rise to a particular expression of queer Christian identity. Among the many implications of these expressions of queer Christian identity is their impact on mainstream Christian congregations and Christian ideologies and practices. I describe these implications briefly in the conclusions.

As I have noted in the Introduction, my original intent was to understand the motivations and experiences of lesbian and gay Catholics and Mormons who wished to be recognised explicitly for both their religiosity and sexuality. I began the project by talking with several such individuals, including my hairstylist, a self-described 'flaming queen with a flair for building miniature houses' who is also active in his local Catholic parish. Larry's openly gay behavior was considered outrageous even by the standards of the gay-friendly hair salon that he worked in. Quite frankly, I could not imagine what his fellow parishioners made of his queerness. Yet Larry seemed to have found quite a home there. He spoke often and enthusiastically about his involvement with the parish. He invited me to attend services and, eventually, several meetings of the lay ministry, to experience for myself what his 'contradictory' world was like. Another point of entry came through a colleague who had granted me a formal interview and then invited me to attend services at

Seattle's First Baptist where he was an active participant. Later his congregation invited me to participate as a speaker in their ongoing 'Adult Education' series—a version of Sunday School. They wanted to explore the theme of sexuality and asked if I would kick-off the topic. Jim, my colleague and interview subject, was instrumental in organising the series and in setting me up with subsequent interviews.

Through participation in these congregational activities I was introduced to more lesbian and gay Christians who granted me interviews and put me in contact with other friends and colleagues throughout the western United States and British Columbia. I also learned first-hand of the tensions taking place within the congregations that were support-ive of lesbian and gay members.[5] The late 1990s was a time of ferment within Christian congregations regarding the presence and affirmation of lesbian and gay members. In this respect, the timing of my research was serendipitous. In recognition of these community and organisational tensions, I expanded my interviews to include heterosexual congregants and clergy members. I also expanded my participation to several regional congregations representing Episcopalian, Methodist, Unitarian, and Presbyterian denominations, in addition to my initial participation with Baptist, Catholic and Mormon groups. My formal research process included 63 open-ended interviews and sustained contact with five congregations and two lesbian/gay Christian groups (Affirmation and Dignity) for a period of three years.

During this time I came to recognise what I term a 'field of relations,' which includes lesbian and gay Christians, the congregations in which they have found a 'spiritual com-munity,' the general membership of these congregations, the congregational ministries, and the relationships between these congregations and their denominational organisa-tions. There is awareness among these congregations that they are part of a historical moment that is fraught with considerable tension and debate regarding the very definition of Christianity. In this regard, I think it accurate to talk in terms of a social movement that is taking place within the pews (with a distinctly different genesis and process from LGBT political movements as they are typically presented in the social movements literature).

My research methods are consistent with ethnographic interpretive methodologies in which the intent is to articulate fields of relations and the intrapersonal and interpersonal relations that occur within these fields. My approach is especially informed by feminist methodologies, according to which my intent is to ascertain what persons within the field of inquiry have to say for themselves while remaining cognisant of my own relationship with these persons and my influence within the field of relations. At the same time, my work is strongly influenced by sociological theories that orient me toward ascertaining patterned discourses regarding how people make sense of themselves—what stories they tell themselves about who they are and what they can do— especially regarding conflict and contradiction (O'Brien 2001a; Plummer 1995). My observations and conclusions are interpretations that reflect my sociological orientation. Throughout the research process I presented myself as a sociologist with special interests in religion and sexuality. Early in the research process people became aware of my project and approached me about being interviewed and/or having me visit their congregations. This awareness and interest confirms my observation that a self-aware field of relations regarding queer Christian identities exists. My interpretations are limited to the specific context of this research project. However, my aim with this in-depth inquiry is to provide empirical insight and grounding for the conceptual frameworks through which scholars attempt to understand the integration of religion and sexuality generally.[6]

THE 'GAY PREDICAMENT': AN IRRECONCILABLE CONTRADICTION

> Homosexuality is intrinsically disordered. (Catechism of the Catholic Church 1994, 566)

The 'question of homosexuality' has been a central focus of discussion in Catholic and Protestant denominations since the 1960s. Historically, homosexuality is forbidden in most Christian doctrines. In these texts the homosexual has been variously defined as 'disordered,' 'evil,' and 'sinful' (Conrad and Schneider 1980; O'Brien 2001b). In many texts homosexuality is rendered as absolutely irreconcilable with the basic tenets of Christianity. Recent revisions of a few doctrines offer a slightly more forgiving interpretation wherein homosexual behavior is separated from homosexual identity.[7] The new Catechism, for instance, defines homosexual inclinations (identity) as a 'condition' that is not chosen and is experienced as a 'trial' (Catechism of the Catholic Church 1994, 566). Grappling with this affliction can be a lifetime struggle and those who are 'successful' in taming the beast of homosexuality can expect the same joys and blessings as other good Catholics.[8] In this rendering the act is the sin, while desire is an affliction. In an accompanying passage, the text admonishes all Catholics to treat persons who suffer the condition of homosexuality with 'respect, compassion and sensitivity' (1994, 566). Progressive Catholics see this doctrine as at least an acknowledgement that homosexuality exists. The separation of act and identity is considered by some to be a statement of acceptance. Still, even in this supposedly progressive statement, the 'homosexual' is rendered as someone (something) lacking, someone whose desires are a potential source of shame and exile.

Doctrines that condemn homosexuality constitute the ideological backdrop against which Christians initially experience their homosexuality. At worst, they are irredeemable sinners: at best, they suffer from problems or afflictions. Given this discourse of rejection, non-Christians might assume that the simplest path would be the renunciation of religion. For many Christians struggling with feelings of homosexuality the path is not so simple.

Psychologists of religion offer a holistic explanation for sustained Christian participation, even when the participation involves conflict. According to this thesis, Christianity is a well-established and deeply meaningful cosmology that weaves together spirit, intellect, body and community (Fortunato 1982). Christianity offers answers to big questions such as the meaning of life and death. Religious participation is also a means of transcending the oppressions and banalities of everyday living. For many Christians, the traditional ceremonies of religious expression are both evocative and comforting. Thus, motivation for participation is not so much the puzzle. In fact, to frame the question this way, as many studies of religion and homosexuality (including my own initial research proposal) do, is arguably to impose a secular perspective on a religious question.[9] Rather, the puzzle becomes: How does the homosexual make sense of the fact that, by definition, he/she is considered an exile who is beyond the promised redemption of Christian theology? Christian therapist John Fortunato refers to this as the 'gay predicament.' The 'gay predicament,' simply put, is that one cannot be a good Christian and also be queer.

The intensity of this contradiction can only be fully understood within a framework of Christian experience. Within a heteronormative culture, lesbians and gays are (often painfully) aware that they are social cast-offs. Within Christianity, active homosexuals are also aware that, in addition to their being social cast-offs, their souls have been cast off as well. This predicament poses a tremendous existential crisis. To experience homosexual desires, and certainly to pursue fulfillment of these desires, will result in being cast out from the cosmology through which one makes sense of one's life. One obvious solution is to cast off Christian theology in favor of the homosexual identity. This is easier said than done, however. Bending the rules is one thing, but shedding an entire structure of meaning may leave one cast adrift in a sea of meaninglessness -which may be even less tolerable than the knowledge that one is potentially damned. This is a defining predicament for lesbian and gay Christians. It is also a profound set of contradictions. Abandoning Christianity may mean losing a sense of meaning and purpose, yet keeping this particular religion means facing the prospect of damnation.

Queer Secularism

In addition to the predicament of exile, lesbian and gay Christians who are open about their religiosity face rejection from other queers. Lesbian and gay political activists, scholars and writers tend to be critical and dismissive of Christianity. The following remark from gay author John Preston (known especially for his anthologies of gay male short stories) is indicative of the discourse of disdain prevalent among lesbian and gay activists and artists. Preston was invited by Brian Bouldrey to write a chapter for his anthology, *Wrestling with the Angel: Religion in the Lives of Gay Men*. This is his response:

> I'd have nothing to say in your anthology. As an atheist I have no angels with which to wrestle, and, to be honest, I think adults who worry about such a decrepit institution as organized religion should drink plenty of fluids, pop an

aspirin, and take a nap, in hopes that the malady will pass. (Quoted in Bouldrey 1995, xi).

Thus, lesbian or gay Christians who seek comfort and insight among fellow queers may be setting themselves up for further disdain and rejection because of their religious affiliation. The queer Christian is doubly damned: according to Christian doctrine, homosexuality is an affliction; among fellow (non-Christian) lesbians and gays, religious affiliation may be the affliction. Not only can one not be a good Christian and be queer, apparently one cannot be a good queer and be religious. Or, as Elizabeth Stuart, author of a guide for LGBT Christians, so aptly phrases it, 'queer Christians find themselves caught as it were between the devil and the rainbow, aliens in both lands' (1997, 13).[10]

Persons who have been 'spun off from their galaxy of meaning' (Fortunato 1982)—in this case, heteronormative acceptance and Christian systems of meaning and purpose—seek reintegration into new systems of meaning. For instance, heterosexual persons who are inclined, for whatever reasons, to denounce their religious roots usually construct new systems of meaning within secular frameworks. Persons who find themselves spun off from heterosexual culture often find meaning in queer groups that have articulated anti-straight philosophies and practices.

Religious Individualism

In her dissertation on members of the Metropolitan Community Church (MCC), Melissa Wilcox chronicles the stories of LGBT Christians and their struggle to reconcile spirituality and sexuality. Her research indicates that even before finding the MCC, which offers a community of like-minded fellows, individuals experienced long struggles around coming out. Wilcox refers to this struggle as an 'immense crisis of identity.' She observes that most members '[forge] their own paths to self-acceptance and spiritual wholeness' prior to joining MCC (Wilcox 2000, 135). Wilcox offers a theoretical interpretation situated in the concept of 'religious individualism' (Roof 1999). There is a double-thread to her thesis. The way in which individual lesbians and gays reconcile their predicament is often a solitary process, one that reflects aspects of a culture of religious individualism rather than community and congregational support. At the same time, the increasing visibility of LGBT members in Christian religions may also reflect a general climate of religious individualism.[11] The title of her dissertation, 'Two Roads Converged,' is a kind of double-play that indicates the road not taken (refusal to renounce forbidden sexuality in this case), and also the manner in which individual reconciliation of this 'immense crisis of identity' converges in similar experiences, expressions and ways of making sense of the contradiction.

This religious individualism is evident in my research as well. Individuals experience an awakening of both religiosity and homosexuality that is very personal and profound. This awakening ushers in a sense of contradiction and a desire to somehow reintegrate themselves into the system of meaning from which they now feel outcast. Interviewees describe this period of initial struggle as very lonely and painful. There is a sense of insurmountable shame and alienation. The path to resolution is a solitary one. Given this, it is especially noteworthy that individual forms of resolution converge in a very similar and particular ways.

Responses to the Gay Predicament[12]

Anecdotal and experiential information suggests three general sorts of responses to the gay predicament: denunciation and flight, acceptance of the doctrine of shame, and articulation of an alternative (queer) religiosity. The first, denunciation and flight, is a well-known story among many lesbians and gay men. Many 'coming out' stories involve a process of renouncing religious roots. These stories can be interpreted as a statement of renunciation and opposition against a system of meaning in which lesbians and gays find no place for themselves. These expressions involve a process of reshaping one's sense of self and identity in opposition to religious teachings and practices. For many individuals, this is a painful and alienating process that involves not only casting off an entire system of meaning and belonging, but forging a new (non-Christian) ideology. As one former Mormon missionary-turned-lesbian put it:

> Non-Mormons don't get that Mormonism answers your questions about everything. Now I have to wonder about every little thing. Do I still believe in monogamy? Or is that something I should throw out along with Mormonism? Do I still believe in life-after-death? Marriage? Commitment? What do I believe in? It's all a big gaping hole for me now. (Lori)[13]

For many the struggle is about how to (re)integrate with society more generally. This is often done through alignment with other queer groups and the articulation of a discourse whereby the religious community, not the individual, is seen as the problem. In this instance, throwing off the cloak of religious shame is seen as an act of liberation:

> Healthy living means finding ways to throw off the guilt. It's not just the guilt of feeling like you've betrayed your family and friends and their expectations for you. It's the guilt that comes from messages all around you that you don't belong. That you're an aberration. Until one day you start to get it and say, hey, I'm here. I'm doing okay. I must belong. When you figure that out you have the courage to walk away from the [church] and realize the problem is them. They're not big enough to let you belong. (Brian)

This group of 'recovering Christians' may be the least tolerant of lesbians and gays who attempt to find a place for themselves within Christianity.

Another familiar, and similarly complex, response is to learn to accept Christian teachings that render homosexuality an affliction. In such instances, the struggle to be a good Christian (and a good person generally as defined through adherence to Christian principles) revolves around the struggle to sustain celibacy. Homosexual reintegration into Christianity involves accepting the definition of an afflicted self, donning a cloak of shame regarding one's homosexuality (or, minimally, a cloak of sickness), and embarking upon the struggle indicated by this affliction. The literature on ex-gay therapies and ministries, most of which consists of personal narratives and 'undercover' participant observation, indicates that those who seek out these 'therapies' are likely to come from strong Christian backgrounds. Often they are referred to the therapies by a Church leader in whom they have confided (see, for instance, Harryman 1991). In these cases, the homosexual Christian who is not 'cured' is encouraged to remain 'closeted' if he/she wishes to maintain a position in the religious community.

My focus is on those individuals who endeavor to maintain both a strong Christian identity and an open and 'proud' lesbian or gay identity. These people recognise their distinct position with respect to those who renounce Christianity and those who accept Christian definitions of affliction. A defining feature of this group is the desire to (re)integrate within a Christian system of meaning while maintaining a queer identity and, ideally, to integrate both identities within a common community. Given this, especially viewed within the framework of the other paths of response, it is possible to assert that lesbian and gay Christians are a distinct group who have at least some awareness that they are forging a unique response to their predicament. It must be noted, however, that, at least initially the responses to this predicament are local and individual. In this regard, the convergence of responses into similar themes is sociologically noteworthy.

In this paper, I am particularly interested in the content of the themes that lesbian and gay Christians have articulated. As I note in the concluding section, it is the expression of these themes and the performance of a queer Christianity within congregations that creates a critical mass, or groundswell, that can be interpreted as a particular form of queer Christian religious movement. In other words, none of the individuals in this project started out with an inclination to reform religion or to make a socio-political statement. Rather, each was primarily interested in the question of (re)integrating within a Christian community. Given this context, meaningful research questions include: how do lesbian and gay Christians make sense of and manage their predicament? What motivates their involvement in a system of meaning from which they have been spun off, socially and spiritually? What (if any) source of (re)integration do they articulate for themselves?

RAISON D'ETRE

Despite the threats of damnation and rejection among other queers, lesbian and gay Christians remain undaunted in their commitment to both a queer identity and Christian religiosity. Each of the 42 lesbian and gay Christians that I interviewed described having a sense of deep spirituality. Many of them offered details of what they felt to be an 'early sense of vocation.' As one interviewee phrased it, 'religion has always been a natural and necessary part of existence for me.'

At the same time, lesbian and gay Christians recognise that these proclamations of Christian spirituality put them at odds with other queers. Detailed statements about religious conviction are usually accompanied by accounts of having to defend this spirituality as a 'thoughtful, meaningful enterprise and not some sort of brain-numbing self-denial' (Sean). He continues, 'When I see it through the eyes of other gays, I often wonder if my religiosity is a character flaw.'

Each of the interviewees articulated an awareness of a secular hegemony in this culture ('educated professional people in general are often embarrassed about their spiritual leanings'). To be religious in a secular society is a struggle. To be religious and queer is to expect ongoing struggle. The theme of struggle is constant throughout my own interviews, in my ethnographic participation in various congregations and in related writings.

The theme of struggle is also familiar and persistent throughout Christian doctrine and teachings. For example, in the Catechism, persons are instructed that appropriate sexual behavior (chastity) is an 'apprenticeship in self-mastery which is a training in human freedom' (Catechism of the Catholic Church 1994: 562). This mastery (which culminates in sexual expression contained within a marriage blessed by the Church) will bring happiness and fulfillment. Failure to achieve it will lead to enslavement by the passions. 'Struggle' may be a definitive trope of Christianity itself. Certainly one of the religion's most enduring themes is that persons will confront challenges and afflictions. The implied lesson is that the way they handle these struggles shapes their character. In this regard, lesbian and gay Christians can be seen as playing out a variation on an old theme: the contradiction of spirituality and sexuality is their particular struggle; the manner in which they engage the struggle defines their character. Struggle is paramount in each of the three responses to the 'gay predicament'—struggle to reinterpret or renounce a dominant system of meaning; struggle to suppress and hide homosexual desire. A common distinction among the lesbian and gay Christians in this study is the extent to which struggle with a contradiction is a definitive aspect of self-understanding and identification (cf. White and White 2004). Two themes in particular emerged from my interviews and observations. First, wrestling the contradiction of spirituality and sexuality defines the self-proclaimed lesbian or gay Christian. Second is the sense among them that they are better Christians—indeed, better persons—as a consequence of this struggle. In other words, the struggle is the crucible in which their character is forged.

Articulating the Self as a Process of Contradiction

There is a version of social psychology that suggests the 'articulated self' develops through the process of managing tensions and contradictions in aspects of life that the person considers most meaningful. In my own work I make the claim that the 'self' can be usefully defined in terms of this process. In other words, the ways in which we make sense of and manage these contradictions are the definitive features of the social self (O'Brien 2001a). One common experience among the persons I interviewed was an early awakening of both spirituality and homosexuality.[14] Several participants indicated that their awareness of both their spirituality and their homosexuality was simultaneous. For each of them this was a profound realisation, and one that was followed almost immediately by a sense of dread and panic:

> I was about 14 or so. I had this heightened sense that I was very special. Very spiritual. God has something special in mind for me. At the same time I had this sense of myself as sexual and that felt so good and so right. And then it occurred to me that these two feelings didn't fit and were going to get me into big trouble. That's when I started trying to figure out what God wanted with me. What was this struggle supposed to teach me? I was really a mess about it for a long time. I think I have some answers now. But I still struggle with it every day. (Jim)

Fortunato remarks that it is 'no surprise that gay people ask an inordinate number of spiritual questions.' For those who fit comfortably within an accepted system of meaning such as Christianity, the extent to which they think about their spirituality is probably in terms of some benign Sunday school lesson, or perhaps something that is mildly comforting in times of need.[15] Christians who have acknowledged their homosexuality do not have the luxury of semi-conscious spirituality. The discovery that one's sexuality is so deeply contradictory 'requires awakening levels of consciousness far beyond those necessary for straight people' (Fortunato 1982, 39). Thus, lesbian and gay Christians may have a more articulated sense of what it means to be a Christian precisely because they have to make ongoing sense of deeply felt contradictions.

For the most part this struggle for articulation is seen as positive and definitive. Every interviewee remarked in some way or another that her/his core sense of being was shaped significantly by the struggle to reconcile homosexuality and religiosity. Comments such as 'I wouldn't be me if I didn't have this struggle' were typical.

> This is what has forged me, my defining battle. I'd probably be a very conservative evangelical Christian if I wasn't gay—everything is different as a result, especially my spirituality. Wrestling this marginality has become the thing that shapes me more than anything else. (Jim)

For these individuals, self-understanding comes through the process of engaging with persistent contradiction. The experience of contradiction is ongoing, both in conversations with oneself and in interactions with others. Lesbian and gay Christians constantly find themselves in situations in which they must explain (and often defend) their seemingly contradictory statuses to others. This experience is seen both as an occasion that can be tiresome and also as an occasion for growth and self-articulation. As one lesbian Baptist put it:

> You can never take yourself for granted. If I go to an event with lesbians and somehow it comes up that I'm an assistant pastor, I have to listen to this barrage of criticism about the history of Christianity and what it's done to us. I get soooo tired of that. What's amazing is that it never seems to occur to them that maybe I've thought about this. Maybe I have complicated reasons for being who I am. But they don't ask. As tiresome as it can be, it's still a good experience for me. I tend to go home and ask myself, why are you doing this? And I find that I understand my own answers better and better. Does that make any sense? (Carol)

Or this comment from a gay Methodist:

> It's like coming out over and over again. Every time someone new joins [the congregation] we're going to go through the same ol' dance about how the Sunday School coordinator is this gay guy. Thankfully, I'm so well-known now that the other members warn the newcomers. But there's always someone who wants to bait you, y'know, corner you at a social or something and quiz you on doctrine. Like they know doctrine! ... I wanted to be able to scoff at their ignorance. The funny thing is, now that I know what I do, it turns out I want to educate them instead of show them up. I guess this whole thing has made me much more conscious of being a good Christian. (Mark)

This comment is from a student of Theology and Ministry:

> It seems like everyday, everywhere I go I'm a problem for somebody. It's a problem for white America that I'm black. It's a problem for gay America that I'm in the ministry. It's a problem for the ministry—a big, big problem—that I'm gay. Always a problem. Weird thing is, and you might think this is funny, but being a problem has made me really strong. I mean, as a person. I'm always having to think about who I am and not let it get to me. That makes you strong in yourself. You really know who you are. (Everett)

Another common feature in these narratives is the prevalence of contradiction.

These experiences are similar in tone and expression to some of the narrative reflections on multiple consciousness (for example, Anzaldua 1987). Persons who occupy contradictory social positions find themselves traversing the boundaries, or borders of multiple worlds. In so doing they develop a consciousness that reflects their marginal position. Persons in such positions usually have a heightened awareness of their own marginality; they are also more likely to be critically aware of expressions and practices that less marginalised persons take for granted. Most individuals perceive this heightened awareness as an advantage. At the very least, as noted in the illustrative quotes, contradictory positions are an occasion for reflection and articulation.

A significant outcome of these reflections among lesbian and gay Christians is the articulation of contradiction itself as useful and worthwhile in the shaping of a Christian identity. Not only is contradiction a catalyst for self-reflection, but ultimately it is a source of challenge for Christian congregations. Lesbians and gays who denounce Christianity and leave often make sense of their departure by recognising that their religion is 'too small' to accept 'the likes of me.' This (re)conception of the church and/or God as being too small to accommodate difference is a common basis for renouncing religious affiliation among lesbians and gays. Among those who remain (or become) active participants in their religious communities, there is a slightly different and highly significant twist to this discourse. The strands of this twist include the articulation of the theme that 'my gay presence in this too small church is an opportunity for members to stretch their own limits of love and acceptance' and the even more radical notion, 'homosexuality is a gift from God.' The articulation and convergence of this uniquely queer response to Christianity is the subject of the next section.

ARTICULATING A QUEER CHRISTIAN IDENTITY

> Biography and faith traditions intersect to produce discursive strategies toward religion. (Wade Clark Roof)

> Homosexuality is a gift from God. (John McNeill, formerly of the Society of Jesus)

In the foregoing comments I have suggested that lesbian and gay Christians are aware that they occupy a unique, marginal and contradictory position with regard to fellow (heterosexual or closeted) Christians and to (former-Christian or non-Christian) lesbians and gays. This contradiction is experienced as a source of insight and as an occasion for articulating a self that these individuals perceive as stronger, more purposeful and, in many cases, indicative of the true meaning of Christianity. In other words, I suggest that rather than attempt to resolve the apparent contradiction of being queer and Christian, these individuals see 'living the contradiction' as a purpose in itself, a raison d'etre.

One additional theme that emerged from my conversations with lesbian and gay Christians is this: 'my contradictory presence is good for the Church.' This revision of the discourse on homosexuality (from problem to useful challenge) serves to reintegrate the homosexual into Christianity (at least in terms of her/his personal articulation of the religion). Further, it renders the homosexual a sort of modern-day crucible with which Christianity must grapple. In doing so, mainline Christian denominations must revisit and redefine the message of love and redemption. In this regard, lesbian and gay Christians redefine 'affliction' as an ability; the ability to embrace contradiction and ambiguity is articulated as a manifestation of Christian goodness and character.

This articulation can be interpreted in terms of Roof's thesis, as quoted earlier. Individuals enter into a 'creative dialogue with tradition' and articulate discursive strategies that enable them to retain significant (often contradictory) aspects of self while maintaining religious commitments.[16] In this instance, the homosexual biography intersects with familiar aspects of Christianity—faith in God's divine wisdom, acceptance of challenge, struggle, oppression, awakening and rebirth—to produce a particularly queer discursive response toward religion. The lesbian and gay Christians who took part in my research, as well as those interviewed by Wilcox (2000), are a unique group in that they have not rejected religion altogether, nor have they accepted the terms of a 'divinely ordered closet' (i.e. donning the cloak of shame and silence in order to maintain Christian commitments and status). Instead, they have articulated a position that can be interpreted as a unique queer Christian identity. This identity merges elements of essentialist reasoning, Christian doctrines of love and acceptance, Christian histories of oppression, and collective struggle to attain godly virtues. The emergence of a common discourse among individuals who are, for the most part, engaged in solitary struggle, is noteworthy. I attribute this emergent queer Christian discourse, in its initial phases, to the common threads in Christianity generally. In articulating a queer Christianity, lesbians and gays take up similar threads regarding the formation of identity and their position within their congregations.

The most common theme I heard among both the lesbian and gay Christians I came to know and the congregants who fully accepted them was that we are 'all God's children.' A point of reconciliation with one's homosexuality and Christianity seems to be the acknowledgement that 'God created me; He must have created me this way for a reason.' This 'realization' is marked by many lesbian and gay Christians as a turning point: 'All of a sudden it hit me, I believe in God, I believe He is perfect and has created a perfect world. Why would I have these desires if they weren't part of a perfect plan?' Or as one lesbian pastor phrased it, 'Yes I've been reborn through my faith in God's love. Turns out I was born queer.'[17]

Coupled with the theme of struggle, this discourse becomes a narrative whereby homosexuality is 'both a gift and my cross to bear.' In this regard, homosexuality becomes a personal crucible for forging character. This discourse is buttressed by the Christian belief that God creates everything for a purpose. The good Christian's task is to nurture faith in God and to live out the purpose evident in her/his own creation—in this case, the creation of homosexuality. Queer Christians find doctrinal support for their homosexuality in the principle, 'God is love.' A loving God loves and accepts all Her/His creations; a Church founded on these principles must make room for all that God has created and loves. From this thread comes the idea that a Church is only as big as its god, and its god is only as big as the extent of her/his love. Thus, a truly Christian church is a church that is big enough to love and accept homosexual members.

The third and most critical thread in this discourse combines with the others to weave the theme whereby the homosexual is a necessary and useful challenge for contemporary Christianity. In the words of former Jesuit and self-declared gay liberation theologian John McNeill, 'God is calling us to play an historical role' (1996, p. 192). This role is to extend to Christian congregations and denominations the challenge of stretching to accept all who enter and wish to belong—in short, to become as big as God's love, which is infinite. This discourse reclaims the proverbial phrase, 'love the sinner but hate the sin,' but it reframes sin as failure to love and accept all God's creations. In this conceptualisation, God and Christianity *per se* are not the problem; rather, the problem is the institution through which God's intent is interpreted. In the words of a gay Methodist minister, 'I never had any doubts about my relationship with God. It's the church that's been a problem for me.' Thus, the institution of Christianity becomes the problem and lesbian and gay Christians become the chosen few whose special calling it is to redeem institutional Christianity by liberating its narrowly defined god.

Articulating a queer Christian identity involves transforming a discourse of shame and silence (with the promise of exile) into a narrative of pride and expression. For lesbian and gay Christians, pride is based on a belief that homosexuality has a place in God's plan. The particular place at this particular moment in history is to foment Christian renewal and reformation. In this way, lesbian and gay Christians manage their original predicament by renaming themselves and their positions within their congregations in terms of a gay Christian activism. This discursive strategy is consistent with both lesbian and gay social movements and a Christian tradition of faith-based struggle and martyrdom. It elevates the homosexual from a position of 'irredeemable problem' to one of 'path to redemption.' In this particular instance, it is institutional Christianity that is in need of redemption. Just as the individual must struggle in order to grow and to achieve character and, ultimately, exaltation, so too must the institution of Christianity struggle. The 'latter-day homosexual' is the occasion for this institutional metamorphosis. Within this discourse, lesbian and gay Christians become both modern-day Christian soldiers and sacrificial lambs.

IMPLICATIONS

In this concluding section I suggest some of the implications of a queer Christian identity with regard to a queer Christian movement. The fullness of the phenomenon that some have referred to as 'the queering of Christianity' is best understood in terms of separate but mutually constitutive fields of relations: individual, communal, organisational, and ideological. My focus in this article is the ways in which individuals who choose to remain in mainstream Christian denominations while being out about their sexuality make sense of and manage the presumed discontinuity of homosexuality and Christianity. For the persons in this study, the journey from feeling ashamed of their sexuality and betrayed by God to articulating a strong queer Christian identity was mostly solitary. Once they achieved this queer Christian identity they became aware that there were many others who shared similar histories.[18]

In this conclusion, I want to discuss briefly some of the shifts taking place at various analytical levels as a consequence of what I would term a social movement within the pews. There are several noteworthy developments, including the proliferation of queer Christian literatures and websites (for example, Stuart 1997; Tigert 1997; see also www.lesbianchristians.com), as well as literatures that attempt to identity, define and 'authorize a specifically gay, lesbian, or queer "spirituality" as an alternative to the restrictions of "organized religion"' (Comstock 1997, 11). Here I address two areas: congregational communities and theology. Another equally noteworthy battle is being waged at the organisational/denominational level. Space does not permit me to comment on this level here (see Hartman 1996).

Congregational Communities

The presence of open lesbians and gays who are active participants in Christian congregations poses tensions and contradictions for their religious communities. Much of my own ethnographic research centers on the responses of congregants to the presence of lesbian and gay members. There is much more complexity in these congregational deliberations than the existing literature indicates (much of this literature assumes, uncritically, a simple, antagonistic dichotomy between straight and queer Christians). Queer Christians who consider themselves a source of challenge for their Christian communities are often correct in this understanding. Numerous Christian congregations throughout the United States, British Columbia and Great Britain[19] have issued formal statements of 'inclusion and affirmation' of lesbian and gay members. In most cases, the creation of these documents, and the position of acceptance implied, has involved considerable debate among members of the congregations.

Significant numbers of members leave a particular parish or congregation because of its acceptance of openly homosexual members (e.g. the outcry among church members whose ministers perform 'gay' wedding ceremonies). Equally significant, but less often discussed, are those who leave a congregation because of its intolerance toward lesbian and gay members. In my research I encountered several heterosexual Catholics and Protestants who had explicitly sought out 'open and affirming' churches after experiencing a 'crisis of faith' in observing the intolerance of their previous congregations.[20] For some churchgoers, an 'open and affirming' marquee is a positive indication that the church also espouses other 'liberal' values.

The process whereby congregations come to terms with openly gay and lesbian members is varied and complex. In some instances, anti-gay activism in the region serves as a catalyst to galvanise support for lesbians and gays. For instance, one Seattle area church notes in the letter announcing its vote 'unanimously to become open and affirming' that the final impetus for this vote was a visit to the city by anti-gay activist Fred Phelps. With a gleeful aside the letter states, 'Pssst… don't tell Fred Phelps that his presence here only served to solidify our support of becoming Open & Affirming on this Lord's Day' (Cornell-Drury 2000). The AIDS epidemic has also forced a focus on members who are in need of the church's services and ministries, many of whom are gay men. In his book, *AIDS, Gays and the American Catholic Church,* Richard Smith (1994) chronicles the elaborate debates that have taken place among American Catholic priests in determining how best to respond to the AIDS crisis. The creation of Catholic AIDS ministries, many of which are staffed by lay Catholics who are themselves gay and living with AIDS, has brought homosexuality directly into the parishes in a way that cannot be ignored.

These events are noteworthy but should not overshadow the everyday presence of, and interactions that take place between, church members. Repeatedly I heard stories from 'straight' members who had struggled with their own definition of Christianity and how best to respond to lesbian and gay members. These narratives converge around similar themes, especially the theme that God is 'unconditional love.' For many of these Christians, a lesbian and gay presence in the church truly is an occasion to examine the meaning of Christianity and how best to 'live' it. For individual members, as well as entire congregations, this is a long and difficult process. For example, Seattle First Christian states in its letter of affirmation notes that 'this is the culmination of three years of listening, dialogue, discernment and unconditional love … [this statement] is indeed a work of faith' (Cornell-Drury 2000). My observation is that there is a growing movement taking place within congregational pews (in addition to the polls and in legislative arenas). This movement is being shaped by the presence of lesbian and gay members, the contradiction they force upon the community, and the discursive strategies that emerge as a way to manage this community-level contradiction. As congregations struggle to manage this contradiction and to articulate their own positions, they are responding more and more to aspects of queer Christian theology. It is possible that this occurrence is also creating more opportunities for placement of lesbian and gay clergy in mainstream congregations. Again, the effects are mutually constitutive and should be studied as such.

Theology

What are the ideological consequences of a gay and lesbian presence in mainstream Christianity? I have suggested that lesbian and gay Christians are authoring a historically specific queer religiosity to make sense of their predicament of exclusion. This queer Christianity is likely to have transformative effects at the individual, community and organisational levels—all of which are mutually constitutive. Similarly, there are implications for Christian ideologies as well. I offer the following as preliminary observations. Whether one is in agreement with it or not, the articulation of a queer Christian theology, especially as it has emerged within the ranks of individuals trying to make sense of their own contradiction, has implications.

Queer Christian theologies resituate and redefine the parameters for discussions of sexuality and morality. Regardless of one's views, the conversation is different as a consequence of acknowledging homosexuality. Another significant implication is the authoring of a 'gay liberation theology' whereby homosexuality is identified as a gift from God. Again, regardless of whether one agrees, this particular discourse is already leading to a re-examination in many denominations of what it means to say that theology should be a 'living guide' that reflects its times.

In my own assessment, one of the most noteworthy ideological considerations is the implication of focusing on 'unconditional love' as a discursive strategy for accepting and affirming a homosexual presence. Concerning the case of homosexuality, the belief that 'god is love' sits in tension with the notion of a patriarchal god who, like the unchallenged parent, sets down rules that are not to be questioned. An ideology of unconditional love implies a love that is growing and stretching; a love that is manifest among members of a community who interpret for themselves the extent and expression of this love. This is a longstanding tension in Christian theology. Deliberations regarding homosexuality that are framed in terms of 'god's unconditional love' tip the equation one degree further toward a rendering of a Christian god who is not an anthropomorphic figure handing down his particular rules. Rather, this god is an expression of agreement and affirmation among a collective body united in spirit and intent. In short, 'god' becomes the extent of the community's expression of love. The larger the reach of the group's love, the bigger their god.

A Final Note Regarding Oppositional Consciousness

In an attempt to explain lesbian and gay involvement in Christian organisations, some lesbian and gay political activists have suggested that religion is one of the 'last citadels' of gay oppression (see Hartman 1996 for a review). These observers see the struggle for inclusion in mainstream religions as a final step toward attaining cultural and political acceptance. In this literature, lesbian and gay Christian involvement is interpreted as a form of political expression whereby queers are taking on traditional homophobia by acting from within. This thesis presumes an 'oppositional consciousness' (Mansbridge 2001) that conflates outcomes (religious reform) with motivation and presumes a motivation (desire to reform religion) that is not necessarily reflective of the actual experiences of lesbian and gay Christians. My research suggests that there are several stages in self-awareness and articulation that occur before any form of 'oppositional consciousness' develops among lesbian and gay Christians. To the extent that such a consciousness is developing, I suggest that it is historically unique and should be understood within the context in which it is developing. Specifically, the motivation should be understood in terms of the homosexual Christian's desire for self-understanding in Christian terms and reintegration into a system of meaning from which he/she has been cast off.

Sociological theses such as Mansbridge's 'oppositional consciousness' or Roof's 'creative dialogue' are useful in providing a general framework of analysis, but they miss the mark in interpreting motivations and commitments. Roof's thesis is intended to explain what he views as a 'shopping' mentality regarding contemporary religion, in which the individual shops around in search of a congregation or denomination that fits personal needs. Queer Christian identities appear to be motivated more by the desire for (re)integration within Christian traditions, at which point the individual may begin to 'shop' for a welcoming congregation. Similarly, while it is certainly possible to view the growing lesbian and gay visibility within Christian organisations as a manifestation of 'oppositional consciousness,' I think it would be inaccurate and misleading to assume a political motivation for this involvement. An intended contribution of this study is to make clear that lesbian and gay Christian participation (and related activism) must be understood on its own terms, in its own context and in terms of the particular historical moment.

NOTES

1. The emergence of businesses, such as GayMart USA, is indicative of both a commodification and a homogenisation of 'gay culture.' See, for example, *Homo Economics* (Gluckman and Reed 1997).
2. The inclusion of this group is highly controversial for many lesbian and gay events.
3. In this paper I use the phrase 'lesbian and gay' because it is the most accurate description of the group about which I am writing. The term lesbian/gay/ bisexual/transgender (LGBT) is politically strategic and meaningful, but often not descriptively accurate in specific case studies.
4. Several colleagues and interviewees have indicated that the experiences of Jewish lesbians and gays are similar. In this project, I have maintained a focus on mainstream Christian denominations because of my familiarity with Christian theology. For studies in Jewish queer experience, see Schneer and Aviv (2002) and Balka and Rose (1991).
5. During the course of my formal research, Seattle First Baptist was one of a handful of recent Baptist denominations in the United States that were threatened with revocation of their

charter for affirming lesbian and gay membership. Other congregations that were the spiritual homes to several of my interviewees struggled with similar tensions within their denominational organisations, especially congregations attempting to appoint lesbian and gay ministers and those that supported standing ministers who had recently 'come out' to the congregation.

6. This ethnography is limited, especially in what it suggests regarding variations of gender, race and geography on the articulation of and circumstances surrounding a queer Christian identity. I expect that there are significant variations in terms of the dimensions of gender and race, and I suspect these interact differently in different geographical regions. This study highlights one variation on the theme of individual reconciliation of homosexuality and Christianity. It should be read in terms of what it can suggest for further research regarding different variations on this theme.

7. There is a notable historical correlation between gay political movements, Christian denominations' heightened discussion of the 'homosexual question'—including the revision of the Catechism—and the removal of 'homosexuality' as a category of pathology in the 1974 *Diagnostic and Statistical Manual* used by the American Psychiatric Association to identify and diagnose psychological disorders.

8. Article Six, section 2359: 'Homosexual persons are called to chastity. By the virtues of self-mastery that teach them inner freedom, at times by the support of disinterested friendship, by prayer and sacramental grace, they can and should gradually and resolutely approach Christian perfection' (Catechism of the Catholic Church 1994, 566).

9. This explanation is consistent with a social psychological literature demonstrating that dominant belief systems are usually not rejected in the face of contradiction. Rather, individuals attempt to make sense of the contradictions through 'secondary elaborations' (Mehan and Wood 1975, 197). The motivation for continued engagement in the belief system is the desire to maintain a coherent system of meaning regarding the meaning and purpose of one's life. Even problematic positions within the system of meaning can be less threatening than having no sense of meaning or basis for self-understanding. This literature can be used to explain seemingly incomprehensible behavior such as attendance at one's own 'degradation ceremony' (e.g. the Mormon who participates in her/his own excommunication process).

10. Stuart also points out the similarities with other Christians, such as Christian feminists or Christian ecologists, who must also explain and justify their religious commitments.

11. Religious individualism as articulated by Roof is a process whereby persons seek individual paths of spiritual fulfillment. In this modern religious turn, individuals select among an array of churches and spiritual paths to fulfill personal needs. Roof and others have referred to this process as a form of religious 'shopping' whereby religion is seen in terms of personal enhancement (what does this church do for me?) rather than as a form of traditional community obligation.

12. I am not implying that these responses are mutually exclusive or fixed. Rather, it is probable that during the course of a queer Christian career individuals try on aspects of each of these responses. It is beyond the scope of this paper to develop an explanation for primary self-expression through one response or another—a settling in to a particular expression of identity. I assume that various reference groups play a part in this process and that, over time, the proliferation of an articulated queer Christianity will in itself serve as one such point of reference for a new generation of queer youth. I offer some suggestions toward such an explanation in the conclusions.

13. All quotes from subjects used in this article are intended to be illustrative (rather than analytically definitive). For this reason I do not give detailed subject descriptions. These descriptions are available on request. All of the interviewees in this study elected to use their real names. For reasons of 'voice' this is my preferred ethnographical practice.

14. Although nothing conclusive can be ascertained from my few interviews, this phenomenon of simultaneous awakening of homosexuality and spiritual vocation may be more prevalent among young men. Nineteen of the 25 men I interviewed spoke of this experience. Only two of the women mentioned a similar feeling. In fact, the women tended to develop a strong sense of spirituality and desire for religious involvement sometime after coming to terms with their homosexuality. Two of the men offered an explanation of their early sense of vocation as being a means of making them feel better about their homosexuality. As one put it, 'God wouldn't have made me this way if he didn't have something special in mind for my life.' Another noted that he considered his experience somewhat normal 'for someone who was meant to be a priest… after all, aren't all priests supposed to be gay? I figured that my attraction to men, including one of the teachers at my [Catholic] school, was just God's way of making it clear that I was meant to be a priest.'

15. Evangelicalism is another domain of Christianity whose members experience struggle and are likely to view this struggle as a definitive aspect of themselves and their religious commitment. Smith, C. 1998. American Evangelicalism: Embattled and Thriving. Chicago: University of Chicago Press.

16. For another interesting example, see Gloria Gonzalez-Lopez's (2004) study of Catholic Mexican immigrant women and their sex lives.

17. In the past two decades, many lesbian and gay Christians embraced the hypothesis that homosexuality is genetic rather than socially determined. This essentialist position was consistent with the idea that if homosexuality exists, God must have intended it. Catholicism has accepted the essentialist proposition of biological determinism explicitly without accepting the corollary that homosexuality is a positive characteristic. The latter is the queer twist on the essentialist proposition. But belonging to a denomination that accepted the initial proposition made it easier to make the case for the possible goodness and purpose of homosexuality. Other denominations, notably Mormonism, state explicitly that homosexuality is a 'lifestyle choice' that a person should resist by every possible means,

no matter how strong the inclination. For a discussion of the intersection of essentialist and constructionist reasoning within Christian considerations of sexuality, see Boswell (1997).

18. The persons in my study range in age from 27 to 63 years. It is likely that a younger generation of lesbian and gay youth are discovering the existence of a queer Christianity in community rather than in isolation.

19. In England, the Lesbian and Gay Christian Movement is considered to be the single largest LGBT movement in the country (Gill 1998).

20. During this research process I gave a talk at a Baptist church and mentioned that I had been raised as a Mormon. Afterward a married couple approached me and remarked that they had left a Presbyterian church and joined this congregation because of its acceptance of homosexuality. Before joining this particular church, they had not known 'anyone who is gay,' but they had 'grave concerns' about a Christian church that would be so exclusive. After hearing this, I was somewhat surprised when they continued with a question for me. What they really wanted to know was whether Mormons were as bad as they had been led to believe. Their daughter had recently begun dating a Mormon man and they were quite overwrought about this.

REFERENCES

ANZALDUA, G. 1987. *Borderlands/La Frontera: the new Mestiza.* San Francisco: Aunt Lute Books.

BALKA, C., and ROSE, A., ed. 1991. *Twice blessed: on being lesbian, gay and Jewish.* Boston, MA: Beacon.

BOSWELL, J. 1997. Concepts, experience, and sexuality. In *Que(e)rying religion: a critical anthology,* ed. G. D. COMSTOCK and S. E. HENKING. New York: Continuum.

BOULDREY, B., ed. 1995. *Wrestling with the angel: faith and religion in the lives of gay men.* New York: Riverhead Books.

Catechism of the Catholic Church. 1994. United States Catholic Conference, *Libreria Editrice Vaticana.* Mahwah, NJ: Paulist Press.

COMSTOCK, G.D. 1997. Que(e)rying Religion: A Critical Anthology. New York: Continuum.

CONRAD, P., and SCHNEIDER, J. 1980. Homosexuality: from sin to sickness to lifestyle. In *Deviance and medicalization: from badness to sickness,* ed. P. CONRAD and J. SCHNEIDER. Philadelphia: Temple University Press.

CORNELL-DRURY, P. 2000. Seattle First Christian Church unanimously becomes 'open & affirming'. Letter to the congregation, 6 November, Seattle, WA.

FORTUNATO, J. 1982. *Embracing the exile: healing journeys of gay Christians.* San Francisco: Harper Collins.

GILL, S., ed. 1998. *The lesbian and gay christian movement: campaigning for justice, truth, and love.* London: Cassell.

GLUCKMAN, A., and REED, B., ed. 1997. *Homo Economics.* New York: Routledge.

GONZALEZ-LOPEZ, G. 2004. *Beyond the bed sheets, beyond the borders: Mexican immigrant women and their sex lives.* Berkeley: University of California Press.

HARRYMAN, DON D. 1991. With all thy getting, get understanding. In *Peculiar people: mormons and same-sex orientation,* ed. R. SCHOW, W. SCHOW and M. RAYNES. Salt Lake City: Signature Books.

HARTMAN, K. 1996. *Congregations in conflict: the battle over homosexuality.* New Brunswick, NJ: Rutgers University Press.

MANSBRIDGE, J. 2001. The making of oppositional consciousness. In *Oppositional consciousness: the subjective roots of social protest,* ed. J. MANSBRIDGE and A. MORRIS. Chicago: University of Chicago Press.

MCNEILL, J. 1996. *Taking a chance on god: liberating theology for gays, lesbians, and their lovers, families, and friends.* Boston, MA: Beacon.

MEHAN, H., and WOOD, H. 1975. Five features of reality. In *Reality of ethnomethodology,* ed. H. MEHAN and H. WOOD. New York: Wiley.

NESTLE, J. 2002. How a 'liberationist' fem understands being a Jew. In *Queer Jews,* ed. D. SCHNEER and C. AVIV. New York: Routledge.

O'BRIEN, J. 2001a. Boundaries and contradictions in self articulation. In *The production of reality,* ed. J. O'BRIEN and P. KOLLOCK. Newbury Park, CA: Pine Forge Press.

O'BRIEN, J. 2001b. Homophobia and heterosexism. In *International encyclopedia of the social and behavioral sciences.* London: Elsevier Science.

PLUMMER, K. 1995. *Telling sexual stories: power, change, and social worlds.* London: Routledge.

ROOF, W.C. 1999. *Spiritual marketplace: baby boomers and the remaking of American Religion.* Princeton, NJ: Rutgers University Press.

SCHNEER, P. and AVIV, C. 2002. *Queer Jews.* New York: Routledge.

SMITH, R.L. 1994. *AIDS, gays and the American Catholic church.* Cleveland, OH: Pilgrim Press.

STUART, E. 1997. *Religion is a queer thing: a guide to the christian faith for lesbian, gay, bisexual and transgendered people.* Cleveland, OH: Pilgrim Press.

TIGERT, L.M. 1997. *Coming out while staying in: struggles and celebrations of lesbians and gays in the church.* United Church Press, Cleveland, Ohio.

WHITE, D. and WHITE, O.K. 2004. Queer Christian confessions: spiritual autobiographies of gay Christians. *Culture and Religion* 5 (2).

WILCOX, MELISSA. 2000. Two roads converged: religion and identity among lesbian, gay, bisexual and transgender Christians. Doctoral Dissertation, University of California Santa Barbara.

Jodi O'Brien (author to whom correspondence should be addressed), Department of Sociology, Seattle University, 900 Broadway, Seattle, WA 98122, USA. E-mail: jobrien@seattleu.edu.

AMERICAN INDIAN ETHNIC RENEWAL: POLITICS AND THE RESURGENCE OF IDENTITY*

By Joane Nagel

University of Kansas

Ethnic renewal is the reconstruction of one's ethnic identity by reclaiming a discarded identity, replacing or amending an identity in an existing ethnic identity repertoire, or filling a personal ethnic void. Between 1960 and 1990, the number of Americans reporting an American Indian race in the U.S. Census more than tripled. This increase cannot be accounted for by simple population growth (increased births, decreased deaths, immigration), or by changing enumeration definitions or techniques. Researchers have concluded that much of this growth in the American Indian population results from "ethnic switching," where individuals who previously identified themselves as "non-Indian" changed their race to "Indian" in a later census. The question posed here is: Why does such ethnic switching occur? Drawing

*Address all correspondence to Joane Nagel, Department of Sociology, 716 Fraser Hall, University of Kansas, Lawrence, KS 66045 (Internet: nagel@falcon.cc.ukans.edu). This research was supported in part by the National Science Foundation (grant SES-8108314) and by a 1994/95 Jensen Lectureship sponsored by Duke University and the American Sociological Association. My thanks to Karl Eschbach and Leif Jensen for their generous technical assistance with this and related work, and to Duane Champagne, Steven Cornell, Karl Eschbach, John W. Meyer, C. Matthew Snipp, Norman Yetman, Carol A. B. Warren for their helpful comments on this and earlier drafts. [The reviewers acknowledged by the author include Gary D. Sanderur and Charles Tilly. — Ed.]

on historical analyses and interview data, I argue that this growth in the American Indian population is one instance of ethnic renewal. I identify three factors promoting individual ethnic renewal: (1) federal Indian policy, (2) American ethnic politics, and (3) American Indian political activism. These three political factors raised American Indian ethnic consciousness and encouraged individuals to claim or reclaim their Native American ancestry, contributing to the observed Indian census population increase. American Indian ethnic renewal contributes to our general understanding of how ethnicity is socially constructed.

This paper examines the phenomenon of ethnic identity change and the role of politics in prompting the reconstruction of individual ethnicity. Specifically, I examine recent demographic trends in the American Indian population to understand the conditions and factors that lead individuals to change their racial identity.[1] Between 1960 and 1990, the number of Americans reporting American Indian as their race in the U.S. Census more than tripled, growing from 523,591 to 1,878,285. This increase cannot be accounted for by the usual explanations of population growth (e.g., increased births, decreased deaths). Researchers have concluded that much of this population growth must have resulted from "ethnic switching," where individuals who identified their race as non-Indian (e.g., White) in an earlier census, switched to 'Indian" race in a later census. Why are more and more Americans reporting their race as American Indian?

My research draws on historical analyses and interview data, and combines a social constructionist model of ethnic identity with a social structural approach to ethnic change. I argue that the increase in American Indian ethnic identification reflected in the U.S. Census is an instance of "ethnic renewal." Ethnic renewal refers to both individual and collective processes. *Individual ethnic renewal* occurs when an individual acquires or asserts a new ethnic identity by reclaiming a discarded identity, replacing or amending an identity in an existing ethnic repertoire, or filling a personal ethnic void. Reclaiming a discarded identity might entail resuming religious observances or "retraditionalization" (e.g., the return to orthodoxy by American Jews). Replacing an identity in an existing ethnic repertoire might involve religious conversion (e.g., the conversion to Islam by Christian African Americans); amending an existing ethnic repertoire might involve exploring a new side of one's family tree and including that nationality or ethnicity among one's working ethnic identities (e.g., the taking on of Armenian ethnicity by an Irish Armenian American already involved in Irish American ethnic life). Filling a personal ethnic void might entail adopting a new ethnic identity for the first time (e.g., Americans reconnecting with their ethnic "roots" and joining ethnic social, political, or religious organizations). *Collective ethnic renewal* involves the reconstruction of an ethnic community by current or new community members who build or rebuild institutions, culture, history, and traditions (Nagel 1994, forthcoming).

My thesis is that ethnic renewal among the American Indian population has been brought about by three political forces: (1) federal Indian policy, (2) American ethnic politics, and (3) American Indian political activism. Federal Indian policies have contributed to the creation of an urban, intermarried, bicultural American Indian population that lives outside traditional American Indian geographic and cultural regions. For these individuals, American Indian ethnicity has been more optional than for those living on reservations. Changes in American political culture brought about by the ethnic politics of the civil rights movement created an atmosphere that increased ethnic consciousness, ethnic pride, and ethnic mobilization among all ethnic groups, including American Indians. The resulting "Red Power" Indian political activist movement of the 1960s and 1970s started a tidal wave of ethnic renewal that surged across reservation and urban Indian communities, instilling ethnic pride and encouraging individuals to claim and assert their "Indianness."

Below I provide a constructionist conceptual framework for interpreting ethnic identity generally; review the demographic evidence and explanations for increases in the American Indian population; outline the role of structural factors, such as political policies, ethnic politics, and ethnic political activism in prompting or strengthening Indian ethnic identification; and explore the meaning and consequences of activism for American Indian ethnic renewal.

BACKGROUND

Negotiating and Changing Individual and Collective Identities

In the past 30 years, our understanding of ethnicity has increasingly stressed the socially constructed character of ethnicity. The pioneering work of Fredrik Barth (1969), shows ethnicity to be situational and variable. Many studies have followed that have found ethnicity to be more emergent than primordial, ethnic group boundaries to be more fluid than fixed, ethnic conflicts to arise more from clashes of contemporary interests than from ancient animosities, ethnic history and culture to be routinely revised and even invented, and the central essence of ethnicity—ethnic identity—to be multifaceted, negotiable, and changeable (see Conzen, Gerber, Morawska, Pozzetta, and Vecoli 1992; Sollors 1989).

It is this last assertion—that one ethnic identity can be exchanged for another—that runs most against the grain of common wisdom. Sociologists have long identified forms of ethnic change associated with intergroup contact, such as assimilation, accommodation, and acculturation (Park 1928; Gordon 1961; Glazer and Moynihan 1963). These processes have been seen as long-term, often intergenerational, frequently involving the dissolution or blending of immigrant or minority ethnicities into a larger dominant ethnicity or nationality (e.g., from "Indian" to "White" or from "Irish" to "American"). In the case of ethnic renewal, however, individuals adopt a nondominant ethnic identity, and thus move from membership in a dominant group to become part of a minority or subnational group (e.g., from "White" to "Indian" or from "American" to "Irish American" or "Jewish American"). This resurgence of nondominant ethnic identity does not fit clearly into traditional models of ethnic change which carry a heavy presumption that ethnic change invariably moves in the direction of assimilation (i.e., from minority to majority).

Opportunities for individual ethnic change vary. Certainly some people, for instance, American Whites, have a wide menu of "ethnic options" from which they are free to choose (Waters 1990). It is more difficult for members of other racial or ethnic groups to change their ethnicity, particularly communities of color. This is because in the United States such groups confront a world of "hypodescent," where one drop of particular blood (African, Asian) dictates a specific ethnic group membership, leaving limited options for individual members (see Harris 1964; Davis 1991). European Americans and African Americans represent two ends of an ethnic ascription continuum, in which Whites are always free to remember their ancestry and Blacks are never free to forget theirs. These ethnic boundaries are maintained and policed by both Blacks and Whites, although their content and location can change over time (see Collas 1994 for a discussion of "transgressing racial boundaries").

Despite such strict racial regimes, and perhaps because of their constructed character, there is constant flux at the edges of individual ethnic identity and ethnic group boundaries. For instance, despite the "one drop rule," Davis (1991) describes centuries of defining and redefining "Blackness" in the United States (also see Stein 1989), and discusses divisions among Americans of African descent based on national origin and skin tone (also see Keith and Herring 1991; Waters 1994). Similarly, many studies describe the shifting and emerging identities of Latinos (Pedraza 1994; Padilla 1985, 1986; Gimenez, Lopez, and Munoz 1992), Asian Americans (Espiritu 1992; Wei 1993), Native Americans (Cornell 1988; McBeth 1989; Forbes 1990), and European Americans (Alba 1990; Waters 1990; Lieberson and Waters 1988; Bakalian 1993; Kelly 1994).

While historical shifts do indeed occur in ethnic boundaries and definitions, is it really possible to change one's *individual* ethnicity? The answer, of course, is yes. Individuals change their ethnic identity often, singly and *en masse*. Perhaps the most common form of ethnic switching is religious conversion. This sort of ethnic change is most likely to occur when a particular religion-based ethnicity is especially stigmatizing. Schermerhorn (1978) reports a common form of ethnic switching in India, where Hindu Untouchables convert to Islam to escape untouchability. Another instance of mass ethnic change occurred in the former Yugoslavia during Ottoman rule, when Christian conversions to Islam created a permanent ethnic boundary; contemporary conflicts between the descendants of these Muslims and the Christian Croat and Serb populations illustrate the resurgent power of ethnicity and nationalism, as these conflicts involve communities marked by varying degrees of intermarriage, residential integration, and religious tolerance (Hodson, Sekulic, and Massey 1994). Another type of ethnic change is "passing"—hiding or camouflaging a disadvantageous ethnicity while adopting the dress or behavior of a more advantaged group. Nayar (1966) notes that in India many instances of passing were motivated by the British colonial preference for Sikh military recruits: Hindus and others identified themselves as Sikhs to qualify for army posts. Sometimes ethnic switching is pursued bureaucratically. Lelyveld (1985) describes how individuals petitioned the South African government to change officially their own or others' racial designations under *apartheid* regulations. Similar challenges to racial designations on birth certificates have been mounted in the United States (Davis 1991).

American Indian Ethnicity: Opting for an Indian Identity

American Indians reside at the intersection of two racial regimes: hypodescent and self-identification. In some portions of the United States Indianness is strongly socially ascribed and often mandatory (e.g., in the Southwest or the Northern Plains). In these settings Indian ethnicity is regulated in two ways. The first is informal and external to Indian communities, and involves ascription mainly, though not exclusively, by non-Indians. In this instance of classic hypodescent, any visible "Indianness" labels an individual as "Indian." The second, more formal way American Indian ethnicity is regulated can be both internal and external to native communities, and involves official membership in Indian tribes. In this case, tribal, state, and/ or federal governments recognize an individual as an "enrolled" member or not.

In much of the United States, however, American Indian ethnicity is largely a matter of individual choice; "Indian" ethnicity is an ethnic option that an individual can choose or not. This is *not* to say that *anyone* can choose to be an Indian or that all observers will unanimously confirm the validity of that choice. Indeed, there is enormous controversy among native people about who should be considered an Indian for purposes of receiving tribal services, federal benefits, affirmative action consideration, or rights to participate in tribal governments (Larimore and Waters 1993; Reynolds 1993; Snipp 1993).

An important point to make here about supratribal "American Indian" ethnicity is that it is purely a social construction. That is, the Native American population is comprised of many linguistic, cultural, and religious groups, more than 300 of which are separately recognized by federal or state governments in the lower 48 states (with many more in Alaska and Hawaii); each group has its own political, legal, and police system, economy, land base, and sovereign authority. Around two-thirds of American Indians identified in the U.S. Censuses are official members of these recognized communities (Snipp 1989). Thus, when we speak of an "American Indian" race or ethnicity, we are of necessity referring to a group of individuals from various tribal backgrounds, some of whom speak native languages, most of whom converse in English, some of whom live on or regularly visit reservation "homelands," most of whom live off-reservation, some of whom participate in tribal community life, most of whom live in urban areas.

Despite this diversity, researchers assert that, indeed, there are 'Indians," and this all-encompassing category can be seen as an "ethnic group."[1] For instance, Deloria (1992a) argues that as American Indians became increasingly involved in off-reservation political and economic life after World War II, they came to see themselves as minority group members and as part of the larger American ethnic mosaic. In fact, many Native Americans carry within their portfolio of ethnic identities (which may include identities based on kin or clan lineage, tribe, reservation, language, and religion) a supratribal or pan-Indian "Indian" identity, which is often reserved for use when interacting with non-Indians. Finally, as further evidence of the existence of an "American Indian" ethnic group, in recent decades increasing percentages of Americans who identify their race as 'Indian" fail to specify a tribal affiliation, suggesting that their primary ethnic identity is supratribal or "Indian" (Masumura and Berman 1987).[2]

DESCRIBING THE "NEW" INDIAN POPULATION

Although researchers seem to agree that individual ethnic change is an important factor in the recent growth of the American Indian population, the reasons remain unclear. Phrased as research questions, we might ask: Who are these "new" Indians? And, what motivates them to change their ethnicity? Compared to the total American Indian population, these Indians are more urban, more concentrated in non-Indian states without reservation communities, more often intermarried, less likely to assign their mixed offspring an Indian race, and more likely to speak only English. These characteristics are all descriptive of a population more "blended" into the American demographic and cultural mainstream than their reservation co-ethnics, more likely to have more flexible conceptions of self, residing in parts of the country that permit a wide range of ethnic options. In other words, under the proper conditions, the fastest growing portions of the American Indian population are available for ethnic renewal.

ACCOUNTING FOR AMERICAN INDIAN ETHNIC RENEWAL

What *are* the conditions that promote American Indian ethnic renewal? Restated, what has motivated these new Indians to change their ethnicity? The answers to this question can be found in policy and politics: federal Indian policy, American ethnic politics, and Native American political activism.

---

1   Some native scholars and commentators have taken offense at the notion that Indians are a "mere" ethnic group, arguing that they are instead, sovereign nations (Trask 1990, 1991; Morris 1989; Deloria and Lytle 1984; Stiffarm and Lane 1992).

2   In 1980, about one-fifth of U.S. Census respondents who identified their race as "American Indian" did not report a tribe (U.S. Bureau of the Census 1981).

Federal Indian Policy

Beginning in the nineteenth century, federal Indian policy was designed to assimilate American Indians into the Euro-American cultural mainstream (e.g., through forced English language acquisition, Anglo-centric education in Indian boarding and day schools, and reservation land reduction programs). Despite a brief pause in federal assimilation programs during the "New Deal" era,[3] the net result of decades of federal Indian policy was the creation of an English-speaking, bicultural, multi-tribal American Indian population living in U.S. cities. World War II also spurred the urbanization and acculturation of the Native American population, as Indians volunteered and were drafted into the military and non-enlisted native workers left reservations for wartime industrial jobs in urban areas. Many of these Indian veterans and workers never returned to the reservation (Nash 1985; Bernstein 1986). Post-World War II programs for job training and urban relocation were specifically designed to reduce reservation populations during the "termination" era of federal Indian policy, and provided a further push in the reservation-urban Indian population stream.[4] For instance, Sorkin (1978) estimates that from 1952 to 1972, federal programs relocated more than 100,000 American Indians to a number of targeted cities, including Chicago, Cleveland, Dallas, Denver, Los Angeles, Oakland, Oklahoma City, Phoenix, Salt Lake City, San Francisco, San Jose, Seattle, and Tulsa (Sorkin 1978:chap. 3). By 1970, nearly half of American Indians lived in cities as a result of relocation programs and other general urbanization processes. The combined result of decades of these federal Indian policies was the creation of an urbane, educated, English-speaking Indian constituency that was available for mobilization when the civil rights era arrived in the 1960s.

Not only did federal Indian policy help urbanize the Indian population, many programs had a major impact on the organizational fabric of urban Indian life. For instance, relocation programs directly funded the creation and operation of a number of Indian centers in both relocation target cities and cities near large reservation populations (Ablon 1965). These centers were established to provide services and meeting places for burgeoning urban Indian populations. Further, as an indirect consequence of relocation efforts, other urban Indian organizations blossomed: intertribal clubs, bars, athletic leagues, beauty contests, powwows, and dance groups, as well as Indian newspapers and newsletters, social service

---

3   For instance, the Indian Reorganization Act of 1934 (IRA) reaffirmed tribal rights. Many critics maintain that the IRA was also an acculturation program of sorts, because it created tribal "councils" with "chairmen" linked to the Bureau of Indian Affairs (Deloria and Lytle 1984; Champagne 1986).

4   The "termination" era in federal Indian policy began in 1946 with the creation of the Indian Claims Commission, which was designed to settle all Indian land claims, and so to begin a process of ending (terminating) the federal-Indian trust relationship. Termination policies were unofficially suspended when the Kennedy administration took office in 1961, although a number of tribes were terminated after that date. A 1970 statement by President Richard M. Nixon that embraced Indian «self-determination» marked the official turning point in federal Indian policy, shifting it from «termination» to «self-determination» (see Cohen [1982] for a summary of federal Indian policy).

agencies, political organizations, and Christian churches (Hertzberg 1971; Guillemin 1975; Steele 1975; Mucha 1983; Weibel-Orlando 1991).

In a few urban areas, some of these organizations had a specific tribal character and were frequented only by members of a particular tribe (Hodge 1971). However, the vast majority of urban Indian organizations were intertribal and had names reflecting their inclusionary character: the Cleveland American Indian Center, the *Inter-Tribal Tribune* (newsletter of the Heart of America Indian Center, Kansas City), the Los Angeles American Indian Bowling League, the Many Trails Indian Club, the First Southern Baptist Indian Church (Weibel-Orlando 1991). In such intertribal organizations, many urban Indians "sought refuge from the terrible loss of identity that marked modern urban existence" (Clark 1988:289). The diverse organizations that populated the urban Indian organizational landscape formed the core of an intertribal network and informal communication system in urban Indian communities. They were important building blocks in the development of a supratribal level of Indian identity and the emergence of a pan-Indian culture, both of which were essential ingredients in the Red Power political mobilization of the 1960s.

American Ethnic Politics

Two forces converged in the 1960s to end the assimilationist thrust of federal Indian policy and to set in motion the contemporary period of American Indian ethnic renewal. One was the civil rights movement and the shifts in American social and political culture that followed in its wake. The other was President Lyndon Johnson's solution to the problem of race in America—the Great Society, the War on Poverty, and the civil rights legislation of the 1960s. The fluctuating currents of cultural change and reform politics that marked the 1960s were responded to by increasingly cosmopolitan and sophisticated American Indians who lobbied successfully to send federal War on Poverty and community development resources into impoverished urban and reservation communities (Witt 1968:68; Deloria 1978:88).

This mix of volatile ethnic politics and an explosion of federal resources, many earmarked for minority programs, combined with earlier federal Indian policies, which had concentrated large numbers of tribally diverse, educated, acculturated, and organizationally connected Indians in American cities. The result: a large-scale mobilization of urban Indians marked by a rapid growth of political organizations, newspapers, and community programs. To grasp fully these dynamic changes in many American communities, Indian and non-Indian, it is important to recall the atmosphere of the 1960s. As Hugh Davis Graham (1990) writes in the Introduction to *The Civil Rights Era*:

> This is a story about a rare event in America: a radical shift in national social policy. Its precondition was a broader social revolution, the black civil rights

movement that surged up from the South, followed by the nationwide rebirth
of the feminist movement. (P. 3)

The demographic changes that underlay the rise of Black militancy in American cities, namely, the "great Black migration" from the rural south to the urban north (Cloward and Piven 1975; Edsall and Edsall 1991; Lemann 1991), were paralleled by the movement of American Indians off the reservations. The federal response to Black protest—civil rights legislation and the War on Poverty— spilled over into other minority communities, including American Indian communities, which were quickly mobilizing in the wake of Black insurgency. The ethnic militancy of the 1960s redefined mainstream America as "White" and exposed and challenged its racial hegemony. For America's ethnic minorities it was a time to cast off negative stereotypes, to reinvent ethnic and racial social meanings and self-definitions, and to embrace ethnic pride. For American Indians it marked the emergence of supratribal identification, the rise of Indian activism, and a period of increased Indian ethnic pride. Despite their often brutal treatment by United States' authorities and citizens throughout American history, American Indians have ironically, but consistently occupied a romanticized niche in the American popular media and imagination (Berkhofer 1978). The durable symbolic value of the American Indian as a cultural icon was further enhanced by the increased ethnic pride characterizing the civil rights era. The result increased the appeal of Indian ethnicity for many individuals, and no doubt contributed to the resurgence of Indian self-identification.

In addition to the symbolic allure of Indian ethnicity, there were also material incentives. Castile (1992) notes the connection between these ideational and material realms, commenting that American Indians were able "to manipulate their symbolic position [in American history and society] in ways that grant[ed] them a political leverage far greater than their numbers justif[ied]. By keeping a sharp eye on the political waves of ethnicity, which they [could] not raise themselves, shrewd timing ... allow[ed] them to ride those waves and maximize their impact in positive ways" (p. 183). American Indians indeed were able to navigate the changing currents of American ethnic politics, and their successes resulted in increased federal spending on Indian affairs, making American Indian identification a more attractive ethnic option for many Americans of Indian descent. The settlement of land claims by the Indian Claims Commission and the U.S. federal court system during the 1970s and 1980s was another important source of funds for Indian communities. Churchill (1992) reports that more than $128 million in Indian land claims awards were disbursed between 1946 and 1970, and by 1978 the total amount of claims awards exceeded $657 million (also see Lurie 1978:101). In addition, a number of major land claims were settled during the early 1980s, some of which involved large controversial settlements. Most notable are the claims of Maine's Passamaquoddy and Penobscot tribes, who in 1980 recovered 300,000 acres of land and received a payment of $27 million (see Jaimes 1992).

Increased federal spending in general and land claim awards in particular, along with the inclusion of Indians in many affirmative action and minority set-aside programs, contributed to the American Indian ethnic resurgence in part because they increased both the symbolic and the potential material value of Indian ethnicity. Individuals of Indian ancestry became more willing to identify themselves as Indians, whether or not such identification was a strategy to acquire a share of real or putative land claims awards or other possible ethnically-allocated rewards (such as scholarships, mineral royalties, employment preference). It was in this atmosphere of increased resources, ethnic grievances, ethnic pride, and civil rights activism that Red Power burst on the scene in the late 1960s and galvanized a generation of Native Americans. The rest of the country watched as the media covered such events as the occupation of Alcatraz Island, the takeover of the Bureau of Indian Affairs headquarters in Washington, D.C., and the siege at Wounded Knee.

American Indian Activism: Red Power

The shifting political culture and protest climate of the 1960s and 1970s spawned many Indian activist organizations, such as the American Indian Movement (AIM) and the National Indian Youth Council, and produced a number of Indian protest actions: the 19-month occupation of Alcatraz Island which began in 1969; the 1972 Trail of Broken Treaties which culminated in a week-long occupation of the Bureau of Indian Affairs in Washington, D.C.; the 71-day siege at Wounded Knee, South Dakota in 1973; the 1975 shoot-out on the Pine Ridge Reservation in South Dakota which resulted in the imprisonment of Leonard Peltier; and numerous protest events in cities and on reservations around the United States, concluding with the 1978 Longest Walk to Washington, D.C. These events and this era stand out boldly in the publications and accounts of Native Americans living at that time, particularly native youth (see Fortunate Eagle 1992; Crow Dog and Erdoes 1990). Red Power played an important symbolic role in motivating individual ethnic renewal on the part of Indian participants and observers; this ethnic renewal took two forms, and both forms are relevant to the argument I present here.

The first type of individual ethnic renewal involves individuals who most likely would have identified themselves as Indians in earlier censuses, and thus is best summarized as a resurgence in ethnic pride which did not involve taking on a new ethnic identity (e.g., does not involve racial switching). Instead, this type of individual ethnic renewal involved a reaffirmation, reconstruction, or redefinition of an individual's ethnicity. For example, the slogan, "I'm Black and I'm proud" reflected such a redefinition of "Negro" in the U.S. in the 1960s. These individuals did not change their race, rather they changed the *meaning* of their race. This parallels the resurgence of Native American ethnic pride among individuals who already identified themselves as "Indian."

The second type of individual ethnic renewal involves individuals who would *not* have identified themselves as Indian in earlier censuses, but rather would have "passed" into the non-Indian race categories. For these individuals, a resurgence of ethnic pride meant not only redefining the worth and meaning of their ancestry, but also involved laying a new claim to that ancestry by switching their race on the census form from non-Indian to Indian. This type of individual ethnic renewal is, I believe, reflected in census data; but currently the data do not exist for evaluating directly the influences of federal Indian policy, the ethnic politics of the civil rights era, or the rise of Indian activism on this kind of ethnic renewal. Such an evaluation would require examining the backgrounds and beliefs of those individuals who changed their race from non-Indian to Indian in the 1970, 1980, and 1990 Censuses. As Sandefur and McKinnell (1986) state, "it is not possible to know from census data who has changed his or her racial identification since a previous census" (p. 348). Indeed, researchers are awaiting such a definitive study. Snipp (1993) notes, while it is plausible that census increases reflect the fact that "more mixed ancestry persons are identifying themselves as American Indians than in the past, ... [it] is virtually impossible to prove" (p. 16; also see Thornton, Sandefur and Snipp 1991:365; Harris 1994:592).

PERSONAL PERSPECTIVES ON ETHNIC POLITICS AND RED POWER ACTIVISM

To begin to understand the role of politics and Red Power activism in promoting increased American Indian ethnic pride and awareness, I interviewed and corresponded with 25 Native Americans who participated in or observed the activist events of the 1970s (or, in the case of the 2 youngest respondents, who had heard accounts of the Red Power period from their parents). Of the 25, 11 were women and 14 were men; on average they were in their mid-40s (the youngest was 21, the oldest 79); 5 resided mainly in reservation communities, 9 were urban Indians, and 11 had lived in both settings for significant portions of their lives; 15 were activists during the 1960s and mid-1970s at the height of Red Power, another 5 became activists in the late 1970s and 1980s, and 5 described themselves as nonactivists. I asked each of the 25 whether the movement had any effect on them or their communities, and if so, what its impact was.

In addition to these interviews, I surveyed a large and growing body of oral histories and published personal accounts of recent Indian history. The responses in the archival material, the published literature, and in my interviews were quite similar: The activist period raised individual ethnic consciousness and prompted dialogues about the meaning of Indianness. These various sources also reflected some interesting regional and generational differences in assessments of the meaning and consequences of Red Power. The remainder of this paper provides an interpretive context for these native voices speaking about their ethnic identity and how it was influenced by the decade of American Indian activism that began with the occupation of Alcatraz Island.

Activism and Identity: Reversing the Causal Connection

The traditionally understood relationship between identity and activism is that identity precedes activism, making particular individuals more likely than others to engage in protest activities (for a review of this literature see McAdam 1988 and Tarrow 1992). Much recent research on social movements questions this assumption, exploring more fully the interrelationships among activism, identity, and culture. Fantasia (1988) points out the capacity of both spontaneous and planned protest action to reshape conceptions of personal and collective identity, redefine notions of fairness and justice, and build community consensus and solidarity. Benford and Hunt (1992), Hunt and Benford (1994), and Snow and Anderson (1993) document the emergence of collective ideologies and identities in social movement organizations and movements, and the interplay between movement-sited interpretative frames and rhetoric and larger political and cultural themes in the emergence of collective identity. Taylor and Whittier (1992) and Groch (1994) focus on the importance of group boundaries and collectively negotiated and defined meaning systems in the emergence of oppositional consciousness among movement participants and constituents.

The resurgence of American Indian ethnic identity in the 1970s and 1980s is consistent with these findings and illustrates the power of activism to inspire individual and collective ethnic pride and to raise ethnic consciousness. My interviews most strongly support the notion that activism has its biggest impact on individuals who themselves personally witness or become directly involved in protest action. The narrative accounts of both activists and nonactivists, however, also suggest that social movements exert a wider impact, affecting the attitudes of nonparticipants as well, though to a lesser extent.

Alcatraz, Red Power, and the Resurgence of Indian Ethnic Pride

The 1960s were characterized by increasing levels of American Indian protest activism, much of which tended to be regional and associated with specific tribal groups and grievances (e.g., the "fish-ins" of the mid-1960s in the Pacific Northwest). The national Red Power movement got fully underway in November 1969, when Richard Oakes led a group of fellow Indian students from San Francisco State University and landed on Alcatraz Island in San Francisco Bay. Calling themselves "Indians of All Tribes," they claimed the island by "right of discovery." The takeover caught the attention of a nation already engrossed in the escalating protest and conflict of the civil rights movement, and the rhetoric and demands of the Alcatraz occupiers captured the imagination of many Native Americans. Indians of All Tribes issued the following proclamation which reflected their supratribal roots and agenda:

> We, the native Americans, re-claim the land known as Alcatraz Island in the name of all American Indians . . . . Since the San Francisco Indian Center burned down,

there is no place for Indians to assemble . ...Therefore we plan to develop on this island several Indian institutions: 1. A CENTER FOR NATIVE AMERICAN STUDIES. ... 2. AN AMERICAN INDIAN SPIRITUAL CENTER. ... 3. AN INDIAN CENTER OF ECOLOGY. ... 4. A GREAT INDIAN TRAINING SCHOOL ... [and] an AMERICAN INDIAN MUSEUM. ... In the name of all Indians, therefore, we reclaim this island for our Indian nations. ... We feel this claim is just and proper, and that this land should rightfully be granted to us for as long as the rivers shall run and the sun shall shine.

Signed, INDIANS OF ALL TRIBES (Blue Cloud 1972:40–42)

During the next 19 months the Alcatraz occupiers negotiated unsuccessfully with local and federal authorities and eventually were removed from the island in June 1971. Despite the failure to achieve their demands, as Haupt man (1986) notes, "the events at Alcatraz were a major turning point in the history of Indian activism ... [and] became the symbol to many young, disillusioned Indians, ... stimulating a rash of similar protests" (p. 227). The occupation highlighted Indian grievances and promoted Indian pride. Deloria (1974) summarizes its importance: "Alcatraz was the master stroke of Indian activism" (pp. 184–85). Writing at the height of Red Power activism in the early 1970s, he recognized the immediate impact of the movement on American Indian ethnicity:

"Indianness" was judged on whether or not one was present at Alcatraz, Fort Lawson, Mt. Rushmore, Detroit, Sheep Mountain, Plymouth Rock, or Pitt River. ... The activists controlled the language, the issues, and the attention. (Deloria 1974:184–85)[5]

The much publicized Alcatraz takeover and the first months of the occupation constituted a powerful symbolic moment both for those Native Americans involved in the protest and for those who witnessed it from more distant points around the country (see Johnson 1993; also see "Alcatraz Revisited: The 25th Anniversary of the Occupation," a special issue of *American Indian Culture and Research Journal* [vol. 18, no.4, 1994]). Just as the civil rights movement challenged prevailing racial hegemony by reframing Black ethnicity through the assertion of Black pride and Black power, Red Power, in the form of the Alcatraz occupation and the decade of Indian activist events that followed, challenged cultural depictions of Indians as victims of history, as living relics, powerless

---

5   In written correspondence with Deloria in the summer of 1993, I asked him about the longer-term impact of the Red Power movement. He wrote: "This era will probably always be dominated by the images and slogans of the AIM people. The real accomplishments in land restoration, however were made by quiet determined tribal leaders" (Deloria 1993, personal communication).

and subjugated. As a result, the Alcatraz occupation stimulated Indian ethnic pride and prompted a resurgence in American Indian ethnic consciousness. LaNada Means, one of the participants in the occupation, comments:

> The protest movement at Alcatraz had positive results. Many individuals were not ashamed to be Indian anymore. People who had relocated in the cities were reidentifying themselves as Indians. (Philp 1986:230; also see Means Boyer 1994)

Wilma Mankiller, who went on to become the Principal Chief of the Cherokee Nation of Oklahoma, visited the island many times during the 19-month occupation. She describes the personal impact of the event as "an awakening that ultimately changed the course of her life" (Johnson 1993:125).

> I'd never heard anyone actually tell the world that we needed somebody to pay attention to our treaty rights, that our people had given up an entire continent, and many lives, in return for basic services like health care and education, but nobody was honoring these agreements. For the first time, people were saying things I felt but hadn't known how to articulate. It was very liberating. (Mankiller quoted in Johnson 1993:125)

My interviews with Native Americans who participated in or observed the events on Alcatraz and later protest events and who were young adults at the time, showed similar reactions. Their reactions affirmed the powerful symbolic meaning of the Alcatraz occupation and its importance in raising ethnic consciousness:

> Alcatraz was a major turning point in my life. For the first time in my life I was proud to be an Indian and an Indian woman. I grew up in an all white area. It was very difficult. You were constantly struggling to maintain any kind of positive feeling, any kind of dignity. Alcatraz changed all that. (Telephone interview with Frances Wise, Oklahoma City, OK, August 24, 1993)

> The movement gave me back my dignity and gave Indian people back their dignity. It started with Alcatraz, we got back our worth, our pride, our dignity, our humanity. If you have your dignity and your spirituality and you can pray, then you can wear a tie, carry a briefcase, work a job. If you don't have those things, then you are lost. (Telephone interview with Len Foster, Ft. Defiance, AZ, September 5, 1993)

When Alcatraz came, suddenly they bloomed—all the Metis said they were French, now suddenly they said they were Indian. Those with Indian blood hid it, saying they were Turks or Mexicans or Armenians. Now Indians were coming out of the woodwork. (Anonymous interview, summer, 1993)

Every once in a while something happens that can alter the whole shape of a people's history. This only happens once in a generation or lifetime. The big one was Alcatraz. (Telephone interview with George Horse Capture, Fort Belknap, MT, May 24, 1993)

These quotes communicate a resurgence of ethnic pride and an increased willingness to claim and assert Indian ethnicity. I have argued that assimilation and relocation policies created the population base for a resurgence of Indian ethnicity in cities. Implicit in these policies was also the not-so-subtle subtext of assimilation—that Indianness was something to be discarded, inferior to the larger Anglo culture. While some argue that termination policy was successful in repressing Indian identity in many older native individuals (for instance Baird-Olson [1994] refers to those over 30 at the time as the "lost generation"), it seems clearly to have backfired among the younger generation of urban Indians caught up in the youth culture of the 1960s. It was on this mostly younger group that Red Power had its strongest impact.

Mary Crow Dog (Crow Dog and Erdoes 1990) describes the response of young people on the Rosebud Sioux reservation in South Dakota as AIM swept through on the Trail of Broken Treaties, a nationwide caravan en route to Washington, D.C. in 1972:

The American Indian Movement hit our reservation like a tornado, like a new wind blowing out of nowhere, a drumbeat from far off getting louder and louder. It was almost like the Ghost Dance fever that had hit the tribes in 1890. … I could feel this new thing, almost hear it, smell it, touch it. Meeting up with AIM for the first time loosened a sort of earthquake inside me. (Pp. 73–74)

Frances Wise was on the Trail of Broken Treaties:

Many of the people with us were like me before Alcatraz. They didn't quite understand what was going on, but they were interested. A lot of people joined us [in the auto caravan from Los Angeles to Washington, D.C.]. I remember driving around a freeway cloverleaf outside of Columbus, Ohio. All I could see were cars in front of us and behind us, their lights on, red banners flying from their antennas. It was hard to believe, really. We were that strong. We were really doing something. It was exciting and fulfilling. It's like someone who's been in bondage. Indian country knew that Indians were on the move. (Telephone interview with Frances Wise, Oklahoma City, OK, Augusta, 1993)

Despite the power of the times, the actions of Red Power activists were not easily or enthusiastically embraced by all Native Americans. Generational differences were evident in attitudes toward the movement:

My parents did not want me to get involved [in activism], they weren't active. They were just struggling to live. When they got involved it was out of dire need. Their generation was almost at the point of being beaten into passivity. They would say, "There's nothing we can do; government's too powerful." The defeatism was very strong. One reason things changed then was that the children of those in power were resisting. (Telephone interview with Leonard Peltier, Leavenworth, KS, June 1, 1993)

Most of the older generation was forced to assimilate and are still in the mode of assimilation. Their attitude toward activism is "don't rock the boat." (Interview with Loretta Flores, Lawrence, KS, May 12, 1993)

The tendency of the younger generation of Native Americans to recapture a fading or suppressed Indian heritage and to reaffirm Indian identity stood in contrast to the skepticism of their elders. The different reactions to Red Power paralleled the "generation gap" so often used to depict 1960s' America, and these differences are consistent with one trend in the 1980 Census data reported by Passel and Berman (1986:173). They observe that "the 'new' American Indians [those from traditionally non-Indian states] are generally young adults" (p. 173)—precisely the generation that participated in and witnessed Red Power.

Activism as a Crucible for Ethnic Pride and Identity

The occupation of Alcatraz Island was followed by dozens of protest actions around the country throughout most of the 1970s. During this and the following decade, many individuals of native ancestry were motivated to reconnect with their ethnic roots. For Z. G. Standing Bear, the events on Alcatraz and his own participation in protests during the 1970s represented a counterpoint to other aspects of his biography, a tension that took him years to resolve, but one that he settled in favor of his native ancestry:

I was in Vietnam when I heard about Alcatraz. I thought "Right on! That's great what those guys are doing." … It was years later, after hearing Russell Means talk at Florida State University in 1981, that there was a major turning point in my life. I had been on a personal journey to come to terms with my service in the army during the Vietnam War, and Means's talk made me finally decide to go back to my grandfather's culture. (Telephone interview with Z. G. Standing Bear, Valdosta, GA, June 25, 1993)[6]

Standing Bear's reference to his "personal journey" is a theme that runs through many oral and written accounts of Red Power and of the individual ethnic renewal that has taken place since that time. The personal journeys described by many Native Americans involve a seeming contradiction: they go forward by going back; or as one native person characterized it to me, "We become what we were." This process of becoming often involves a spiritual component that for many Indians, perhaps for most, represents the symbolic core of Indianness and is a central part of the ethnic renewal process. Deloria (1992b) acknowledges the cardinal importance of spiritual matters in native life and identifies an underlying spiritual agenda in Indian activism. Indeed, activist Frances Wise noted the direct importance of Red Power activism in changing policies and creating a climate that permitted and supported individual ethnic renewal through traditional dress and spiritual practices. In the early 1970s she was involved in organizing a successful challenge to an Oklahoma school board's restriction on men's hair length. She noted the changes that resulted:

> It had a big impact. People now wear long hair, people who said back then, "Are you sure you know what you're doing with this [protest]?" Now they can wear their hair long—and they do. … Another outcome is we have greater numbers of people who have both traditional Indian educations and are also educated in white ways. (Telephone interview with Frances Wise, Oklahoma City, OK, August 25, 1993)

During and since the Red Power period, the religious and spiritual dimension of tribal life has become a focal concern among many of the Indian people with whom I spoke. Many reported becoming Sun Dancers for the first time as adults, many spent time with tribal elders seeking instruction in tribal history and traditions, many learned more of their tribal language, many abandoned Christian religions and turned to native spiritual traditions,[7] and some have returned to their home reservations. In recounting his decision

---

6   To affirm this change, Z. G. reclaimed his family name of Standing Bear. His family's reaction revealed the continuing generation gap: "'What are you trying to prove?' one said, 'all that stuff is over and done with'" (Standing Bear 1988).

7   This return to traditional spirituality has been particularly evident in prisons, where there has been a legal battle over Native American prisoners' rights to engage in particular spiritual practices (e.g., the building of sweatlodges on prison grounds or the wearing of braids and medicine bundles). These disputes led to the introduction in 1993 of Senate Bill 1021, the Native American Free Exercise of Religion Act (see Reed 1990).

to return to the reservation, Horse Capture (1991) believes that he is not the only one embarked on such a journey back to what he was:

> Originally I thought I was alone on this quest. But as time has passed, a whole generation and more were influenced by these same forces, and we traveled the same course. (P. 203)

CONCLUSION

The rise in American Indian ethnic identification during the last three decades has resulted from a combination of factors in American politics. Assimilationist federal Indian policies helped to create a bicultural, intermarried, mixed race, urban Indian population living in regions of the country where ethnic options were most numerous; this was a group "poised" for individual ethnic renewal. The ethnic politics of the civil rights era encouraged ethnic identification, the return to ethnic roots, ethnic activism, and provided resources for mobilizing ethnic communities; thus, the climate and policies of civil rights provided individuals of native ancestry (and others as well) symbolic and material incentives to claim or reclaim Indian ethnicity. Red Power activism during the 1960s and 1970s further raised Indian ethnic consciousness by dramatizing long held grievances, communicating an empowered and empowering image of Indianness, and providing Native Americans, particularly native youth, opportunities for action and participation in the larger Indian cause. Together then, federal Indian policies, ethnic politics, and American Indian activism provided the rationale and motivation for individual ethnic renewal.

The overall explanation of the resurgence of American Indian ethnicity I offer here can be seen as part of a general model of ethnic renewal. The impact of federal Indian policies on American Indian ethnic renewal represents an instance of the political construction of ethnicity (i.e., the ways in which political policy, the structure of political opportunity, and patterns of political culture shape ethnic boundaries in society). The impact of events in this larger political arena on Indian ethnic activism and identity illustrates the role of politics and political culture in ethnic mobilization (i.e., the power of political *Zeitgeist* and shifting political definitions to open windows of opportunity for ethnic activists and to affirm and render meaningful their grievances and claims). The impact of Red Power on American Indian ethnic consciousness reveals the role of human agency in individual and collective redefinition and empowerment (i.e., the power of activism to challenge prevailing policies, to encourage ethnic awareness, and to foster ethnic community-building). This model of ethnic renewal suggests that, given the capacity of individuals to reinvent themselves and their communities, ethnicity occupies an enduring place in modern societies.

Joane Nagel is Professor of Sociology at the University of Kansas. Her research focuses on the politics of ethnicity. Her publications include "Constructing Ethnicity: Creating and Recreating Ethnic Identity and Culture" (Social Problems, 1994, *pp. 152–76) and* American Indian Ethnic Renewal: Red Power and the Resurgence of Identity and Culture *(forthcoming, Oxford University Press). She is currently working on a book, titled* Masculinity and Nationalism: The Global Politics of Gender and Ethnicity.

REFERENCES

Ablon, Joan. 1965. "American Indian Relocation: Problems of Dependency and Management in the City." *Phylon* 66:362–71.

Alba, Richard D. 1990. *Ethnic Identity: The Transformation of White America.* New Haven, CT: Yale University Press.

Baird-Olson, Karren. 1994. "The Survival Strategies of Plains Indian Women Coping with Structural and Interpersonal Victimization on a Northwest Reservation." Ph.D. dissertation, Department of Sociology, University of New Mexico, Albuquerque, NM.

Bakalian, Anny. 1993. *Armenian-Americans: From Being to Feeling Armenian.* New Brunswick, NY: Transaction Books.

Barth, Fredrik. 1969. *Ethnic Groups and Boundaries.* Boston, MA: Little, Brown.

Benford, Robert D. and Scott A. Hunt. 1992. "Dramaturgy and Social Movements: The Social Construction and Communication of Power." *Sociological Inquiry* 62:36–55.

Berkhofer, Robert F. 1978. *The White Man's Indian: Images of the American Indian from Columbus to the Present.* New York: Alfred A. Knopf.

Bernstein, Alison Ricky. 1986. "Walking in Two Worlds: American Indians and World War Two." Ph.D. dissertation, Department of History, Columbia University, New York.

Blue Cloud, Peter, ed. 1972. *Alcatraz Is Not an Island.* Berkeley, CA: Wingbow Press.

Castile, George P. 1992. "Indian Sign: Hegemony and Symbolism in Federal Indian Policy." Pp. 163–86 in *State and Reservation: New Perspectives on Federal Indian Policy,* edited by G. P. Castile and R. L. Bee. Tucson, AZ: University of Arizona Press.

Champagne, Duane. 1986. "American Indian Values and the Institutionalization of IRA Governments." Pp. 25–34 in *American Indian Policy and Cultural Values: Conflict and Accommodation* (Contemporary American Indian Issues Series No. 6), edited by J. R. Joe. Los Angeles, CA: American Indian Studies Center, UCLA Publications Services Department.

Churchill, Ward. 1992. "The Earth Is Our Mother: Struggles for American Indian Land and Liberation in the Contemporary United States." Pp. 139–88 in *The State of Native America: Genocide, Colonization, and Resistance,* edited by M. A. Jaimes. Boston, MA: South End Press.

Clark, Blue. 1988. "Bury My Heart in Smog: Urban Indians." Pp. 278–91 in *The American Indian Experience. A Profile: 1524 to the Present,* edited by P. Weeks. Arlington Heights, IL: Forum Press.

Cloward, Richard A. and Frances Fox Piven. 1975. *The Politics of Turmoil: Poverty, Race, and the Urban Crisis.* New York: Vintage Books.

Cohen, Felix S. *Felix S. Cohen's Handbook of Federal Indian Law.* 1982. Charlottesville, VA: Michie Bobbs-Merrill.

Collas, Sara. 1994. "Transgressing Racial Boundaries: The Maintenance of the Racial Order." Paper presented at the annual meeting of the American Sociological Association, August 8, Los Angeles, CA.

Conzen, Kathleen N., David A. Gerber, Ewa Morawska, George E. Pozzetta, and Rudolph J. Vecoli. 1992. "The Invention of Ethnicity: A Perspective from the U.S.A." *Journal of American Ethnic History* 12:3–41.

Cornell, Stephen. 1988. *The Return of the Native: American Indian Political Resurgence.* New York: Oxford University Press.

Crow Dog, Mary and Richard Erdoes. 1990. *Lakota Woman.* New York: Grove Weidenfeld.

Davis, James F. 1991. *Who Is Black? One Nation's Definition.* University Park, PA: Pennsylvania State University.

Deloria, Vine, Jr. 1974. "The Rise of Indian Activism." Pp. 179–87 in *The Social Reality of Ethnic America,* edited by R. Gomez, C. Collingham, R. Endo, and K. Jackson. Lexington, MA: D.C. Heath.

-------. 1978. "Legislation and Litigation Concerning American Indians." *The Annals of the American Academy of Political and Social Science* 436:88–96.

--------. 1981. "Native Americans: The American Indian Today." *The Annals of the American Academy of Political and Social Sciences* 454:139–49.

-----. 1986. "The New Indian Recruits: The Popularity of Being Indian." *Americans Before Columbus* 14:3, 6–8.

-------. 1992a. "American Indians." Pp. 31–52 in *Multiculturalism in the United States: A Comparative Guide to Acculturation and Ethnicity,* edited by J. D. Buenker and L. A. Ratner. Westport, CT: Greenwood Press.

-------. 1992b. *God Is Red: A Native View of Religion.* 2d ed. Golden, CO: North American Press.

Deloria, Vine, Jr. and Clifford Lytle. 1984. *The Nations Within: The Past and Future of American Indian Sovereignty.* New York: Pantheon Books.

Edsall, Thomas B. and Mary D. Edsall. 1991. *Chain Reaction: The Impact of Race, Rights, and Taxes on American Politics.* New York: W. W. Norton.

Eschbach, Karl. 1992. "Shifting Boundaries: Regional Variation in Patterns of Identification as American Indians." Ph.D. dissertation, Department of Sociology, Harvard University, Cambridge, MA.

-------. 1995. "The Enduring and Vanishing American Indian: American Indian Population Growth and Intermarriage in 1990." *Ethnic and Racial Studies* 18:89–108.

Espiritu, Yen Le. 1992. *Asian American Panethnicity: Bridging Institutions and Identities.* Philadelphia, PA: Temple University Press.

Fantasia, Rick. 1988. *Cultures of Solidarity.* Berkeley, CA: University of California Press.

Forbes, Jack D. 1990. "Undercounting Native Americans: The 1980 Census and the Manipulation of Racial Identity in the United States." *Wicazo Sa Review* 6:2–26.

Fortunate Eagle, Adam. 1992. *Alcatraz! Alcatraz! The Indian Occupation of 1969–71*. San Francisco, CA: Heyday Books.

Giago, Tim. 1991. "Big Increases in 1990 Census not Necessarily Good for Tribes." *Lakota Times*, March 12, p. 3.

Gimenez, Marta E., Fred A. Lopez, and Carlos Munoz, Jr. 1992. *The Politics of Ethnic Construction: Hispanic, Chicano, Latino?* Beverly Hills, CA: Sage Publications.

Glazer, Nathan and Daniel P. Moynihan. 1963. *Beyond the Melting Pot*. Cambridge, MA: Harvard University Press.

Gordon, Milton. 1961. "Assimilation in America: Theory and Reality." *Daedalus* 90:263–85.

Graham, Hugh Davis. 1990. *The Civil Rights Era: Origins and Development of National Policy, 1960–1972*. New York: Oxford University Press.

Groch, Sharon A. 1994. "Oppositional Consciousness: Its Manifestations and Development: A Case Study of People with Disabilities." *Sociological Inquiry* 64:369–95.

Guillemin, Jeanne. 1975. *Urban Renegades: The Cultural Strategy of American Indians*. New York: Columbia University Press.

Harris, David. 1994. "The 1990 Census Count of American Indians: What Do the Numbers Really Mean?" *Social Science Quarterly* 75:580–93.

Harris, Marvin. 1964. *Patterns of Race in the Americas*. New York: Norton. Hauptman, Laurence M. 1986. *The Iroquois Struggle for Survival: World War II to Red Power*. Syracuse, NY: Syracuse University Press.

Hertzberg, Hazel. 1971. *The Search for an American Indian Identity: Modern Pan-Indian Movements*. Syracuse, NY: Syracuse University Press.

Hodge, William H. 1971. "Navajo Urban Migration: An Analysis from the Perspective of the Family." Pp. 346–92 in *The American Indian in Urban Society*, edited by J. O. Waddell and O. M. Watson. Boston, MA: Little, Brown and Company.

Hodson, Randy, Dusko Sekulic, and Garth Massey. 1994. "National Tolerance in Yugoslavia." *American Journal of Sociology* 99:1534–58.

Horse Capture, George P. 1991. "An American Indian Perspective." Pp. 186–207 in *Seeds of Change*, edited by H. J. Viola and C. Margolis. Washington, DC: Smithsonian Institution Press.

Hunt, Scott A. and Robert D. Benford. 1994. "Identity Talk in the Peace and Justice Movement." *Journal of Contemporary Ethnography* 22:488–517.

Jaimes, M. Annette. 1992. "Federal Indian Identification Policy: A Usurpation of Indigenous Sovereignty in North America." Pp. 123–28 in *The State of Native America: Genocide, Colonization, and Resistance*, edited by M. A. Jaimes. Boston, MA: South End Press.

Johnson, Troy. 1993. "The Indian Occupation of Alcatraz Island, Indian Self-Determination, and the Rise of Indian Activism." Ph.D. dissertation, Department of History, University of California at Los Angeles, Los Angeles, CA.

Keith, Verna M. and Cedric Herring. 1991. "Skin Tone and Stratification in the Black Community." *American Journal of Sociology* 97:760–78.

Kelly, Mary E. 1994. "Ethnic Pilgrimages: Lithuanian Americans in Lithuania." Paper presented at the annual meeting of the Midwest Sociological Society, March 13, St. Louis, MO.

Larimore, Jim and Rick Waters. 1993. "American Indians Speak Out Against Ethnic Fraud in College Admissions." Paper presented at a conference sponsored by the American Council on Education: "Educating One-Third of a Nation IV: Making Our Reality Match our Rhetoric," October 22, Houston, TX.

Lelyveld, Joseph. 1985. *Move Your Shadow: South Africa, Black and White.* New York: Penguin.

Lemann, Nicholas. 1991. *The Promised Land: The Great Black Migration and How It Changed America.* New York: A. A. Knopf.

Lieberson, Stanley and Mary C. Waters. 1988. *From Many Strands: Ethnic and Racial Groups in Contemporary America.* New York: Russell Sage Foundation.

Lurie, Nancy O. 1978. 'The Indian Claims Commission." *The Annals of the American Academy of Political and Social Science* 436:97–110.

Masumura, William and Patricia Berman. 1987. "American Indians and the Census." Unpublished manuscript.

McAdam, Doug. 1988. *Freedom Summer.* New York: Oxford University Press.

McBeth, Sally. 1989. "Layered Identity Systems in Western Oklahoma Indian Communities." Paper presented at the annual meeting of the American Anthropological Association, November 17, Washington, DC.

Means Boyer, LaNada. 1994. "Reflections on Alcatraz." *American Indian Culture and Research Journal* 18:75–92.

Morris, Glenn T. 1989. "The International Status of Indigenous Nations within the United States." Pp. 1–14 in *Critical Issues in Native North America* (Document No. 62), edited by W. Churchill. Copenhagen, Denmark: International Work Group for Indigenous Affairs.

Mucha, Janosz. 1983. "From Prairie to the City: Transformation of Chicago's American Indian Community." *Urban Anthropology* 12:337–71.

Nagel, Joane. 1994. "Constructing Ethnicity: Creating and Recreating Ethnic Identity and Culture." *Social Problems* 41:1001–26.

——Forthcoming. *American Indian Ethnic Renewal: Red Power and the Resurgence of Identity and Culture.* New York: Oxford University Press.

Nash, Gerald D. 1985. *The American West Transformed: The Impact of the Second World War.* Bloomington, IN: Indiana University Press.

Nayar, Balde Raj. 1966. *Politics in the Punjab.* New Haven, CT: Yale University Press.

Padilla, Felix. 1985. *Latino Ethnic Consciousness: The Case of Mexican Americans and Puerto Ricans in Chicago.* Notre Dame, IN: University of Notre Dame Press.

——. 1986. "Latino Ethnicity in the City of Chicago." Pp. 153–71 in *Competitive Ethnic Relations,* edited by S. Olzak and J. Nagel. New York: Academic Press.

Park, Robert E. 1928. *Race and Culture.* Glencoe, IL: The Free Press, 1950.

Passel, Jeffrey S. and Patricia A. Berman. 1986. "Quality of 1980 Census Data for American Indians." *Social Biology* 33:163–82.

Pedraza, Silvia. 1994. "Ethnic Identity: Developing a Hispanic-American Identity." Paper presented at the annual meeting of the American Sociological Association, August 5, Los Angeles, CA.

Philp, Kenneth R. 1986. *Indian Self-Rule: First-Hand Accounts of Indian-White Relations from Roosevelt to Reagan.* Salt Lake City, UT: Howe Brothers.

Reed, Little Rock. 1990. "Rehabilitation: Contrasting Cultural Perspectives and the Imposition of Church and State." *Journal of Prisoners on Prisons* 2:3–28.

Reynolds, Jerry. 1993. "Indian Writers: Real or Imagined." *Indian Country Today,* September 8, pp. Al, A3.

Sandefur, Gary D. and Trudy McKinnell. 1986. "American Indian Intermarriage." *Social Science Research* 15:347–71.

Schermerhorn, Richard A. 1978. *Ethnic Plurality in India.* Tucson, AZ: University of Arizona Press.

Snipp, C. Matthew. 1989. *American Indians: The First of This Land.* New York: Russell Sage Foundation.

——. 1993. "Some Observations about the Racial Boundaries and the Experiences of American Indians." Paper presented at the University of Washington, April 22, Seattle, WA.

Snow, David A. and Leon Anderson. 1993. *Down on Their Luck: A Study of Homeless Street People.* Berkeley, CA: University of California Press.

Sollors, Werner, ed. 1989. *The Invention of Ethnicity.* New York: Oxford University Press, 1989.

Sorkin, Alan L. 1978. *The Urban American Indian.* Lexington, MA: Lexington Books.

Standing Bear, Z. G. 1988. "Questions of Assertion, Diversity, and Spirituality: Simultaneously Becoming a Minority and a Sociologist." *The American Sociologist* 20:363–71.

Steele, C. Hoy. 1975. "Urban Indian Identity in Kansas: Some Implications for Research." Pp. 167–78 in *The New Ethnicity: Perspectives from Ethnology,* edited by J. W. Bennett. St. Paul, MN: West Publishing Company.

Stein, Judith. 1989. "Defining the Race, 1890–1930." Pp. 77–104 in *The Invention of Ethnicity,* edited by W. Sollers. New York: Oxford University Press.

Steiner, Stanley. 1967. *The New Indians.* New York: Harper and Row.

Stiffarm, Lenore A. and Phil Lane, Jr. 1992. "The Demography of Native North America: A Question of American Indian Survival." Pp. 23–53 in *The State of Native America: Genocide, Colonization, and Resistance,* edited by M. A. Jaimes. Boston, MA: South End Press.

Taliman, Valorie. 1993. "Lakota Declaration of War." *News from Indian Country* 7:10.

Tarrow, Sidney. 1992. "Mentalities, Political Cultures, and Collective Action Frames." Pp. 174–202 in *Frontiers in Social Movement Theory,* edited by A. D. Morris and C. M. Mueller. New Haven, CT: Yale University Press.

Taylor, Verta and Nancy E. Whittier. 1992. "Collective Identity in Social Movement Communities: Lesbian Feminist Mobilization." Pp. 104–20 in *Frontiers in Social Movement Theory,* edited by A. D. Morris and C. M. Mueller. New Haven, CT: Yale University Press.

Thornton, Russell. 1987. *American Indian Holocaust and Survival.* Norman, OK: University of Oklahoma Press.

——— 1990. *The Cherokees: A Population History.* Lincoln, NE: University of Nebraska Press.

Thornton, Russell, Gary D. Sandefur, and C. Matthew Snipp. 1991. "American Indian Fertility Patterns: 1910 and 1940–1980." *American Indian Quarterly* 15: 359–67.

Thornton, Russell, C. Matthew Snipp, and Nancy Breen. 1990. "Appendix: Cherokees in the 1980 Census." Pp. 178–203 in *The Cherokees: A Population History,* edited by R. Thornton. Lincoln, NE: University of Nebraska Press.

Trask, Haunani-Kay. 1990. "Politics in the Pacific Islands: Imperialism and Native Self-Determination." *Amerasia* 16:1–19.

———. 1991. "Natives and Anthropologists: The Colonial Struggle." *The Contemporary Pacific* 3:159–67.

U.S. Bureau of the Census. 1981. *American Indian Population Estimates by Tribe.* U.S. Bureau of the Census, Washington, DC. Unpublished tables.

———. 1988. *We, the First Americans.* Washington, DC: Government Printing Office.

———. 1989. *Census of Population, Subject Reports, Characteristics of American Indians by Tribes and Selected Areas, 1980.* Washington, DC: Government Printing Office.

———. 1991. "Census Bureau Releases 1990 Census Counts on Specific Racial Groups" (Census Bureau Press Release CB91–215, Wednesday, June 12). U.S. Bureau of the Census, Washington, DC.

———. 1992. *Census of the Population, General Population Characteristics, American Indian and Alaskan Native Areas, 1990.* Washington, DC: Government Printing Office.

Waters, Mary C. 1990. *Ethnic Options: Choosing Identities in America.* Berkeley, CA: University of California Press.

——. 1994. "Ethnic and Racial Identities of Second Generation Blacks in New York City." *International Migration Review* 28:795–820.

Wei, William. 1993. *The Asian American Movement.* Philadelphia, PA: Temple University Press.

Weibel-Orlando, Joan. 1991. *Indian Country, L·A.: Maintaining Ethnic Community in Complex Society.* Champaign, IL: University of Illinois Press.

Witt, Shirley Hill. 1968. "Nationalistic Trends among American Indians." Pp. 53–75 in *The American Indian Today,* edited by S. Levine and N. O. Lurie. Deland, FL: Everett/Edwards, Inc.

UNDERSTANDING DOGS

Caretakers' Attributions of Mindedness in Canine-Human Relationships

BY CLINTON R. SANDERS

This article focuses on the criteria used by dog owners to define their animals as minded individuals with whom they maintain viable and satisfying social relationships. The discussion is based on field data drawn from a study in a veterinary clinic, interviews with dog owners, and autoethnographic materials compiled by the author as he observed and interacted with his own dogs. Special attention is directed at caretakers' understandings of their dogs' thought processes, emotional experiences, and unique personalities. The significance of investigations of animal-human interaction to enlarging sociological views of mindedness and the construction of social identities is emphasized.

Words are the source of misunderstanding.
—Antoine de Saint Exupery (from The Little Prince)

AUTHOR'S NOTE: An earlier version of this discussion was presented at the International Conference on Science and the Human-Animal Relationship, Amsterdam, March 1992. I am indebted to Patti Adler, Peter Adler, Arnold Arluke, Emma, Ann Goetting, Isis, Eleanor Lyon, Raven, Gaye Tuchman, Françoise Wemelsfelder, and two anonymous reviewers for their assistance. JOURNAL OF CONTEMPORARY ETHNOGRAPHY, Vol. 22 No. 2, July 1993 205-226 © 1993 Sage Publications, Inc.

Few associations are as intense and emotionally involving as those we have with companion animals. Despite the frequency and importance of relationships between humans and animals, analyses of interspecies interaction are noticeably rare in the social scientific literature (for exceptions, see Arluke 1988; Bryant 1991; Crist and Lynch 1990; Helmer 1991 ; Hickrod and Schmitt 1982; Mechling 1989; Nash 1989; Sanders 1990; Robins, Sanders, and Cahill 1991; Wieder 1980).

To a major degree, this lack of attention to animal-human exchanges is due to the conventional sociological belief that "authentic" interaction is premised on the abilities of social actors to employ conventional linguistic symbols. Language enables interactants to construct and share a mutually defined reality and provides the vehicle for the internal conversation that constitutes mind.

Because they are presumed to lack the ability to understand and use shared linguistic symbols, animals are, in the conventional sociological view, excluded from all but the most simple social exchanges. Mead ([1934] 1964) presented nonhuman animals as ongoingly involved in communicative acts involving the use of natural signs. He conceived of animal exchanges as immediately situated and involved in direct references to physically present objects or intentions. The only connection between the sign/gestures presented by animals and the subsequent behaviors of their cointeractants was due, according to Mead, to instinct or conditioning.

In establishing this phonocentric view, Mead effectively excluded the routine encounters of people with their nonhuman companions from all but the most cursory of examinations. Because animals are not full-fledged social actors from the Meadian point of view, their encounters with humans are oneway exchanges, lacking the intersubjectivity at the heart of true social interaction. People interact with animals as objects. From the conventional perspective, dog owners[1] babbling endearments to their canine companions are simply taking the role of the animals and projecting humanlike attributes onto them (see Pollner and McDonald-Wickler 1985). Interpreting the behavior of dogs as authentic social responsiveness is the same form of anthropomorphic projection in which people engage when they "interact" with a computer (Turkle 1984), automobile, or other inanimate object (Cohen 1989).

In contrast, caretakers of companion animals and others who live in everyday situations entailing frequent and intimate interaction with nonhuman animals and who have practical interests in making ongoing sense of their behavior consistently see animals as subjective actors and define interactions with them as being "authentic" and reciprocal social exchanges (see Crist and Lynch 1990; Griffin 1984; Hearne 1987; Shapiro 1990; Ristau 1990). People grant this (at least, limited) mindedness to animals even when the situation in which they encounter the animal-other is formally constrained by a reductionist ideology demanding that they be seen and dealt with as scientific objects. Arluke's (1988, 1990) studies of animal care technicians in medical research facilities and Wieder's (1980) work with chimpanzee researchers, for example, amply illustrate the persuasiveness of everyday encounters in prompting people to regard nonhuman animals as minded coactors.

This discussion focuses on dog owners' definitions of the companion animals with whom they have ongoing relationships. Based on routine, intimate interactions with their dogs, caretakers come to regard their animals as unique individuals who are minded, empathetic, reciprocating, and well aware of basic rules and roles that govern the relationship. Caretakers come to see their dogs as consciously behaving so as to achieve defined goals in the course of routine social exchanges with people and other canines. The dogs are regarded, in short, as possessing at least a rudimentary ability to "take the role of the other." This interpretation of the dogs' actions and reactions as "expressions of competence" (Goode 1992)—as thoughtfully constructed and reciprocating—requires owners, in turn, to take the role of the animal other in order to establish the "natural rituals" (Collins 1989) that constitute their ongoing relationship.

Following a brief presentation of the various sources of data on which this discussion is grounded, I expand on the key elements outlined above. Drawing parallels to the sociological work on interactions between able-bodied people and ostensibly less competent human others (e.g., Bogdan and Taylor 1989; Goode 1992; Gubrium 1986), I first describe how owners construct perspectives on their dogs as minded actors and what they see to be the nature of their subjective experience. Next, I present the owners' definitions of their animals as possessors of unique, historically grounded personalities. I then focus on the central emotional component of the canine-human relationship. Owners typically view their canine companions as having an emotional life and as being ongoingly aware of and appropriately responsive to the emotional experience of their human companions. The substantive discussion closes with a description of how caretakers incorporate their dogs into the social networks and key routines that encompass and comprise their intimate lives. The article's conclusion points to areas of further research and focuses on how investigations of animal-human relationships can expand sociological perspectives on such central issues as mind, identity construction, and interpersonal intimacy.

THE RESEARCH

The data on which this discussion is based are drawn from three sources. First, I call on material included in an "auto-ethnography" constructed as I systematically observed and recorded personal experiences with my own dogs (three Newfoundland females) over a 4-year period. As the term implies, autoethnography is a combination of autobiography and ethnography. As such, it rejects the traditional ethnologic convention of positioning the researcher as an objective outsider describing and interpreting observed events. Instead, autoethnography emphasizes the value of information drawn from the systematic examination of personal experiences, emotions, and interpretations (see Denzin 1989; Ellis 1991 ; Hayano 1979; Shapiro 1990).[2]

The second body of data was amassed during 9 months of participant observation in a large veterinary clinic located in the Northeast. The field data of central importance to this article consist of detailed observations of owners and their dogs as they waited for a veterinarian to come into the examination room, the conversations that owners had with me during this time, and the exchanges that occurred between clients and veterinarians in the course of the service encounter. Unless asked directly who I was, I did not identify myself as a sociologist to the clients. In general, clients assumed that I was a veterinary student or a technician employed by the clinic. As a participant in the setting, I routinely made myself generally useful, holding animals for various procedures, fetching equipment and supplies, helping clean examination rooms, offering nonmedical advice, and in a variety of other ways assisting with the business of the clinic.

Finally, information is drawn from relevant portions of a series of in-depth, semi-structured interviews conducted with 24 dog owners initially contacted when they presented themselves at the veterinary hospital or who agreed to be interviewed following their involvement in an 8-week-long puppy-training class sponsored by the clinic. These interviews averaged between 60 and 90 minutes in length and were tape-recorded with the interviewee's permission. All interviews were conducted in the interviewee's homes, and in all cases the owner's dog was present during the encounter, thereby allowing me to observe exchanges between the informant and his or her animal in their most familiar interactional setting.

I do not maintain that this description of owners' orientations toward and interactions with their dogs encompasses all such exchanges. It is certainly the case that owners construct a variety of identities for their dogs—from object through make-believe person to surrogate child—and consequently treat them in a variety of ways. I do contend, however, that the interactants and canine-human exchanges presented here are fairly typical of the people, dogs, and relationships one finds in the average American household.

The informants were drawn from and observations were made in a veterinary practice that provided services for a largely middle-class clientele. A recent national survey commissioned by the Veterinary Medical Association (1988) reveals that approximately 38% of American households include an average of 1.5 dogs and that close to 78% of dog owners visit a veterinarian an average of about 2.5 times a year. People with canine companions encountered in a veterinary clinic, therefore, can reasonably be seen as fairly typical dog owners. Certainly, one would expect to encounter rather different orientations and relationships (probably more on the functional/object end of the continuum; see e.g., Jordon 1975) were research done with lower-class owners and/or those who never seek veterinary services.[3]

ASSIGNING THE DOG A HUMANLIKE IDENTITY

The designation of another as "human" is an eminently social activity. The exclusion of certain people from this category has been a fairly common sociohistorical phenomenon. "Primitives," African Americans, and members of various other human groups routinely have been, and continue to be, denied the status of human (see Spiegel 1988), and studies of interactions in total institutions (e.g., Bogdan et al. 1974; Goffman 1961; Goode 1992; Vail 1966) are filled with descriptions of the "dehumanization" of inmates by staff members, principally on the grounds that the inmates do not possess the requisite level of mind.

In their study of the interactions of nondisabled people with severely disabled family members, Bogdan and Taylor (1989) discussed the ways in which the social meaning of humanness is created and the criteria used by "normals" to assign a human identity to severely disabled intimates.[4] This definitional activity entails attending to four basic factors. First, the nondisabled *attribute thinking* to disabled others. The latter are seen as minded—able to reason, understand, and remember. The caretakers regard the disabled individuals as partners in the inter-subjective play of social interaction, interpret their gestures, sounds, postures, and expressions as indicators of intelligence, and are adept at taking the role of the disabled others.

Second, the nondisabled see the others as *individuals.* They regard the disabled persons as having distinct personalities, identifiable likes and dislikes, authentic feelings, and unique personal histories.

Third, the disabled persons are seen as *reciprocating,* as giving as much to the relationship as they receive from it. For nondisabled associates, the others are true companions who help to expand their lives by providing companionship, acting as objects of caring, and opening up situations in which they can encounter new people (see Messent 1983; Robins, Sanders, and Cahill 1991).

Finally, Bogdan and Taylor (1989) described how disabled persons are humanized by being *incorporated into a social place.* Through defining the disabled persons as integral members of the family and involving them in ongoing domestic rituals and routines, the nondisabled actively situate the others into the intimate relational network.

The owners I interviewed and encountered in the veterinary hospital engaged in a process of identity construction very similar to that described by Bogdan and Taylor. They routinely used their day-to-day experience with their dogs to define their animals as minded social actors and as having, at least, a "person-like" status.[5] Caretakers typically saw their dogs as reciprocating partners in an honest, nondemanding, and rewarding social relationship.

The skeptical reader of what follows may well discount caretakers' identity construction of their dogs as "mere" anthropomorphic projections. Even if this were the case, we should not disregard people's definitions of the other as the central element in understanding how human-animal relationships—or relationships between "normals" and alingual others more generally— are organized (see Pollner and McDonald-Wickler 1985).

Evaluating the subjective experience of others is always a tricky procedure (Schutz 1970; Goffman 1959). Most basically, the chaining of interactions is a practical endeavor; estimations of coactors' perspectives are assumed, altered, or discarded with regard to what works. Intimate familiarity with others—animal or human—is an effective teacher.

As I write these words, for example, one of my dogs comes to my study and stares at me. She then walks back down the hall to the door opening onto the porch and rings the bell she uses to signal her desire to go outside. Because I am not immediately responsive, she returns to my study, pokes me with her nose, and returns to the door. Grumbling about the intrusion, I get up, open the door, and she goes out to lie down in her usual spot.

I maintain, and the dog owners presented below would maintain, that the most reasonable interpretation of this mundane sequence of events is to see it as an authentic social exchange. My dog has encountered a problem, realized on the basis of remembered past events that my actions hold the potential for solving her problem, purposefully behaved in a manner that effectively communicated her "request," and, in so doing, shaped my behavior to her defined ends.

Seeing this simple encounter as involving communication of a definition of the situation, mutual taking the role of the other, and projection of a short-term future event does not, however, require that we *literally see* dogs as people. Defining companion animals as "people in disguise" (Clark 1984,24) is as degrading to them as is the view that they are mere behaviorist automatons. My informants, in describing their dogs' humanlike qualities and actions, did not regard them as literally human. Nor did they facilely place them in a "keyed frame" as "pretend" people (Hickrod and Schmitt 1982). The point they were making, and the focus of this discussion, is that their animal companions were far more than objects; they were minded, creative, empathetic, and responsive. The animal-human relationships they shared were authentically social.

THE DOG AS MINDED ACTOR

The owners with whom I spoke had little doubt of their dogs' cognitive abilities, and all could recount examples of what they defined as minded behavior. Dogs' thought processes were generally seen as fairly basic ("He's not exactly a Rhodes scholar"), and, to a certain extent, thoughtful intelligence was seen as varying from animal individual to individual and from breed to breed. Because they were dogs and not humans, the companion animals were typically described as engaging in thought processes that were "wordless" (Terrace 1987). Thought was characterized as being nonlinear, composed of mental images, and driven largely by emotion (see Gallistel 1992). When asked if she thought that her malamute cross could think, an interviewee replied,

> Yes I do. I don't think [dogs'] heads are empty. I think their thinking process is different from ours. I think they think on emotions. If the environment is

happy and stable, they are going to act more stable—pay more attention to
what you are doing. They are going to be more alert. If everything is chaotic,
they would not be thinking externally but be more concerned with themselves
internally—protecting themselves and not paying attention to my cues. I would
call that thinking, but it is not what you would call linear thinking. ... They are
making decisions based on emotional cues.

No matter what the mode of mental representation defined by caretakers, most agreed
that the issues *thought about* were rather basic. The dog's mind was focused predominantly
on immediate events and matters of central concern to his or her ongoing physical and
emotional experience:

I think that [my dogs] are here just to get approval. [They are here for] feeding
or to get petted or get their ears rubbed. I think they think enough not to get
yelled at, not to get into trouble. That's the way dogs are. I don't think they can
reason like people.

On the other hand, some owners did see their animals as going beyond these basic
physiological and emotional concerns. One typical type of example offered by informants
focused on their dogs' play activities and the adjustments they made while being trained.
The dog's purposive modification of behavior was seen as indicating a basic ability to
reason. For example, one owner described the actions of his hunting dog in the course of
learning to retrieve objects from the water:

This is the smartest dog I have ever had. We are having him trained profession-
ally, and we were with the trainer with my dog and some of the other dogs he
was training. He said, "Look here. I'll show you how smart your dog is." He
threw the retrieving dummy out into the middle of this long pond there. My
dog jumped in and swam to the thing, grabbed it in his mouth, and took a
right turn. He swam to the land and walked back to us with the dummy in his
mouth—all proud. He was the only one smart enough to walk back. The other
dogs all swam out, retrieved the thing, and swam all the way back.

While watching my own dogs play, I was struck by the adjustments they made—
behavioral alterations that, were they made by hairless bipeds, clearly would be seen as
demonstrating thought. Soon after the introduction of a new puppy into my household,
I made the following entry in my autoethnographic notes following a walk in the woods:

Today Isis [my 3 year old Newfoundland] appeared to come to a realization
about how she had been attempting to play "chase" and this prompted her to

alter the play process somewhat— essentially altering the assumption of roles. On each of the walks so far, Isis has attempted to initiate chase by acting as the chaser. She runs off at a rapid pace, turns back, runs toward Raven [the puppy], bowls her over, runs past, etc. This doesn't work because of the size and strength difference. Raven just cowers, runs to one of us for protection, cries out. So, this time when Raven made a run at her at one point in the walk, Isis ran off a little ways until Raven followed. Isis then ran further and soon Raven was in hot pursuit. Isis led her on a merry chase over fallen trees, through thickets, into gullies. It was particularly interesting to watch because Isis was adjusting the game on the basis of her knowledge of Raven's, as yet, limited abilities. She would run just fast enough so that Raven wouldn't get more than a few feet behind and would occasionally slow down enough that Raven could grab hold of some hair on her side or legs. Isis would also toy with the other player by jumping over larger falls or into gullies with deep, vertical sides—obstacles she knew were beyond Raven's limited abilities.

Owners frequently offered stories in which their dogs acted in ways that were thoughtfully intended to shape the owners' definitions of the situation and to manipulate their subsequent behavior to desirable ends. A number of informants told of dog behavior such as the following:

> We have a beanpot that we keep filled with dog cookies. Every time the dogs go out and "do their business" they get a cookie. They have interpreted this as "all we have to do is cross the threshold and come back and we get a cookie." So it will be raining and they won't want to go out and they will just put one foot outside the door and then go over to where the cookies are kept: "Well, technically we went out."

Though rarely successful, this sort of behavior indicated for the owners an attempt by the dog to deceptively manipulate their definition of the situation (dog went out) so as to shape their behavior (give cookie). Caretakers also provided descriptions of situations in which they observed their dogs engaging in deceptive actions while playing with other dogs. For example, a veterinarian offered the following story when we were discussing the issue or whether or not dogs think:

> I believe that dogs think. My dogs play a game called "bone." One of them will get the rawhide bone and take it over to the other one and try to get him to try and get it. Or one will try to get the bone if the other one has it. One day I was watching and the youngest one was trying to get the bone without much luck. So he goes over to the window and begins to bark like someone is coming up

the driveway. The other dog drops the bone and runs over to the window and the puppy goes and gets the bone. There wasn't anyone in the driveway—it was just a trick. Maybe it was just coincidence but...[6]

THE DOG AS AN INDIVIDUAL

Although many caretakers did see certain personality characteristics as breed related, they regularly spoke of their own dogs as unique individuals. Few informants had any trouble responding at some length to my routine request that they describe what their dog "was like." Owners currently living with multiple dogs or those who had had serial experience with dogs often made comparisons in presenting their animals' unique personal attributes. For example, an interviewee with two springer spaniels responded to my question about his dogs' personalities as follows:

> It's interesting. A good way to look at this is to compare her with my other dog. I look at my older springer and she is always begging for attention. Sometimes I misinterpret that as wanting something to eat. I'll just be studying and she is happy just to sit there and have her head in my lap while I scratch her behind the ears. On the other hand, Ricky really likes attention and she seeks it. But if you're not willing to give it to her, she'll go find something else to entertain herself. She's bold, she's aggressive. At the same time she is affectionate—willing to take what you will give her.

Owners also were adept at describing their dogs' unique personal tastes. Informants typically took considerable pleasure in talking about individual likes and dislikes in food, activities, playthings, and people. For example, when asked by the veterinarian whether her dog liked to chew rocks (he had noticed that the dog's teeth were quite worn), a woman described her female Doberman's special passion:

> She just loves big rocks—the bigger the better. When she finds a new one she is so happy she howls. She'll lie and chew them all day. She puts them in her water bucket, and sometimes it takes two hands to get them out.

Owners also attributed individuality to their dogs by embedding them in a readily recountable narrative history. Interviewees took great pleasure in telling stories about their dogs' exploits and how they were acquired. In somewhat more abstract terms than those used by my informants, Shapiro (1990) presented the individuality of his own dog, stressing its embeddedness in their shared historical experience:

History informs the experience of a particular animal whether or not it can tell that history. Events in the life of an animal shape and even constitute him or her. ... [My dog] is an individual in that he is not constituted through and I do not live toward him as a species-specific behavioral repertoire or developmental sequence. More positively, he is an individual in that he is both subject to and subject of "true historical particulars". ... I can not replace him, nor, ethically, can I "sacrifice" him for he is a unique individual being, (p. 189)

THE DOG AS EMOTIONAL AND RECIPROCATING

As mentioned above, owners typically understood their dogs as having subjective experiences in which some form of reasoning was linked with emotion. The most common theme that emerged from the encounters in the clinic and interviews with owners was that dogs are eminently emotional beings. Dogs were, for example, described as experiencing loneliness, joy, sadness, embarrassment, and anger. Interviewees often focused on this last emotional experience—anger—because it was linked to incidents in which dogs responded in ways which owners saw as indicating vindictiveness. For example, one owner described her Shar Pei puppy's displeasure at being abandoned and his playfully vengeful response to her absence:

It's funny. Usually after I have been at work all Friday I don't go out unless I am sure that somebody is going to watch him. But one time I left him alone and when I got home HE WAS ANGRY. He just let me know. [How did he let you know?] He'd follow me around and he would look up at me and he would just bark. It was like he was yelling at me. And I would say, "What is it with you?" and when I would stop talking he would look at me and bark—like "You left me. How could you do that?" You could read it in his face. When he was younger and I would go to work and leave him during the day, he would find some way to let me know that he wasn't pleased—like he would shred all his newspapers. Every day was something new. He would move his crate, or he would flip his water dish, or something like that.

In the course of my research, I routinely asked owners whether they thought that their dogs had a "conscience." Although there was some considerable difference of opinion among informants about how effective their animals' consciences were in constraining unwanted behavior, all saw their dogs as possessing a basic sense of the rules imposed by the human members of the household. In turn, they all could offer descriptions of incidents where their animals violated the rules and subsequently responded in ways that indicated the subjective experience of guilt. Typical guilt responses entailed clearly readable body language—bowed head, tucked tail, ears down, sidelong glances. For example:

> Some major problems existed with Diz when he was younger and learning the house rules—what's proper and what's not proper. [Do you think Diz has a conscience?] He knows what he should and shouldn't do. If he gets into something. … He came up the stairs with a big old flower in his mouth, this silk flower, and his ears go forward. That's his look, "Am I doing something I'm not supposed to be doing?" He'll get something in his mouth and he'll put his head down and his ears go down and his little tail is kind of wagging. It is a body language that says to me, "Am I supposed to be doing this?"

Because caretakers saw their dogs as experiencing a subjective world in which emotion played a central role, they frequently understood their relationships with the animals as revolving around emotional issues. The chief pleasure they derived from the animal-human relationship was the joy of relating to another being who consistently demonstrated love— a feeling for the other that was honestly felt and displayed and not contingent on the personal attributes or even the actions of the human other. One indication of the intensely positive quality of their relationship with their animals were the owners' perceptions that their dogs were attuned to their own emotions and responded in ways that were appropriate and indicated empathy. A man and his teenage daughter, for example, spoke of their dog's ability to read their emotions and his attempts to comfort them when they felt sad:

> 1. Daughter: He's just fun. He keeps us lightheaded. And he certainly senses our moods. If you're sad and crying he will come snuggle next to you.
> 2. Father: He just seems to sense it somehow, you can be in a different room and be down. Recently when Mary was in her room he just seemed to know where to go He sensed that somewhere in this house—his doghouse—there was something that was not quite right. He sought Mary out and was just there. One day I was sitting on the front porch kind of blue about some things and he just snuggled in there—totally noninvasive, just "If you want to pet me, pet me. I'm here if you need me."

Owners saw their intimate relationship with their dogs as premised on intersubjectivity and shared emotion. However, caretakers defined the animal-human relationship as unique because it was free from the criticism and contingent feelings that typified relationships with human intimates. This prompted owners to feel intense emotional ties to their dogs. The centrality of emotional connectedness is obvious in this story offered by a client in the veterinary clinic as she responded to my request for her to tell me about how she acquired her dog:

A lady down the street had a litter. I went in and immediately he came right over to me. It was love at first sight—he chose me. I remember it was really snowing that night and we couldn't get to the grocery store. My mother made him chicken soup. To this day he goes wild when he smells chicken soup. Every time I make it he gets half. Sometimes this annoys my roommate— "Hey, I wanted some of that." But he is more important. He's not a dog to me. He's my best friend. He loves me and I love him. When I come home from work he's happy to see me and I am happy to see him. I try to spend quality time with him every day. … He gives me love. He can't live without me and I can't live without him. It's so hard to see him getting old. I just don't know what I would do without him.

AFFORDING THE DOG A SOCIAL PLACE

Because their dogs were regarded by owners as displaying these essentially humanlike attributes, they actively included their animals in the routine exchanges and the special ritual practices of the household. The dogs typically were considered as being authentic family members.[7] Shared family routines commonly centered around feeding and food preparation, playing with or exercising the dog, and some more idiosyncratic routines that evolved in the course of the shared relationship. One interviewee, for example, referred to her own childhood experiences while describing the daily breakfast routine she shared with her newly acquired puppies:

I love these dogs. They are people dogs. We do have a set course of activities during the course of the day. We seem to meld very nicely with one another. Anywhere from 5:30 on, the dogs will start to bark which means to me that it is time to get up—the activities of the day have begun. I come downstairs and they are on the back porch waiting to come in for breakfast. I bring them in the house and I talk to them. We talk about what we are going to do today and what do you want for breakfast? Of course, they have no choice—they get the same thing every meal. But it is very important for me to talk to them, and I'm sure they know what I am saying because they will go into the pantry and get a biscuit. So I go in and get the bag of Purina®, and I show it to them and say, 'This is what we're having for breakfast." They'll sit down and look, and I will go the refrigerator and get the … yogurt out, and I will put a spoonful in each dish, and I will always be sure that I leave a little on the spoon so the kids can lick it. I do that because it reminds me of when I was a kid, and whenever my mother made frosting she would leave a little on the spoon. That was always the highlight of frosting a cake— licking the spoon. Then I take the dishes out and they eat. I go get my coffee and read the paper and talk to them. They will walk around and poop. They will play for a while. The day has begun.

Informants regularly spoke of key ritual activities they shared with their animals. Most, for example, celebrated their dogs' birthdays. Cakes were baked, presents were bought, parties were organized, favorite foods were prepared, and other special steps were taken by owners to ritually commemorate their animals' births. The other typical ritual in which the dogs were included was that surrounding Christmas or other religious holidays. A young woman, for example, described her puppy's first Christmas:

He just loved Christmas. Somehow he figured out which were his presents under the tree and he happily opened them all himself. He had his own ornaments on the tree—I got some that were unbreakable and put them on the bottom branches. He would take one carefully in his mouth and come running into the other room with it all proud to show it off. He loved the tree. He thought we had brought it in from the outside just for him.

At the same time that owners presented their dogs as thinking, emotional, creative, role-taking individuals they realized that conventional social definitions tended to situate dogs outside the bounds of humanness. Companion canines are customarily regarded as objects, toys, or creatures whose ostensibly human characteristics are "actually" the result of anthropomorphic projection on the part of overinvolved owners. However, intimate experience and the practical recognition that treating their animals as minded and competent coactors *worked* as an effective context in which to understand and accomplish ongoing collective action convinced owners that rigidly placing dogs outside the social category of "person" was unwarranted. The recognition that their views of their dogs violated conventional boundaries between humans and "others" and could potentially be seen as stigmatizing was apparent in the discomfort often expressed by my interviewees when I asked them if they regarded their dogs as "people." For example:

In a sense they are [people]. They have feelings. There is a mutual caring for one another and although they may hurt one another it is done in a playful manner. Yeah, they are people, but I hesitate to say that to too many individuals because they would think I am nuts. Because I don't think many people think of animals as being people. The majority of people think of animals as pets and they are to be kept at a distance. It is very important to me to have these "kids" portrayed as part of my family. Because they are part of my family. I do treat them as people. I care about them and I would never deliberately hurt them. It is very important for me to convey to them that I do care very much for them. I'm sure they understand that.

CONCLUSION

This discussion has focused on the categories of evidence used by dog owners to include their animals inside the ostensibly rigid but actually rather flexible boundaries that divide minded humans from mindless others. The picture that emerges is of the person experiencing his or her companion dog as an authentic, reciprocating, and empathetic social actor. Canine companions are effectively involved with their caretakers in routine social exchanges premised on the mutual ability of the interactants to take the role of the other, effectively define the physical and social situation, and adjust their behavior in line with these essential determinations. In much the same way as the able-bodied construct identities of intimate human others who have severely limited abilities, caretakers use the evidence at hand to define their dogs as possessing minds, emotional lives, unique personalities, and readily identifiable tastes. These humanlike characteristics qualify dogs to be incorporated into the rituals and routines that symbolize and constitute owners' daily lives and intimate social networks.

This discussion of people and their dogs has touched on only one small segment of human interactions with nonhuman animals. Sociological attention could be directed at a wide variety of related issues and situations—for example, people's interactions with species other than canines; occupational and recreational settings incorporating animals; class, ethnic, and racial variations in human-animal interactions; and intensely interdependent relationships, such as those between people and guide dogs or other assistance animals.

Within the larger context of how animal "humanness" is constructed as a practical accomplishment, this discussion has presented mind as similarly constituted. Much like those who intimately and regularly interact with Alzheimer's patients (Gubrium 1986), the owners on whom I focused regarded their dogs as possessing minds revealed in the knowledge drawn from intimate experience. The import of this view is that it moves away from the Meadian orientation toward mind as an individual internal conversation/object. Instead, mind is reconceived as more fully social, enduring in its social classification by those who are most connected to and knowledgeable of the alingual other. Like Gubrium's (1986) Alzheimer's patient caregivers, dog owners actively engage in "doing mind": They act as agents who identify and give voice to the subjective experience of their animals. Dog caretakers also make claims for the minds of their animals because they, like the intimates of the severely retarded and those with Alzheimer's disease, can "listen with their hearts." Owners foster and value the emotional connections that bind them to their dogs. To a major degree, the intimate relationship and interaction that the owner shares with his or her animal is, as Gubrium put it, an "emotive discourse" (p. 47).

The generative context within which this emotionally focused construction of animal mind takes place involves the accretion of mutual experience of what Collins (1989) referred to as "natural rituals." Caretakers and their dogs ongoingly share activities, moods, and routines. Coordination of these natural rituals requires human and animal participants to assume the perspective of the other and, certainly in the eyes of the owners and ostensibly on the part of the dogs, results in a mutual recognition of being "together."

Most broadly then, this discussion has been about how identities are constructed. Sociogenic identities (Goode 1992) are created and projected in immediate interactional contexts. Perspectives on the other and evaluations of his/her/its capabilities are affected centrally by preexisting expectations and ideologies. Those who routinely interact with alingual companions draw from their ongoing experience information about the other, effectively disconfirming folk beliefs, occupational ideologies, or academic doctrines that present the inability to talk as rendering one mindless and incompetent. Investigations of people's relationships with companion animals, like those focused on affiliations with speechless humans, emphasize the undue emphasis traditionally placed on language as the foundation of intimate interaction, mind and thoughtful behavior, and the generation of social identities.

This, then, is part of the promise of the investigation of people's relationships with companion animals—expansion of sociological perspectives on mind and modes of mental representation ("iconographic mind"), illumination of procedures whereby minded identities are socially generated and the interactional contexts which constrain these procedures, extension of analyses of "the other," and the opportunity to further develop our views of intimate relationships and the emotional elements which are central to these essential social bonds. Seen in this light, systematic attention to animal-human relationships offers symbolic interactionists a challenging and rewarding prospect.

NOTES

1. Despite the significant power difference symbolized by the terms "owner" and "caretaker," I use these designations interchangeably throughout the article.

2. The focus of this discussion on people's relationships with dogs flows, in part, from my own lifelong experience with dogs, my respect for them as a species, and the ready access afforded by my currently living intimately with them. Further, dogs are the nonhuman animals with which humans have the longest history of intimate association (Budiansky 1992; Porter 1989) and for whom people have the most intense attraction (Endenburg 1991). The dog's highly social nature accounts, in part, for this lengthy and emotional relationship with people and also means that human interaction with dogs lends itself ideally to sociological analysis.

3. My informants were not, as one anonymous reviewer skeptically put it, "wacky and lonely people who are over-involved with their pets, dress them in silly outfits, etc." At the veterinary clinic in which I participated, clients with this sort of overinvolved orientation were identified as such, were commonly referred to as "animal nuts," and were frequently the focus of gentle derision. None of the data on which this discussion is based are drawn from observations of or conversations with this readily identifiable category of client.

4. One reviewer of an earlier version of this article expressed some concern with the apparent implication that dogs are "like" severely disabled human beings. Some discussions (e.g., Regan 1983) emphasize that infants, the mentally retarded, and others with limited or nonexistent verbal and social capacities are regarded as human and afforded a consequently appropriate moral place, whereas animals are typically denied similar considerations (see Frey 1980). I do not intend to imply necessarily that because dog owners consistently define their animal companions as minded and humanlike that, therefore, dogs and their interests are morally equivalent to those of humans. This discussion is about the social construction of the companion animal's identity in the context of intimate relationships. While not irrelevant to the issue of animal rights, this description focuses on a sociological phenomenon. The rights of companion animals and the attendant responsibilities of humans are matters of philosophical and legal debate beyond the scope of this article.

5. Of the owners interviewed by Cain (1985), 72% said that their dog usually or always had "people status" (see also Veevers 1985).

6. For interesting discussions of play interactions between dogs and people, see Mitchell and Thompson (1990,1991) and Mechling (1989).

7. The most common categories used by caretakers to situate their relationships with their dogs was to regard them as either family members or close friends. General studies of pet owners show that this is extremely common. Somewhere between 70% (Beck and Katcher 1983) and 99% (Voith 1983) of pet caretakers define their animals as members of the family and from 30% (Nieburg and Fischer 1982) to 83% (Bryant 1982) consider the pet a "special" or "close" friend.

REFERENCES

Arluke, A. 1988. Sacrificial symbolism in animal experimentation: Object or pet? *Anthrozoos* 2:98–117.

------. 1990. Moral evaluation in medical research. *Advances in Medical Sociology* 1:189–204.

Beck, A. and A. Katcher. 1983. *Between pets and people*. New York: Putnam.

Bogdan, R., and S. Taylor. 1989. Relationships with severely disabled people: The social construction of humanness. *Social Problems* 36:135–48.

Bogdan, R., S. Taylor, B. deGrandpre, and S. Haynes. 1974. Let them eat programs: Attendants' perspectives and programming on wards in state schools. *Journal of Health and Social Behavior* 15:142–51.

Bryant, B. K. 1982. Sibling relationships in middle childhood. In *Sibling relationships: Their nature and significance across the lifespan*, edited by M. E. Lamb and B. Sutton-Smith, 87–122. Hillsdale, NJ: Lawrence Erlbaum.

Bryant, C. 1991. Deviant leisure and clandestine lifestyle: Cockfighting as a socially disvalued sport. *World Leisure and Recreation* 33:17–21.

Budiansky, S. 1992. *The covenant of the wild: Why animals chose domestication*. New York: Morrow.

Cain, A. 1985. Pets as family members. In *Pets and the family,* edited by M. Sussman, 5–10. New York: Haworth.

Clark, S. 1984. *The nature of the beast.* New York: Oxford University Press.

Cohen, J. 1989. About steaks liking to be eaten: The conflicting views of symbolic interactionists and Talcott Parsons concerning the nature of relations between persons and nonhuman objects. *Symbolic Interaction* 12:191–214.

Collins, R. 1989. Toward a neo-Meadian theory of mind. *Symbolic Interaction* 12:1–32.

Crist, E., and M. Lynch. 1990. The analyzability of human-animal interaction: The case of dog training: Paper presented at the annual meeting of the International Sociological Association, Madrid, Spain.

Denzin, N. 1989. *Interpretive interactionism.* Newbury Park, CA: Sage.

Ellis, C. 1991. Sociological introspection and emotional experience. *Symbolic Interaction* 14:23–50.

Endenburg, N. 1991. *Animals as companions.* Amsterdam: Thesis.

Frey, R. G. 1980. *Interests and rights: The case against animals.* Oxford: Clarendon.

Gallistel, C. R., ed. 1992. *Animal cognition.* Cambridge: MIT Press.

Goffman, E. 1959. *The presentation of self in everyday life.* Garden City, NY: Doubleday.

------. 1961. *Asylums.* Garden City, NY: Doubleday.

Goode, D. 1992. Who is Bobby? Ideology and method in the discovery of a Down syndrome person's competence. In Interpreting *disability: A qualitative reader,* edited by P. Ferguson, D. Ferguson, and S. Taylor, 197–213. New York: Teachers College Press.

Griffin, D. 1984. *Animal thinking.* Cambridge, MA: Oxford University Press.

Gubrium, J. 1986. The social preservation of mind: The Alzheimer's disease experience. *Symbolic Interaction* 9:37–51.

Hayano, D. 1979. Auto-ethnography: Paradigms, problems, and prospects. *Human Organization* 38:99–104.

Hearne, V. 1987. *Adam's task.* New York: Alfred A. Knopf.

Helmer, J. 1991. The horse in backstretch culture. *Qualitative Sociology* 14:175–95.

Hickrod, L.J.H., and R. L. Schmitt. 1982. A naturalistic study of interaction and frame: The pet as "family member." *Urban Life* 11:55–77.

Jordon, J. 1975. An ambivalent relationship: Dog and human in the folk culture of the rural south. *Appalachian Journal* 2:68–77'.

Mead, G. H. [1934] 1964. *George Herbert Mead on social psychology.* Edited by Anselm Strauss. Chicago: University of Chicago Press.

Mechling, Jay. 1989. "Banana cannon" and other folk traditions between human and nonhuman animals. *Western Folklore* 48:312–23.

Messent, P. 1983. Social facilitation of contact with other people by pet dogs. In *New perspectives on our lives with companion animals,* edited by A. Katcher and A. Beck, 37–46. Philadelphia: University of Pennsylvania Press.

Mitchell, R., and N. Thompson. 1990. The effects of familiarity on dog-human play. *Anthrozoos* 4:24–43.

---------. 1991. Projects, routines, and enticements in dog-human play. In Perspectives in ethology: Human understanding and animal awareness, edited by P.P.G. Bateson and P. Klopfer, 189–216. New York: Plenum.

Nash, J. 1989. What's in a face? The social character of the English bulldog. *Qualitative Sociology* 12:357–70. Nieburg, H., and A. Fischer. 1982. *Pet loss.* New York: Harper & Row.

Pollner, M., and L. McDonald-Wickler. 1985. The social construction of unreality: A case of a family's attribution of competence to a severely retarded child. *Family Process* 24:241–54.

Porter, V. 1989. *Faithful companions: The alliance of man and dog.* London: Methuen. Regan, T. 1983. *The case for animal rights.* Berkeley: University of California Press.

Ristau, C, ed. 1990. *Cognitive ethology: The minds of other animals.* Hillsdale, NJ: L Erlbaum.

Robins, D., C Sanders, and S. Canili. 1991. Dogs and their people: Pet-facilitated interaction in a public setting. *Journal of Contemporary Ethnography* 20:3–25.

Sanders, C. R. 1990. Excusing tactics: Social responses to the public misbehavior of companion animals. *Anthrozoos* 4:82–90.

Schutz, A. 1970. *On phenomenology and social relations.* Chicago: University of Chicago Press.

Shapiro, K. 1990. Understanding dogs through kinesthetic empathy, social construction, and history. *Anthrozoos* 3:184–95.

Spiegel, M. 1988. *The dreaded comparison: Human and animal slavery.* Philadelphia: New Society.

Terrace, H. 1987. Thoughts without words. In *Mindwaves: Thoughts on intelligence, identity and consciousness,* edited by C. Blakemore and S. Greenfield, 123–37. New York: Blackwell.

Turkle, S. 1984. *The second self.* New York: Simon & Schuster. Vail, D. 1966. *Dehumanization and the institutional career.* Springfield, IL: Charles C Thomas.

Veevers, J. 1985. The social meaning of pets: Alternative roles for companion animals. In *Pets and the family,* edited by M. Sussman, 11 -30. New York: Haworth.

Veterinary Medical Association. 1988. *The veterinary services market for companion animals.* Overland Park, KS: Charles, Charles Research Group.

Voith, V. 1983. Animal behavior problems: An overview. In *New perspectives on our lives with companion animals,* edited by A. Katcher and A. Beck, 181–86. Philadelphia: University of Pennsylvania Press.

Wieder, D. L. 1980. Behavioristic operationalism and the life-world: Chimpanzees and chimpanzee researchers in face-to-face interaction. *Sociological Inquiry 50:7SA* 03.

CLINTON R. SANDERS is Professor of Sociology at the Greater Hartford Campus of the University of Connecticut. He is author of *Customizing the Body: The Art and Culture of Tattooing* (Temple University Press) and editor of *Marginal Conventions: Popular Culture, Mass Media and Social Deviance* (Bowling Green University Popular Press). Current work is directed at building a symbolic interactionist perspective on the relationships between people and nonhuman animals.

A Model of Animal Selfhood: Expanding Interactionist Possibilities

By Leslie Irvine

University of Colorado, Boulder

Interaction between people and companion animals provides the basis for a model of the self that does not depend on spoken language. Drawing on ethnographic research in an animal shelter as well as interviews and auto-ethnography, this article argues that interaction between people and animals contributes to human selfhood. In order for animals to contribute to selfhood in the ways that they do, they must be subjective others and not just the objects of anthropomorphic projection. Several dimensions of subjectivity appear among dogs and cats, constituting a "core" self consisting of agency, coherence, affectivity, and history. Conceptualizing selfhood in this way offers critical access to animals' subjective presence and adds to existing interactionist research on relationships between people and animals.

The notion that animals, like people, have selves is controversial for sociology. The field has defined its subject matter as that which is uniquely human. Along with culture, rationality, and language, the self is one of the entities for which animals purportedly lack the tools. The word *tool* is important here, for tool use and, later, tool making long served

Direct all correspondence to Leslie Irvine, Department of Sociology, University of Colorado, 219 Ketchum, 327 UCB, Boulder CO 80309–0327; e-mail: irvinel@colorado.edu.

Leslie Irvine, "A Model of Animal Selfhood:Expanding Interactionist Possibilities," from *Symbolic Interaction*, Vol. 27 No. 1, Pp. 3-21. Copyright © 2004 by University of California Press. Permission to reprint granted by the publisher.

to distinguish humans from (and portray them as superior to) other animals. When Jane Goodall (1990) observed the chimpanzee David Greybeard not only *using* a tool but also *making* one, her observation called for redefining the existing boundary between humans and animals. If some animals have the ability to make and use various *physical* tools, perhaps they also possess the *conceptual* tools required for selfhood. In other words, if we humans were wrong about tool use among animals, there are likely other things we have underestimated and overlooked, such as their capacity for selfhood. Perhaps the boundary of self-consciousness that has long divided humans from animals is also illusory. If so, then how can sociologists, in particular, interactionists, study animal selfhood? What might we gain from and contribute to the task?

Scholars from a range of disciplines have repeatedly challenged the once-distinct boundary between human and nonhuman animals by showing that the latter can feel emotions (e.g., Bekoff 2000; Darwin [1872] 1998; Goodall 1990; Masson 1997; Masson and McCarthy 1995; Tabor 1983; Thomas 1993, 1994, 2000) and communicate with symbols (e.g., Patterson and Linden 1981; Pepperberg 1991). In humans, emotions and symbol use indicate the presence of capacities that constitute selfhood. In interactionist sociology, Sanders (1990, 1991, 1993, 1999) draws on everyday interaction between people and dogs to illustrate the construction of personhood and the sharing of basic emotions and intentions. Likewise, Alger and Alger (1997) examine attributions of selfhood among cat owners. Following Sanders, they observed cats engaged in taking the role of the others, defining situations, choosing courses of action, and having memories of past events. In addition, Alger and Alger's research in a cat shelter reveals that cats have culture, in that they transmit behaviors socially, as well as instinctually, through symbolic interaction (1999, 2003; see also Bonner 1980; Dawkins 1998).

The interactionist paradigm is well suited to the study of animal selfhood, and applying it expands the notion of what it means to be social. Using interactionism in this way requires moving beyond Mead's ([1934] 1962) language-driven model of selfhood. For Mead, spoken language constituted the social psychological barrier between humans and nonhumans because it enables humans to understand and communicate the symbols for self, such as our names and the names of objects. Mead acknowledged that animals have their own social arrangements but claimed that their interaction involves a "conversation of gestures." This term denotes primitive, instinctual acts, such as when a dog growls at another who threatens to steal his bone or a cat hisses at a rival. Mead considered the conversation of gestures insignificant because it allegedly has only one meaning. As Hewitt (2000:9) explains, "[I]n no sense does either [animal] 'decide' or 'make up its mind' to act in a certain way." In this perspective, the behavior of animals may be goal directed in that it aims at getting food, a mate, or defending territory, but it lacks the negotiated meaning that characterizes human behavior. According to Mead, animals, lacking the capacity to use significant symbols, were incapable of having any meaningful social behavior. From Mead's perspective, "the animal has no mind, no thought, and hence there is no meaning [in animal behavior] in the significant or self-conscious sense" (Strauss 1964:168).

In making spoken language the key to what distinguishes humans from other animals, Mead (and, consequently, social psychology) established two states of consciousness: one for those who could converse about it and another, lesser form for those who could not. Mead thus advanced the anthropocentric, rationalist tradition of Descartes, whose claim *I think, therefore I am* required the ability to *talk* about thinking. The pitfalls in Mead's view are numerous, and other scholars have reviewed them in detail (see Arluke and Sanders 1996; Myers 1998; Sanders 1999; Sanders and Arluke 1993). My intention here is to offer a model of animal selfhood that expands the possibilities of empirical interactionist research. In doing this, I build on previous work by Sanders and Alger and Alger that examines how we come to know animals as conscious, purposeful partners in interaction. Whereas Sanders and Alger and Alger have demonstrated animals' capacity for intersubjectivity, I examine the capacities that animals must have in order to achieve this shared experience. My conclusions apply only to companion animals, by which I mean the dogs and cats with whom so many of us share our homes and our daily lives.[1] Although some of my arguments might well apply to other animals, I have studied only dogs and cats. I leave it to other researchers to incorporate other species.

Before proceeding, I want to anticipate an objection and emphasize that I have taken care to avoid overanthropomorphizing. Note that I said "overanthropomorphizing," for we cannot entirely escape our human perspective. As Shapiro (1997) points out, this perspective is not something we take *only* when we try to understand animals. Rather,

> all understanding is anthropomorphic (from *anthropo*, meaning "man" and *morphe*, "form" or "shape") for it is partly shaped by the human investigator as subject. However, since this is a perspective or "bias" inherent in all experience, it is not an occasional attributional error to which we are particularly prone when we cross species' lines. It is a condition of science which prevents it from reaching certainty and, therefore, from supporting a positivistic philosophy. (P. 294)

Those who use the term *anthropomorphism* usually intend to discredit someone's claims about animals by suggesting they are sentimental and inaccurate projections. However, in describing animals, our choices are not limited simply to the "unconstrained use of anthropomorphism on one hand and the total elimination of anthropomorphism on the other" (Bekoff 2002:49–50). A middle ground involves informed, systematic interaction with and observation of animals known as "critical" or "interpretive" anthropomorphism (Burghardt 1998; Fisher 1991; see also Crist 1999; Mitchell, Thompson, and Miles 1997; Sanders 1999). Critical anthropomorphism aims to do for the understanding of animal life what *Verstehn* (Weber 1949) tries to capture in human life, which is to understand the meanings that people give to their actions. *Verstehn* involves placing oneself in the position of another person to see what purpose his or her actions might have, or, more accurately, to see what that person believes his or her actions will accomplish. Critical anthropomorphism tries to do the same for the experiences of nonhuman animals. Bekoff (2002:48) refers to it as "humanizing animals with care," for it respects the "natural history, perceptual and learning capabilities, physiology, nervous system, and previous individual history" of animals (Burghardt 1998:72). In what follows, I strive to recognize the differences between animals and people while exploring what we share in common.

METHODS

The evidence presented here draws on several sources of data collected and analyzed through continuous, emergent inductive techniques (see Becker and Geer 1960; Charmaz 1983; Glaser 1978; Glaser and Strauss 1967; Stewart 1998; Strauss and Corbin 1997). I conducted more than three hundred hours of research in what Adler and Adler (1987) call a "complete membership role" at a humane society that I refer to as "the Shelter." This private, nonprofit organization offers adoptions, veterinary services, humane education, dog training, and cat behavior consultations and serves as the headquarters for the city's animal control services and welfare investigations. In 1998 I began working as one of the Shelter's volunteers. I have served in many volunteer roles; this article draws chiefly but not exclusively on that of adoption counselor. This position involves introducing people to animals whom they are considering for adoption, providing information about behavior and training, and answering questions. Moreover, it involves determining whether the animal and the person will be a good "match." As an adoption counselor, I became curious about people's interactions with animals in the adoption area and began taking notes. I recorded how long they looked at particular animals, whether they adopted an animal that day or just visited, and what, if anything, they said to the animals or to the people with them. I also took extensive notes about the interaction that occurred when a person (or persons) and a particular animal were introduced.

My volunteer service on what I call the Adoption Mobile, a thirty-foot recreational vehicle that serves as a traveling branch of the Shelter, produced an additional one hundred fifty hours of observation. Five days a week, a volunteer and a staff member take a selection of adoptable cats, rabbits, rodents, and a dog to various sites throughout the county. The locations include shopping centers, libraries, and local festivals. On board, people can adopt animals, make donations, and obtain answers to their questions about animal care and behavior or the Shelter's services. The Adoption Mobile spends four hours at a given site, and an average of one hundred people visit during this time. The work entails intense interaction with the public, and I took notes about the interaction in a small notebook while on site.

In spring 1999 I began developing another source of data through autoethnography. Because the term suggests several different meanings, let me be clear about how I use it.[2] In particular, I want to distinguish it from autobiographical research. The sense of the term as I intend it originated with Hayano (1979), who used it to refer to the study of a group with which one is involved (in Hayano's case, professional card players). In this sense, autoethnography offers an "insider's" view that can only come through immersion in and intimate knowledge of the group's interaction. The approach dates back at least to Charles Horton Cooley ([1902] 1964), who described a version of "sympathetic introspection." More recent practitioners include Denzin (1989), Ellis (1991, 1997, 1998), Rambo Ronai (1992, 1996), and Sanders (1999). In all these works the researcher puts himself or herself into the inquiry, but the result is much more than a report on the ethnographer.

I began the autoethnographic phase of this research by taking notes about my interactions with my own companion cats. I had lived with cats all my adult life, but I stopped taking our lives together for granted and became a participant-observer of our daily routines. Then, in summer 1999, I adopted a dog from the Shelter. As the cats and I adjusted to life with him, I wrote it all down. I examined my autoethnographic notes and those from the Shelter regularly, searching for emergent themes and patterns. Over repeated readings, one idea—the way in which animals communicate their personalities, emotions, preferences, and knowledge to people—came through clearly. To explore this idea further, I began interviewing those who adopted and surrendered animals. The Shelter generously helped me to recruit interviewees by attaching an information and consent form to their adoption paperwork for one month in 2001. I conducted forty semistructured interviews that focused on how people made decisions to adopt, how they had chosen particular animals, and how everyday life and activities with the animal unfolded after adoption.

RETHINKING THE SELF

Observations of the interactions between people and animals in the adoption areas revealed three themes. The first is seeking relationships with the animals. A steady stream of people, most having no intention to adopt, came to visit the animals. Some even came regularly, to visit long-term Shelter residents. They often came in pairs or groups, making the visit a social event. Their interaction with animals was not limited to looking at them but also involved talking to them and about them. Everyone wanted to touch the animals, know their names and their stories, and, whenever possible, hold and play with them outside of their kennels or cages. Moreover, many people who had browsed the Shelter's Web site wanted to meet the animals whom they had seen in thumbnail photos. In other words, they did not simply want to know that the animals existed; they wanted to interact with them face-to-face. In other words, they wanted relationships with the animals.

The second theme has to do with concern for animals' well-being. Shelter clients wanted to learn the animals' histories and, in the case of adoption, provide what he or she needed.

This concern appeared in phrases I heard frequently, such as "I feel so sorry for them" and "I wish I could take them all home." People were genuinely concerned when animals seemed afraid or were obviously recovering from an operation or injury. For example, the Shelter's male dogs routinely wear E-collars (Elizabethan collars) after they are neutered to prevent them from licking at their sutures. They wear these for only a few days, but people consistently ask what happened to the "poor dog" with the cone around his head. Similarly, when longhaired cats arrive with their coats badly matted, the only solution is a full-body shave, usually leaving fur on the head, paws, and tail. Shelter staff and volunteers grow so accustomed to the barrage of questions about what happened to the "poor kitty" that we often add notes explaining the "bad hair day" on the cats' kennel cards.

The third theme involves increasing complexity of interaction. In the adoption areas, I found that people who had had animals previously, some for most of their lives, interacted with a wider range of animals and did not fuss as much over the puppies and kittens. Moreover, with repeated or sustained interaction, people began to explore more facets of the animal's character and capabilities. For instance, a first visit might involve strolling past the kennels and cages, just looking. Then, when a particular animal captured someone's attention, the person might begin talking to the animal, perhaps squatting down to get closer. When this offered an opportunity for an animal to display some unique trait, such as playfulness or attentiveness, the person then engaged the animal further. This, in turn, revealed additional aspects of the animal's "personality" and continued in a reciprocal process, allowing the person to discover more about the animal as interaction grew more complex, albeit within the confines of the kennels. Moreover, animals served as "social facilitators," sparking conversations among visitors and thus encouraging the use of interactional skills with other people as well (see Messent 1983; Sanders 1999, 2000).

The interaction in the adoption areas thus suggests that people seek relationships with animals, express concern for their well-being, and engage in increasingly complex behaviors with them. These three themes, I argue, have one thing in common: they point in the direction of the self. More specifically, they are behaviors or activities that manifest goals of the self (see Myers 1998). For instance, we know from Mead and others that the self emerges through relationships. Once the self has developed, it can exist without relationships, so that the person in solitary confinement continues to have a sense of self. However, relationships allow us to develop a mutual history that is simultaneously a history of the self (see Irvine 1999).

If we can agree that relationships are essential for the self, it would be important to increase the skills that make relationships possible. Maintaining relationships requires the use of the interactional skills that foster relationships in the first place. One of the signs that a relationship is "good for" the self is that it exercises and improves our interactional skills. Good relationships stretch our interactional abilities by requiring us to see things in new ways. Good relationships offer "new information— incongruities, interruptions of expectations, challenges—in the context of familiar otherness" (Myers 1998:78). They challenge our interactional skills *just enough* and consequently increase our abilities to have relationships. As with physical exercise, we build "muscle" that equips us for further challenges. Eventually, the exercise itself becomes intrinsically rewarding. Moreover, concern for the well-being of others, expressed through an interest in their needs, ensures the continuity that provides the relationships on which the self depends.

In sum, the structure of interaction between people and animals (seeking relationships with animals, demonstrating concern for their well-being, and engaging in increasingly complex interaction) revealed that animals mean something for the experience of selfhood. The question that arises has to do with *how* they "mean something." Related to this, how do animals differ from the other "objects" in our environment that contribute to our sense of self?

Sensing Subjectivity

The key, I argue, is the subjective presence of the Other. The interaction must seem to have a source, and we must see the Other as having a mind, beliefs, and desires, just as we do. This not only confirms the Other's sense of self to us; it also confirms our own. How do we sense an Other's subjective presence? With people, we can rely on self-reports. However, these reveal more about the norms of self-reports than about anything else. Self-reports reveal the influence of what people know to be good, desirable, acceptable depictions of the self. They reveal a self digested in consciousness and shaped by language. They indicate how people talk and think about the self, not how they experience it. A stronger objection is that, even with other people, we simply do not rely on language first or foremost for information about selfhood. As Goffman (1959) wrote, only *part* of the self is conveyed through "impressions given." Other aspects appear through "impressions given off."

Relying on language eliminates a considerable amount of interaction as a source of information that contributes to selfhood. Moreover, it restricts the significant interactants to other people. If we can agree that factors beyond spoken language matter for the creation of the self, then animals can participate in the process. In the model of the self that I am using, in order for animals to do so, they must themselves *be* subjective Others. How can we sense their subjective presence? As with other people, we cannot observe subjectivity directly. We perceive it *indirectly*, during interaction. To illustrate how this is so, I turn to a model of self that originates in William James's ([1890] 1950, [1892] 1961) efforts to gain access to the "I," or the subjective sense of self. Along the way, James distinguished four facets that underlie and make us aware of subjectivity. Others have since refined these into a set of basic self-experiences that manifest themselves in infancy, before the acquisition of language (see Myers 1998; Stern 1985). Therefore, the case can be made for the presence of these experiences among animals, who have the same structures of the brain, nervous system, musculature, and memory. Whereas human development takes us into a stage of language acquisition that adds to these basic experiences, the experiences themselves are preverbal. The four self-experiences consist of

1. a sense of *agency,* meaning that you are the author of your actions and movements and not the author of the actions and movements of others;
2. a sense of *coherence,* meaning that you understand yourself as a physical whole that is the locus of agency;
3. a sense of *affectivity,* meaning patterned qualities of feelings that are associated with other experiences of the self; and
4. a sense of *self-history,* meaning that you maintain some degree of continuity, even while changing.

Human beings attain these four senses of self through interaction with others, beginning at birth. They not only underlie our *own* senses of subjective experience, but, as we shall see, they also form the basis for distinguishing self from Other. Combined, these four senses compose a "core" self that is considered necessary for normal psychological functioning (Stern 1985:71). The absence of one of them manifests itself in psychosis and other pathologies. Granted, there are additional senses of self, many of which require the acquisition of language, but the four I draw attention to here are prior to and essential for additional senses. Here, I offer illustrative examples of how these aspects of core self are manifested among dogs and cats.

Agency

In sociology, the term "agency" is used (and misused) in many ways.[3] I use it to refer to the capacity for self-willed action. Agency implies subjectivity, in that an agentic being, by definition, has desires, wishes, and intentions, along with a sense of having those things. In other words, it is the actor's awareness of having desires or wishes that is an element of selfhood, not simply having them. Agency also implies having control over one's own actions (i.e., I can sit when I decide to, and if you push me into a chair, that is something different) and awareness of the felt consequences of those actions. For example, my intention to sit brings the *felt consequence* of sitting. Fortunately, the connection occurs mostly outside of consciousness, for evaluating every action in these terms would be tedious indeed.

Several indicators of a sense of agency appear in the first months of life (Stern 1985). Examples include reaching for objects and hand-to-mouth skills. At about four months, infants begin to use visual information to shape the fingers to accommodate objects of particular sizes. Since agency does not depend on verbal ability, it is therefore feasible among other species. Some of the best examples of animals' agency come from the arena of dog training, even at the beginner's level. As Sanders (1999) explains, the main thing that trainers teach dogs is to exercise *self-control*— and they use precisely this term. Self-control implies that the dog has a sense that he or she can initiate action, since in order to *control one's self* one must first *have* a sense of will or volition. At the Shelter, I saw frequent examples of this when I worked with staff members to make undersocialized dogs more adoptable. A typical case involved a young, mixed-breed dog who jumped up on the gate of his kennel and barked wildly for attention whenever anyone came near, making most potential adopters think twice. The key to modifying the dog's behavior was to change his understanding of the cause of the rewards he receives. Changing his understanding in this way highlights the nonverbal capacity to distinguish self from Other.

A dog who jumps up on his kennel and barks receives two kinds of rewards. To the extent that the behavior is *self-directed* (i.e., aimed at releasing energy), it is constantly rewarding. However, to the extent that it is *directed at others,* as an attempt to gain their attention, there is only a probabilistic chance that it will be rewarded. Many people will avoid such a dog—as was the case with the dog in this example. As long as the reward of attention depends on others, it will be unpredictable. The dog does not control that reward. The only thing he controls (or should) is his behavior. We had to make the dog aware of this and show him how to increase the probability of rewards from others. To do so, we removed him from the adoption area for a few days to reduce the foot traffic past his kennel. We scheduled regular exercise to reduce his need for the jumping. Most important, we stopped reinforcing his bad behavior. We paid attention to him only when he was quiet and had all four paws on the floor. If he stood up on his hind legs or barked, we moved away from his kennel. Because he had released some of his pent-up energy through exercise, the reward of attention quickly became a higher priority. Moreover, because attention depended on *others,* he soon learned to control himself to get it. This subtle act of behavior modification helped the dog to distinguish self from Other by distinguishing different reinforcement schedules. Infants develop this ability as early as three months of age; the same probably holds for other highly social animals, with the same implications for discriminating between self and Other.

One day, as a staff member and I discussed our work with the above-mentioned dog, she said, "We have to get him to be able to show people that he'll be worth it." It occurred to me that although our explicit task was to help him to learn basic canine manners, our larger, albeit implicit, goal was to enable him to demonstrate to people that he had something *underneath,* or *other than,* the problem behaviors. In other words, we had to help him to develop the control over his own behavior that would show people that he had—or was—a self.

Coherence

If agency provides a sense of self versus Other, then coherence provides the boundaries of the self. We acknowledge coherence when "we say of some others that they seem to 'have their act together,' or of our own Self, that some particular line of endeavor is 'very much part of me'" (Bruner and Kalmar 1998:311). Coherence gives agency somewhere to "live." Several indicators of coherence do not rely on language, making their presence likely in nonhuman animals.

Infancy research indicates that the capacity to recognize distinct others, such as primary caregivers, becomes available as early as two or three months of age. Animals, too, can recognize distinct others. At the Shelter, volunteers who regularly work with certain animals for weeks or even months find that these animals begin to recognize them. More relevant for the discussion of coherence is how animals are able to understand that parts of people belong together. For example, at the Shelter's veterinary clinic, I had regular contact with a dog who required several surgeries and diagnostic tests. I often held him while a technician drew blood, and I sat with him as he woke up after his first surgery. When he recovered and went into the adoption area, other volunteers spent more time with him, but whenever he saw me, he brightened up. One day, when an E-collar obscured his vision, I approached him from behind as he stood next to another volunteer who was conversing with a third person. As I passed an adjoining hall, I greeted someone in that direction. As I did, the dog's tail wagged and he turned as if to confirm that the physical form matched the voice. Although some might dismiss this as simply a conditioned response (that is, my voice had been programmed into his behavioral repertoire), critical anthropomorphism calls for a more contextualized and sympathetic understanding. Familiarity with dogs' behavior, and with this dog's behavior, leads me "to discount perspectives that rely on instinctual or rigidly behavioristic explanations" (Arluke and Sanders 1996:43; see also Alger and Alger 2003:47).

Animals indicate the capacity for coherence in the act of hiding, which requires a sense of self as an object to conceal from others. According to Sanders (1999:137), hiding "shows an awareness that the 'embodied self' is in danger and that concealment is in order" (see also Allen and Bekoff 1997). Cats, having evolved as skilled predators, relied on the ability to hide in order to hunt. Those mechanisms did not disappear with domestication. As one guardian explains: "Anyone who has lived around cats has seen this: they hide, they watch, and they attack. They also have very strong notions of when it's okay for them to be seen and any cat-person knows that cats have got to have hiding places." Alger and Alger (2003:58) found that cats can adapt their hiding into games of peek-a-boo and hide and seek.

Coherence has generated the cultural practice of naming animals, which "underscores the animal's particularity—the sense of uniqueness between subjective self and other" (Myers 1998:71; see also Alger and Alger 2003; Masson and McCarthy 1995; Phillips 1994). One of the things people do on adoption is name—or rename— their animals. Some guardians have a name in mind already; others take some time to decide on one, emphasizing the extent to which the name has to suit the animal. The act of changing an animal's name reflects the degree to which an animal's identity emerges through interaction. For instance, a dog who arrived with the name Rowdy became Sadie in her new home, indicating vastly different perceptions of her demeanor.

Phillips, in her study of researchers' conduct toward laboratory animals, finds that naming reflects individuality and coherence:

> [I]n giving an animal a name and using that name to talk to and about the creature, we interactively construct a narrative about an individual with unique characteristics, situated in a particular historical setting, and we endow that narrative with a coherent meaning. (1994:121)

Proper names, Phillips writes, "are linked to the social emergence of personality, which engenders a matrix of ideas and behaviors unique to one individual" (p. 123). Scientists do not name laboratory animals because they see them as parts, rather than whole, coherent beings. They are sources of cells or tissue or "containers" for responses and reactions. Because naming acknowledges coherence, lab animals must remain nameless if researchers are to use them in the ways that they do.[4]

Affectivity

Another dimension of the core self that makes animals' subjectivity available to us is their capacity for emotions. In interviews, guardians reported two ways that they read the emotions of their dogs and cats, and these correspond to two dimensions of feeling.

The first dimension encompasses what are called "categorical affects." Most of the time when we think of "emotions," we think of discrete *categories* of feelings, such as sadness, happiness, fear, anger, or shame. Anyone who lives around animals has seen manifestations of various categorical affects. For example, I have seen cats display grief. Two of my cats, a male and a female, formed a very close bond. They slept together, ate and played together, and groomed each other. When the male had to be euthanized, his companion went through a distinct period of grieving. Indeed, her sadness started before her friend died, when he gradually became withdrawn and disinterested. When the male was gone, the female searched their favorite places for him and stopped eating for a few days. She did not become "herself" again until we moved into a new house. Granted, the behaviors I characterize as feline grief may not be the same as human grief; this is irrelevant. However, I do know that she behaved differently after her friend's death than she behaves when she is sunning herself (a state I would call happiness or contentedness) or inspecting my belongings after I return at the end of a day (curiosity). Along the same lines, Alger and Alger (2003) describe displays of happiness, affection, frustration, irritability, depression, empathy, and jealousy among sheltered cats.

A second dimension of emotions comprises "vitality affects." These are *ways* of feeling, rather than discrete emotions, and they give the behavior of human and nonhuman animals much of its texture. Bruner and Kalmar (1998:311) point out that vitality affects "signal the 'feel' of a life—mood, pace, zest, weariness, or whatever." Long before I knew the term "vitality affects," I knew *about* them. This is so for most of us, for the perception of vitality affects occurs early in infancy. When my niece, Amanda, now a teenager, was very young, I entertained her by making my index and middle fingers into the "legs" of a character whose "body" was my hand. This character could make her laugh by walking up her arm, but we both had more fun when it danced the can-can. This little "person"—it did seem to have what it takes for personhood—could act as if exhausted or take a jaunty walk.

Instances such as these work because we can read vitality affects.[5] We know when the character portrayed by fingers "feels" chipper or bedraggled, and it has nothing to do with facial expressions, for there are no faces to do the expressing. This is an important way in which the comparison applies to animals. Animals' limited ability to change their facial expressions (relative to humans) makes their expressions an unreliable means by which we can infer their emotional states. The vitality affects of animals inform us more than their facial expressions do. In our interaction with animals, we read vitality affects and perceive certain individuals as "sweet," "mellow," "hyper," and so on. These are characteristics of *individual* animals, that is, the core self, rather than the expressions of particular emotions. In other words, when we describe an animal (or a person), we usually include some reference to vitality affects. We might describe someone as "a happy person," but what we mean by that has more to do with vitality affects than with a discrete emotional state. We do the same with animals. Vitality affects are important vehicles of the core self. A woman who described her dog as "sweet," for example, was referring to the dog's overall calmness and submissive tendencies. Likewise, a couple who called their cat a "character" used the phrase as shorthand for his confidence and curiosity, the combination of which often sent him rushing in where more angelic cats would not dare to tread.

Self-History

Self-history, or continuity, makes *interactions* into *relationships*. As Stern (1985:90) writes, "a sense of a core self would be ephemeral if there were no continuity of experience." The capacity that makes continuity possible is memory. Events, objects, others, and emotions gain their meaning and are preserved in memory, in the context of relationships. There are many different modalities of memory, some of which begin to operate very early. The memory required for self-history is preverbal, and several aspects of it appear in animals.[6]

Anyone who has ever taken a dog or a cat to a veterinarian knows that animals remember places. The cat who loves affection at home now hisses and scratches the vet's offending hand. Skeptics might say that the animal "just smells fear," thereby dismissing the reaction as instinctual. However, even if it were "only" instinct, the consistent ability to register a particular emotion in a particular setting nevertheless implies a sense of continuity. Others have also documented animals' "place memory" (Alger and Alger 2003; Lerman 1996;

Sanders 1999). Indeed, Shapiro (1990, 1997) suggests that the lives of dogs are oriented in terms of place, rather than time, as ours are. Feline examples abound in the work of Alger and Alger (1997, 2003). For instance, they recount how one of their own cats always went to a certain throw rug when she wanted to play, and one of their interviewees described how her cat associated their home's radiator with receiving affection (1997:78). In the Algers's research in the cat shelter, they observed that the cats designated certain places such as cage tops and beds as "not just comfortable places for sleeping, but also safe places to relax, to find intimacy with others, and to explore their need for affection" (2003:110). The sheltered cats learned to define these areas in the same terms, suggesting a coherent system of memory created through symbolic interaction.

A behaviorist would characterize these examples not as memory but as simple conditioned responses. In behaviorist terms, the animal who feels fear at a veterinary clinic or pleasure in another setting merely perceives an impulse associated with previous positive or negative reinforcement. To be sure, in light of Occam's razor, which favors behavioristic accounts, cognitive explanations seem implausible. However, just as it is unwise to attribute simple behaviors to complex mental processes, it is equally unwise to dismiss, ignore, or deny the possibility that some behaviors may be best explained in cognitive terms. The question is *which* behaviors are best explained this way, and the answer is far from clear.

Allen and Bekoff (1997:56–62) make a distinction that is useful in this context. They distinguish between behavior that is "stimulus bound," meaning an invariable (or nearly so) response to external stimulus, and behavior that is "stimulus free," or motivated by internal factors. When external factors are seen to dominate internal factors, behaviorist explanations are preferred. However, in many instances, behaviorist conclusions have been drawn from research that ignores or disregards internal factors. For example, many laboratory studies of allegedly stimulus-bound behaviors must modify conditions so that animals will be sufficiently motivated to perform according to behaviorist expectations. This is especially the case in experiments involving food rewards, in which researchers must keep animals motivated to eat even when internal responses perceive satiation. Laboratory researchers introduce protocols that interfere with metabolism in order for the animals to eat beyond satiety. In such cases, stimulus-bound conclusions are drawn from behaviors that under normal circumstances would be stimulus-free. Drawing on an example closer to home, two of my cats regularly sleep on a fleece blanket. It is not stretching the point to say that they find this blanket comforting. This comfort has been to some degree conditioned. Nevertheless, if I were to produce the same blanket while the cats were being examined at the vet's office, I can confidently say that neither cat would respond with kneading and napping. The behavioral explanation becomes inadequate in contexts that involve various inputs. A more complex explanation is needed, and the possibility of memory seems a reasonable alternative.

Animals may have no sense of today, tomorrow, and next week, but they do remember what happened to them in the past. They do not need the sense of past, present, and future that gives purpose to human lives. Consequently, their memory skills differ from ours, but they differ in degree rather than kind. In interaction with humans, animals' memories give humans a sense of the animal as having a concrete history.

In sum, we know the selves of animals in much the same way we know the selves of other people. Two things occur simultaneously. First, animals' subjectivity becomes available to us because elements of a core self become visible through interaction. Granted, the kinds of selves that animals have, or at least those that are visible to humans, are less sophisticated in many ways than human selves are, but the core elements are nonetheless the same. Second, we know the selves of animals because, as this core self becomes present to us, it confirms our own sense of subjectivity. Certain animals' selves, like certain people's selves, mesh with ours in ways that feel comfortable. The feeling is one of being able to "be ourselves," and it occurs with animals through the same basic processes as it occurs with other people.

CONCLUSION

The structure of people's interaction with adoptable animals (seeking relationships with them, demonstrating concern for their well-being, and engaging in increasingly complex interaction with them) suggests that animals contribute something to the experience of human selfhood. Understanding *how* they "mean something" requires examining further interactions, such as those that take place when an animal is part of a human home and family. This type of interaction reveals aspects of the animal's subjective presence. Subjectivity, in turn, accounts for what makes animals different from the other factors that contribute to our sense of self.

Evidence of subjectivity appears in the core dimensions of self. If we think of self as a system of experiences having the features of agency, coherence, affectivity, and history, then our interaction with others will reflect our perception of those features. For example, agency evokes agency. When I perceive it in an animal or another person, doing so confirms my own sense of agency. My interaction with the Other will manifest my expectation and recognition of that agency, along with my response to it. The assumption that the Other can initiate action gives our interaction a particular structure. The Other and I will act toward each other as two beings who are authors of their own conduct. Moreover, when I assume agentic qualities in an Other, I assume the Other's subjectivity. At the same time, I understand myself as agentic, albeit without dwelling on the matter. A helpful example comes from Myers's (1998) study of children and animals. He observed instances in which a child provoked an animal to react, such as when one chased a pigeon and reported, "I made it fly." As Myers explains, "[T]hese children focused on their own agency, but agency means something only with an animate other. In flying away, the action of the pigeon confirms the child's own agency in a way that an inanimate thing cannot" (p. 82).

In the case of coherence, an Other's recognition of me as an embodied, bounded being confirms my own sense of myself in that way. When I come home, for example, the dogs and cats recognize me and greet me in ways that they would not extend to someone else. Their doing so confirms my sense of myself, although this occurs unconsciously, for I seldom pause to check that I am indeed "me." The animals' (and other people's) consistent recognition of me makes this unnecessary. In the case of affectivity, people who live with animals regularly respond to the qualities and intensity of animals' emotions. Moreover, our recognition of animals' affectivity usually occurs in particular contexts, which provides another avenue to confirming our own experience. For example, Sanders describes his experience with his dogs:

> The joy my dogs communicate to me offers an important lesson. When I see the happiness they derive from a walk in the woods, a meal provided at the usual time, the warmth of a body to press against on a cold evening, I realize that the basic and immediate pleasures are the most important and should be treasured. (Quoted in Bekoff 2000:128)

Finally, animals' capacity for memory, which enables self-history, confirms our own sense of history, albeit in a more limited way than the confirmation we experience with other people. With other people, we can create a shared narrative, which is an undeniably more complex account of mutual experience. However, animals use bodies, gestures, preferences, and habits to demonstrate that they share a history with us. For instance, for the past thirteen years, I have slept with my grey, female cat, Pusskin, at my side. Regardless of what she is doing when I go to bed, she joins me. She and I nestle close in a way that I share with none of the other cats. After thirteen years, this way of sleeping together defines our relationship. I cannot imagine sleeping without the warmth and weight of her beside me, and I dread the time when she will no longer be there. Whatever reasons she has for seeking me out at night, I cannot be certain. What I can say is that she remembers where she likes to sleep, and she and I have built a history because she does so.

In this article, I have worked inductively, moving from observations to a model of selfhood instead of beginning with a particular notion of the self. However, the result is an incomplete picture of selfhood for animals, as it would be for humans. Research by Sanders and Alger and Alger completes the model I offer here. Whereas I have focused on the *subjective* presence of animals, these scholars illuminate *intersubjectivity* by documenting animals' ability to share intentions, feelings, and other mental states with their human companions. By interpreting the content of other minds—whether human or nonhuman—we develop a sense of self-in-relation. The selves of animals, evinced through agency, affectivity, coherence, and history, acquire another dimension through interaction that reveals their capacity to share thoughts and feelings. Although we humans can put our accounts of this experience into words, the capacity for intersubjectivity does not depend on language. Animals and people can share thoughts, intentions, and feelings, albeit at a less complex level than that which occurs between two people.

The point of this article has been to show that there is something to animal selfhood and that this "something" becomes apparent during interaction. Our attributions of animals' selves are not merely wishful anthropomorphic projection. Because animals have agency and the other dimensions of the core self, they can choose courses of action that do not always coincide with our projections of what they "should" be like. Humans and animals *can* share meanings and emotions, but that does not imply that they always *will* share them. Nevertheless, in much of human-animal interaction, the features of agency, coherence, self-history, and affectivity coalesce, with memory helping to integrate them. Together, these give the animal an organizing, subjective perspective, or a core self, and concurrently make core Others available. Interactionist research offers a way to capture evidence of these features. Combined with critical anthropomorphism, interactionism allows us to recognize that animals' ways of being in the world are different, while it also honors those ways by attempting to understand them. To do so is to see animals differently, which is to see ourselves differently.

By expanding our field of vision in this way, the model of the self presented here has implications beyond the realm of human-animal interaction. In particular, the model extends interactionist possibilities past the limits of spoken language, opening up avenues of research on selfhood among "alingual" humans. Scholars have already broken ground in the case of the mentally disabled (Bogdan and Taylor 1989; Pollner and McDonald-Wikler 1985), Alzheimer's patients (Gubrium 1986), infants (Brazelton 1984; Stern 1985), deaf and blind children (Goode 1994), and autistic children (Rocque 2003). This literature concurs that those who provide care for people who have no capacity for verbal expression "literally 'do' the minds and selves of those who cannot speak" (Holstein and Gubrium 2000:152). For instance, Bogdan and Taylor explain how nondisabled family members assign personhood to the severely disabled. First, family members attribute thinking to the disabled person, granting him or her abilities to reason and understand. Consequently, the disabled person is considered a partner in interaction, with his or her gestures, body postures, and facial expressions doing what spoken language would otherwise have done. The disabled are seen as having preferences, feelings, and other characteristics that make us individuals. In addition, the disabled are incorporated into household routines and rituals, thus having their own places in the narrative history of the family. In this way, lived experience, which is at the heart of interactionism, provides the material through which the disabled attain the status of "person."

The relationship between selfhood and personhood has far-reaching implications. At the risk of raising questions I cannot answer, I will close with a controversy. Biologist Marc Bekoff (2002), renowned for his work on animal consciousness, emotions, and selfhood, captures the situation well. Marc's elderly mother has lost most of her cognitive, physiological, and locomotor capacities. She receives round-the-clock care. She does not recognize or even acknowledge Bekoff when he visits, and she manifests little if any awareness of her self, her surroundings, or her physical body. In short, she meets few of the criteria that we use to designate personhood. Yet few of us would deny that she has every right to be considered a person. In contrast, Bekoff points out that Jethro, his companion dog at the time, exhibited more of the qualities of personhood than his mother was able to. Jethro demonstrated the components of self that I have outlined here, but many people would nevertheless refuse to call Jethro a person, in any meaningful sense. To be sure, people who knew and loved Jethro granted him personhood, just as the dog owners in Sanders's (1999) study did for their canine companions. But apart from this circle of friends, the objections to doing so would be strong. Nonhuman beings who meet the criteria for personhood are simply not considered persons.

Expanding interactionism to acknowledge selfhood outside the realm of spoken language has tremendous consequences. The meaning of the self has not been established in stone. It remains fluid enough to allow for theoretical and conceptual surprises. And it will take theoretical and conceptual innovation to study it, no matter where it appears.

NOTES

1. The term "companion animal" is currently preferred over "pets," as "guardian" is preferable to "owner." Although birds, fish, rabbits, reptiles, and other species can also be companions, I focus on dogs and cats, which are numerically the most popular as well as those with which I am most familiar. For data on companion animals in American households, see AVMA 2002.

2. Particularly helpful discussions of autoethnography appear in Wolcott 1999 and Goodall 2000.

3. "Agency" usually appears with its putative antithesis, "structure." This is an argument (in my view, an unnecessary one) about whether sociological (external) or psychological (internal) factors are more valuable for explaining human action. For a discussion of the history and a potential resolution of the debate, see Emirbayer and Mische 1998; see also Côté and Levine 2002; Rubenstein 2001.

4. Although animals do not name one another, there is evidence that some species recognize other individuals' signature calls or whistles. See Masson and McCarthy 1995:36–37.

5. To illustrate vitality affects, Stern (1985:56) offers the example of puppets, who "have little or no capacity to express categories of affect by way of facial signals, and their repertoire of conventionalized gestural or postural affect signals is usually impoverished. *It is from the way they move in general that we infer the different vitality affects from the activation contours they trace.* Most often, the characters of different puppets are largely defined in terms of particular vitality affects; one may be lethargic, with drooping limbs and hanging head, another forceful, and still another jaunty" (emphasis added).

6. Victims of early childhood abuse offer other convincing evidence of preverbal memory. Although the child lacks words to describe what occurred, and perhaps cannot even recall distinctly, memories nevertheless endure.

REFERENCES

Adler, Patricia A. and Peter Adler. 1987. *Membership Roles in Field Research*. Newbury Park, CA: Sage.

Alger, Janet M. and Steven F. Alger. 1997. "Beyond Mead: Symbolic Interaction between Humans and Felines." *Society & Animals* 5:65–81.

———. 1999. "Cat Culture, Human Culture: An Ethnographic Study of a Cat Shelter." *Society & Animals* 7:199–218.

———. 2003. *Cat Culture: The Social World of a Cat Shelter*. Philadelphia: Temple University Press.

Allen, Colin and Marc Bekoff. 1997. *Species of Mind: The Philosophy and Biology of Cognitive Ethology*. Cambridge, MA: MIT Press.

American Veterinary Medical Association (AVMA). 2002. *U. S. Pet Ownership & Demographics Sourcebook*. Schaumburg, IL: AVMA.

Arluke, Arnold and Clinton R. Sanders. 1996. *Regarding Animals*. Philadelphia: Temple University Press.

Becker, Howard and Blanche Geer. 1960. "The Analysis of Qualitative Field Data." Pp. 652–60 in *Human Organization Research*, edited by R. Adams and J. Preiss. Homewood, IL: Dorsey.

Bekoff, Marc, ed. 2000. *The Smile of a Dolphin: Remarkable Accounts of Animal Emotions*. New York: Random House/Discovery.

———. 2002. *Minding Animals: Awareness, Emotions, and Heart*. Oxford: Oxford University Press.

Bogdan, Robert and Steven Taylor. 1989. "Relationships with Severely Disabled People: The Social Construction of Humanness." *Social Problems* 36:135—48.

Bonner, J. T. 1980. *The Evolution of Culture in Animals*. Princeton, NJ: Princeton University Press.

Brazelton, T. Berry. 1984. "Four Stages in the Development of Mother-Infant Interaction." Pp. 19–34 in *The Growing Child in Family and Society*, edited by N. Kobayashi and T. B. Brazelton. Tokyo: University of Tokyo Press.

Bruner, Jerome and David A. Kalmar. 1998. "Narrative and Metanarrative in the Construction of Self." Pp. 308–31 in *Self-Awareness: Its Nature and Development*, edited by M. Ferrari and R. J. Sternberg. New York: Guilford.

Burghardt, Gordon M. 1998. "The Evolutionary Origins of Play Revisited: Lessons from Turtles." Pp. 1–26 in Animal Play: Evolutionary, Comparative, and Ecological Perspectives, edited by M. Bekoff and J. Byers. Cambridge: Cambridge University Press.

Charmaz, Kathy. 1983. "The Grounded Theory Method: An Explication and Interpretation." Pp. 102–26 in *Contemporary Field Research: A Collection of Readings*, edited by R. M. Emerson. Boston: Little, Brown.

Cooley, Charles Horton. [1902] 1964. Human Nature and the Social Order. New York: Schocken.

Côté, James E. and Charles G. Levine. 2002. *Identity Formation, Agency, and Culture: A Social Psychological Synthesis*. Mahwah, NJ: Erlbaum.

Crist, Eileen. 1999. *Images of Animals: Anthropomorphism and Animal Mind*. Philadelphia: Temple University Press.

Darwin, Charles. [1872] 1998. *The Expression of the Emotions in Man and Animals*. 3d ed. New York: Oxford University Press.

Dawkins, Marian Stamp. 1998. *Through Our Eyes Only? The Search for Animal Consciousness*. Oxford: Oxford University Press. Denzin, Norman. 1989. *Interpretive Biography*. Newbury Park, CA: Sage.

Ellis, Carolyn. 1991. "Sociological Introspection and Emotional Experience." *Symbolic Interaction* 14:23–50.

———. 1997. "Evocative Autoethnography: Writing Emotionally about Our Lives." Pp. 115–39 in *Representation and the Text: Re-framing the Narrative Voice*, edited by W. G. Tierney and Y. S. Lincoln. Albany: State University of New York Press.

———. 1998. "'I Hate My Voice': Coming to Terms with Minor Bodily Stigmas." *Sociological Quarterly* 39:517–37.

Emirbayer, Mustafa and Ann Mische, 1998. "What Is Agency?" *American Journal of Sociology* 103:962–1023.

Fisher, John Andrew. 1991. "Disambiguating Anthropomorphism: An Interdisciplinary Review." Pp. 49–85 in *Perspectives in Ethology*, vol. 9: *Human Understanding and Animal Awareness*, edited by P. Bateson and P. Klopfer. New York: Plenum.

Glaser, Barney. 1978. *Theoretical Sensitivity*. Mill Valley, CA: Sociology Press.

Glaser, Barney G. and Anselm L. Strauss. 1967. *The Discovery of Grounded Theory*. Chicago: Aldine.

Goffman, Erving. 1959. *The Presentation of Self in Everyday Life*. Garden City, NY: Anchor Books.

Goodall, H. L., Jr. 2000. *Writing the New Ethnography*. Lanham, MD: AltaMira.

Goodall, Jane. 1990. *Through a Window:My Thirty Years with the Chimpanzees of Gombe*. Boston: Houghton Mifflin.

Goode, David. 1994. *World without Words: The Social Construction of Children Born Deaf and Blind*. Philadelphia: Temple University Press.

Gubrium, Jaber. 1986. "The Social Preservation of Mind: The Alzheimer's Disease Experience." *Symbolic Interaction* 6:37–51.

Hayano, David. 1979. "Auto-Ethnography: Paradigms, Problems, and Prospects." *Human Organization* 38:99–104.

Hewitt, John P. 2000. *Self and Society: A Symbolic Interactionist Social Psychology*. 8th ed. Needham Heights, MA: Allyn and Bacon.

Holstein, James A. and Jaber F. Gubrium. 2000. *The Self We Live By: Narrative Identity in a Postmodern World*. Oxford: Oxford University Press.

Irvine, Leslie. 1999. *Codependent Forevermore: The Invention of Self in a Twelve Step Group*. Chicago: University of Chicago Press.

———. Forthcoming. *If You Tame Me: Understanding Our Connection with Animals*. Philadelphia: Temple University Press.

James, William. [1890] 1950. *The Principles of Psychology*. New York: Dover.

———. [1892] 1961. *Psychology: The Briefer Course*. New York: Harper.

Lerman, Rhoda. 1996. *In the Company of Newfs*. New York: Henry Holt.

Masson, Jeffrey Moussaieff. 1997. *Dogs Never Lie about Love: Reflections on the Emotional World of Dogs*. New York: Three Rivers/Crown.

Masson, Jeffrey Moussaieff and Susan McCarthy. 1995. *When Elephants Weep: The Emotional Lives of Animals*. New York: Delta.

Mead, George Herbert. [1934] 1962. *Mind, Self and Society*. Chicago: University of Chicago Press.

Messent, Peter. 1983. "Social Facilitation of Contact with Other People by Pet Dogs." Pp. 37–46 in *New Perspectives on Our Lives with Companion Animals*, edited by A. Katcher and A. Beck. Philadelphia: University of Pennsylvania Press.

Mitchell, Robert W., Nicholas S. Thompson, and H. Lyn Miles, eds. 1997. *Anthropomorphism, Anecdotes, and Animals*. Albany: State University of New York Press.

Myers, Gene. 1998. *Children and Animals: Social Development and Our Connections to Other Species*. Boulder, CO: Westview Press.

Patterson, Francine and Eugene Linden. 1981. *The Education of Koko*. New York: Holt, Rinehart and Winston.

Pepperberg, Irene. 1991. "A Communicative Approach to Animal Cognition: A Study of Conceptual Abilities of an African Grey Parrot." Pp. 153–86 in *Cognitive Ethology: The Minds of Other Animals*, edited by C. A. Ristau. Hillsdale, NJ: Lawrence Erlbaum.

Phillips, Mary T. 1994. "Proper Names and the Social Construction of Biography: The Negative Case of Laboratory Animals." *Qualitative Sociology* 17:119–42.

Pollner, Melvin and Lynn McDonald-Wikler. 1985. "The Social Construction of Unreality: A Case Study of a Family's Attribution of Competence to a Severely Retarded Child." *Family Process* 24:241–54.

Rambo Ronai, Carol. 1992. "The Reflexive Self through Narrative: A Night in the Life of an Erotic Dancer/Researcher." Pp. 102–24 in *Investigating Subjectivity: Research on Lived Experience*, edited by C. Ellis and M. Flaherty. Newbury Park, CA: Sage.

———. 1996. "Multiple Reflections of Child Sex Abuse: An Argument for a Layered Account." Pp. 24–43 in *Private Sociology: Unsparing Reflections, Uncommon Gains*, edited by A. B. Shostak. Dix Hills, NY: General Hall.

Rocque, William. 2003. "Body Talk: Identity and Narratives of Self in Families with Autistic Members." Unpublished manuscript.

Rubenstein, David. 2001. *Culture, Structure, and Agency: Toward a Truly Multidimensional Sociology*. Thousand Oaks, CA: Sage.

Sanders, Clinton R. 1990. "Excusing Tactics: Social Responses to the Public Misbehavior of Companion Animals." *Anthrozoös* 4:82–90.

———. 1991. "The Animal 'Other': Self-Definition, Social Identity, and Companion Animals." Pp. 662–68 in *Advances in Consumer Research*, vol. 17, edited by M. Goldberg et al. Provo, UT: Association for Consumer Research.

———. 1993. "Understanding Dogs: Caretakers' Attributions of Mindedness in Canine-Human Relationships." *Journal of Contemporary Ethnography* 22:205–26.

———. 1999. *Understanding Dogs: Living and Working with Canine Companions*. Philadelphia: Temple University Press.

———. 2000. "The Impact of Guide Dogs on the Identity of People with Visual Impairments." *Anthrozoös* 13:131–39.

Sanders, Clinton R. and Arnold Arluke. 1993. "If Lions Could Speak: Investigating the Animal-Human Relationship and the Perspectives of Nonhuman Others. *Sociological Quarterly* 34:377–90.

Shapiro, Kenneth J. 1990. "Understanding Dogs through Kinesthetic Empathy, Social Construction, and History." *Anthrozoös* 3:184–95.

———. 1997. "A Phenomenological Approach to the Study of Nonhuman Animals." Pp. 277–95 in *Anthropomorphism, Anecdotes, and Animals*, edited by R. Mitchell, N. Thompson, and H. Miles. Albany: State University of New York Press.

Stern, Daniel N. 1985. *The Interpersonal World of the Infant: A View from Psychoanalysis and Developmental Psychology*. New York: Basic Books.

Stewart, Alex. 1998. *The Ethnographer's Method*. Thousand, Oaks CA: Sage.

Strauss, Anselm, ed. 1964. *George Herbert Mead on Social Psychology*. Chicago: University of Chicago Press.

Strauss, Anselm and Juliet Corbin, eds. 1997. *Grounded Theory in Practice*. Thousand Oaks, CA: Sage.

Tabor, Roger. 1983. *The Wild Life of the Domestic Cat*. London: Arrow Books.

Thomas, Elizabeth Marshall. 1993. *The Hidden Life of Dogs*. New York: Houghton Mifflin.

———. 1994. *The Tribe of Tiger: Cats and Their Culture*. New York: Simon & Schuster.

———. 2000. *The Social Lives of Dogs: The Grace of Canine Company*. New York: Simon & Schuster.

Weber, Max. 1949. *The Methodology of the Social Sciences*. Edited by H. H. Gerth and C. W. Mills. Glencoe, IL: Free Press.

Wolcott, Harry F. 1999. *Ethnography: A Way of Seeing*. Walnut Creek, CA: AltaMira.

The Self

Clues from the Brain

By JOSEPH LeDOUX

Center for Neural Science, New York University,
New York, New York 10003, USA

ABSTRACT: Can we find a way of thinking about the self that is compatible with modern neuroscience? I think we can. First of all, we have to recognize that "the self" is not the same as "the conscious self," since much of who we are as individuals takes place out of conscious awareness. Second, we have to accept that some aspects of the self, especially the unconscious aspects, occur in and can be studied in other species, allowing us to relate these aspects of the self to detailed brain mechanisms. Finally, it also helps to think of the self in terms of memory. Obviously, much of who we are is based on memories learned through personal experience, including both conscious or explicit memories and unconscious or implicit memories. This is particularly important since much progress has been made in relating memory to the cells and synapses of the brain. By viewing the self as a network of memories the effort to relate the self to the brain can build on this progress. Emphasizing memory and experience does not take away from the fact that our genetic history also contributes to who we are. In fact, genes and experience, or nature and nurture, are, in the end, not different things, but different ways of doing the same thing—wiring the synapses of our brain. In many ways, the self is synaptic. This synaptic view of the self is not meant as a

Address for correspondence: Joseph E. LeDoux, Ph.D., Henry and Lucy Moses Professor of Science, Center for Neural Science, New York University, 4 Washington Place, Room 1108, New York, NY 10003–6621. Voice: 212-9983930 or 3937; fax: 212-995-4704. ledoux@cns.nyu.edu challenge to other views, such as spiritual, cultural, or psychological views. It is instead, just a way of understanding how these other aspects of who we are relate, deep down, to the brain.

KEYWORDS: self; personality; consciousness; unconscious; memory; learning; brain; neurons; synapses; genes

Who are you and why are you that way? The answer, of course, lies in your brain. But accepting this statement and understanding it are two different matters. Let's begin with a simple definition of what I mean by "you." I am using "you" to refer to the slightly more formal term, your "self," and more generally to the even more formal term, "the self." However, this refinement is still not sufficient to allow us to ask questions about the brain because existing concepts about the self are not very compatible with what we know about the workings of the brain.

REFINING THE SELF

In modern psychology the notion of the self is closely tied in with consciousness, in the sense of being self-aware, possessing agency or conscious control, having self-knowledge, a self-concept and self-esteem, of being self-critical, of feeling self-important, and striving towards self-actualization. Carl Rogers, a pioneer self-psychologist, summed up this view early on, defining *the self* as "the organized, consistent conceptual gestalt composed of perceptions of the characteristics of the "I" or "me" (Hall et al., 1998). For Rogers, these perceptions are "available to awareness, though not necessarily in awareness." Many contemporary "self" psychologists have a similar focus on self-consciousness, emphasizing the self as an active agent in the control of mental states and behavior (Markus and Kitayama, 1991; Cantor et al., 1986).

Philosophers, too, have tended to focus on the importance of consciousness in selfhood. Descartes, for example, emphasized the ability to know oneself as the defining feature of human nature. John Locke had also had something like this in mind, arguing that one's self or "personality extends itself beyond present existence to what is past, only by consciousness" (Dennett, 1976). Perhaps the best-known modern philosophical treatment of this topic is an article by Peter Strawson (1959) called "Persons." To define a person, Strawson distinguished between two kinds of statements: those that can obviously be applied to material bodies that exhibit consciousness ("is in pain," "is thinking," "believes in God") and those that can be applied equally to material bodies that are conscious and that are not ("is heavy," "is tall," "is hard"). In the tradition of Descartes, Locke, and Strawson, many contemporary philosophers take the view that personhood is a characteristic of intelligent, conscious creatures, and that consciousness defines personhood. Daniel Dennett, for example, says that, among other things, a being is a person if it is rational, verbal, conscious, in fact, self-conscious."

In spite of the long tradition of emphasis on the self as a conscious entity in philosophy and psychology, there is a growing interest in a broader view of the self (Gallagher, 2000; Sorabji, 2001; Churchland, 2002), one that recognizes the multiplicity of the self (Gallagher, 1996; Rochat, 1995; Bernaldez, 1996; Neisser, 1988; Damasio, 1999; James, 1890; Elster, 1985) and emphasizes distinctions between different aspects of the self, especially conscious and non-conscious aspects (Gallagher, 2000). This movement argues that the self that we are aware of and strive to improve, that is, the self that we have a sense of, is too narrow a view of what the self really is. Non-conscious aspects of the self were central to early psychodynamic theories of personality (e.g., Freud, Jung, and the neo-Freudians) and have long been part of the Buddhist attempt to eliminate the conscious self (Kolm, 1985; Epstein, 1995). Particularly relevant is the new wave of research in social psychology showing that many important aspects of human social behavior, including decision making and the way we react to members of racial and ethnic groups, to name but a few examples, are mediated without conscious awareness (Bargh, 1990; Greenwald and Banaji, 1995; Bargh and Chartrand, 1999; Higgins et al., 1985; Wilson et al., 2000; Wilson, 2002).

In sum, it would appear that any discussion of the self and the brain needs to recognize that the self is multifaceted, and especially that it has conscious and unconscious aspects. But so far I've emphasized the self of *people.* Do other creatures also have selves?

THE SELF IN EVOLUTION

Strawson's seminal distinction between things that are conscious (people) and things that are not (rocks and chairs) does not leave much room for other animals. Consciousness, at least the kind of consciousness we have in mind when we talk about our own mental states, was very likely added to the brain recently in evolutionary history. It was layered on top of all the other processes that were already there in our animal ancestors. Nevertheless, although other animals are not conscious in the human sense, they are not simply objects, like rocks or chairs.

Non-human animals are living creatures with nervous systems that represent external events internally and that allow their bodies to interact with and change the material world in ways that rocks and chairs do not. The concept of a conscious person, a conscious self, while useful as a way of evaluating issues related to being human, is less valuable as a general-purpose concept for understanding existence in the context of our animal ancestry—only people can be persons. Because we must pursue many aspects of how the brain works through studies of non-human organisms, we need a conception of who we are that recognizes the evolutionary roots of the human body, including the brain.

244 | The Self in Society

Unlike the notion of a person, the notion of the self can be thought of along an evolutionary continuum. While only humans have the unique aspects of the self made possible by the human brain, other animals have the kinds of selves made possible by their brains. To the extent that many of the systems that function non-consciously in the human brain function similarly in the brains of other animals, there is considerable overlap in the non-conscious aspects of the self between species. Obviously, the more similar the brains, the more overlap that will exist. Once we accept that the self of a human can have conscious and non-conscious aspects, it becomes easy to see how other animals can be thought of as having selves, so long as we are careful about which aspects of the self we are ascribing to each species in question.

The existence of a self thus comes with the territory of being an animal. All animals, in other words, have a self, regardless of whether they have the capacity for self-awareness. As a result, the self consists of more than what self-aware organisms are aware of. These differences within organisms (conscious vs. unconscious aspects) and between organisms (creatures with and without consciousness) are not captured by an undifferentiated notion of the self, but can be accounted for by recognizing the self as a multifaceted entity, consisting of both explicit (conscious) and implicit (unconscious) aspects. So how do we get from the multiplicity of self to the brain?

SELF AND MEMORY

Because you are a unique individual, the particular multifaceted aspects of the self that define "you" are present in your brain alone. And in order for you to remain who you are from minute to minute, day to day, and year to year, your brain must somehow retain the essence of who you are over time. In the end, then, the self is essentially a memory, or more accurately, a set of memories.

That one word, "memory," is the key to our ability to begin to understand the self in terms of how the brain works. Few research topics in neuroscience have been more successful than the study of the brain mechanisms of memory, and its companion, learning. If the self is encoded as memories, then we have a way of beginning to understand how the self is established and maintained in the brain.

One of the greatest achievements of modern neuroscience has been the elucidation of the manner in which memories are formed. Across many different kinds of studies, the conclusion has arisen that memories are synaptic in nature (Squire and Kandel, 1999).

Synapses are the tiny spaces, the connections, between neurons, but more important they are the means by which the brain does its business. For example, your memory of a particular experience involves changes in the synaptic connections among the neurons that are engaged by the stimuli that constitute the experience. To the extent that the self is a set of memories, the particular patterns of synaptic connections in an individual's brain and the information encoded by these connections are the keys to who that person is (LeDoux, 2002).

It was once thought that memory was a single capacity mediated by a single brain system. We now know that many different systems in the brain are able to learn during experiences and to store information about different aspects of the experience (Squire and Kandel, 1999; Eichenbaum, 2002; LeDoux, 2002). While some aspects of the experience are stored in a system that makes it possible to consciously recall the experience, most of the learning occurs in systems that function unconsciously or implicitly. When viewed in terms of memory, the multiplicity of the self becomes less mysterious and, in fact, becomes approachable through the brain.

GENES AND THE SELF

But what about genes? Don't they also make important contributions to personality and the self by shaping the brain? Absolutely! All of the capacities that we have as *Homo sapiens,* including our capacities to learn and remember, are made possible by the genetic makeup of our species. What we put in memory systems as individuals is up to experience, but the existence and basic mode of operation of these systems is due to our species' genes. At the same time, we each have a family genetic history that is a variation on the theme of being a human, and a personal set of genes that is a variation on our family's, and these variations also influence who we are.

The most well-articulated view of the role of genes in shaping behavioral and mental characteristics comes from biological trait theories of personality, which propose that one's enduring qualities are due to their genetic background (Hall et al., 1998). Considerable evidence has been amassed to support the view that some traits, such as the extent to which one is extroverted (gregarious) vs. introverted (shy, fearful, withdrawn), are highly influenced by one's genetic history. Nevertheless, genes have been found to account for at most 50% of any particular personality trait (Tellegen et al., 1988). For many traits the influence is far less and often not measurable. Further, life's experiences, in the form of learning and memory, shape how one's genotype gets expressed. There is a relatively new concept known as phenotypic plasticity, which refers to the fact that genes can give rise to different outcomes in different environmental circumstances (Pigliucci, 2001). Even the most ardent proponents of genetic determination of behavior admit that genes and environment interact to shape trait expression. It's a matter of how much, not whether, both are important.

While the fact that both nature and nurture contribute to who we are is widely acknowledged, less recognized is that, from the point of view of how the brain works, nature and nurture are not different things but different ways of doing the same thing: wiring synapses (LeDoux, 2002). That is, both genes and experiences have their effects on our minds and behavioral reactions by shaping the way synapses are formed. Moreover, in many ways, the genetic influence on personality can also be thought of as memory—a memory encoded across generations and species rather than one encoded by individual experience. From this perspective, synapses are the key to both genetic and learned influences on who we are. Without genes, we would have to relearn all the lessons achieved in evolutionary history by our species. Without learning and memory, personality would be an empty, impoverished expression of our genetic constitution. Learning allows us to transcend our genes.

SYNAPTIC SICKNESS

Given the fact that our self is encoded in the synaptic connections of systems that function consciously and unconsciously, will we know what a person is when we figure out how these systems function? Actually, no. Figuring out the synaptic mechanisms underlying each mental process is going to be quite a challenge. But we need to go beyond the mere explanation of how each process works in isolation. We need to understand how the many processes interact, and how the particular interactions that take place inside each of our brains gives rise to and maintains who we are. We are not our perceptions, memories, or emotions, but all of these combined, and synaptic interactions between the systems that underlie the individual processes are key to keeping the self integrated in space (across brain systems) and time (across the days of our lives).

Synaptic connections are also at the core of mental disorders. These were long thought of simply as chemical imbalances. While chemical changes are important, the key is not the chemicals themselves, but the circuits in which the chemicals act. For example, many drugs used to treat mental disorders alter the monoamine class of chemicals in the brain (serotonin, dopamine, norepinphrine, acetylcholine). These chemicals are widely distributed throughout the brain, but the alterations that affect a particular problem, such as schizophrenia, are now believed to be restricted to a select subset of the many circuits that use the chemical in question. And, as with normal brain function, pathological brain function can arise because synaptic circuits are altered by genetic or experiential factors, or some combination of the two.

Treatment of mental illness, whether by drugs or psychotherapy, is a process of changing one's mental states and behaviors. Changing of mental states and behaviors is, by definition, a process of learning and memory, which, as we've seen, are ultimately due to synaptic plasticity. Breakthroughs in understanding the synaptic basis of learning and memory are also relevant to the learning and memory that occurs during therapy. What is particularly interesting is the fact that many of the drugs used to treat depression and anxiety disorders affect the same molecular cascades that have been implicated in learning and memory. This suggests that drug therapy may be a way of placing the brain in a state conducive to learning, enabling patients to alter their behavior in adaptive ways.

THE PARADOX OF PARALLEL PLASTICITY

The fact that so many systems in the brain are able to change during experience raises the paradox of parallel plasticity. How is it that a coherent personality, a self, is ever established and maintained if different systems are able to learn and store information on their own? Why, in other words, don't the systems come to function completely independent of one another?

One reason is that although the different systems have different functions (e.g., seeing and hearing; controlling movements; detecting and responding to food, mates, and predators; and planning and decision making), they experience the same world. Thus, they process information differently, but about the same life events.

Another reason is that brain systems do not exist in synaptic isolation. They are connected with other systems. And just as the inputs to a particular system can serve as the basis for learning and memory within a system, connections between systems can serve as the basis for coordinated learning between systems.

A third factor is the existence of convergence zones, regions that are able to integrate the activity of other regions. Convergence zones tend to engage in so-called higher-order processing since they integrate the activities of areas devoted to specific functions. Not only can convergence areas put information together, but they can also send commands back to the lower-order systems, allowing some high-level control of and coordination across the specific systems.

Then there is the widespread nature of certain chemical systems, such as monoamines. When these systems are turned on, they release their chemicals throughout the brain. These chemicals can then serve as signals that facilitate learning across widely distributed systems.

Monoamine systems tend to be activated during significant experiences, such as ones that are emotionally charged. Indeed, activation of emotion systems is one of the key ways that parallel plasticity is coordinated and the self glued together. The brain has a number of emotion systems, including networks involved in the identification of sexual partners and food sources, as well as detecting and defending against danger. When one of these systems is active, the others tend to be inhibited. For example, other things being equal, animals will hang out in areas where they feel safe. So when it comes time to search for food, their fear of certain places, like wide open spaces, or places where they've encountered a predator before, might have to be overcome, if that's where food is likely to be found. The hungrier the animal is, the more it will tolerate fear and anxiety and take risks to get food. Similarly, both eating and sexual arousal are decreased by activation of systems involved in fear and stress. But once aroused, sexual desire can override many other brain systems—people risk all sorts of adverse consequences for a sexual fling. Not only does the arousal of an emotional state bring many of the brain's cognitive resources to bear on that state, it also shuts down other emotion systems. As a result, during intense emotional arousal, learning is coordinated across systems in a very specific manner, ensuring that the learning that occurs is relevant to the current emotional situation.

Obviously, the broader the range of emotions that a child expresses, the broader will be the emotional range of the self that develops. This is why childhood abuse is so devastating. If a significant proportion of the early emotional experiences one has are due to activation of the fear system rather than positive systems, then the characteristic personality that begins to build up from the parallel learning processes coordinated by the emotional state is one drenched in negativity and hopelessness rather than in affection and optimism.

The wide influence of emotional arousal results in many brain systems being activated at the same time, many more than if you are engaged in quiet cognitive activity. And because more brain systems are typically active during emotional than purely cognitive states, and the intensity of arousal is greater, the opportunity for coordinated learning across brain systems is greater during emotional states. By coordinating parallel synaptic plasticity throughout the brain, emotional states promote the development and unification of the self.

Most of us, most of the time, are able to piece together synaptic connections that hold our self together. Sometimes, though, thoughts, emotions, and motivations come uncoupled. When this happens, the self is likely to begin to disintegrate, and mental health to deteriorate. When thoughts are radically dissociated from emotions and motivations, as in schizophrenia, personality can in fact change drastically. When emotions run wild, as in anxiety disorders or depression, you are no longer the person you once were. And when motivations are captured by drug addiction, the emotional and intellectual aspects of life suffer.

SYNAPTIC AND OTHER SELVES

Given the importance of synaptic transmission in brain function, it's practically a truism to say that the self is synaptic. What else could it be? But not everyone will be happy with this conclusion. Many people will surely counter that the self is psychological, social, or spiritual, rather than neural, in nature. My assertion that synapses are the basis your personality does not assume that your personality is determined by synapses; rather, it's the other way around. Synapses are simply the brain's way of receiving, storing, and retrieving our personalities, as determined by all the psychological, cultural, and other factors, including genetic ones. So as we begin to understand ourselves in neural, especially synaptic, terms, we don't sacrifice the other ways of understanding existence. We don't, in other words, have to think more narrowly about people once we find out that synapses are important. A neural understanding of human nature in fact broadens rather than constricts our sense of who we are (LeDoux, 2002).

REFERENCES

Bargh, J.A. (1990). Auto-motives: Preconscious determinants of social interaction. In T. Higgins & R.M. Sorrentino (Eds.), *Handbook of motivation and cognition* (pp. 93–130). New York: Guilford.

Bargh, J.A. & Chartrand, T.L. (1999). The unbearable automaticity of being. *American Psychologist, 54,* 462–479.

Baumeister, R.F. (1998). The Self. In D.T. Gilbert, S.T. Fiske & G. Lindzey (Eds.), *The handbook of social psychology.* Boston: McGraw-Hill.

Bermudez, J. (1996). The moral significance of birth. *Ethics, 106,* 378–403.

Cantor, N., H. Markus, P. Niedenthal & P. Nurius. (1986). On motivation and the self concept. In R.M. Sorrentino & E.T. Higgins (Eds.), *Handbook of motivation and cognition: Foundations of social behavior.* New York: Guilford.

Churchland, P.S. (2002). Self-representation in nervous systems. *Science 296,* 308–310 [reprinted in this volume. Ed.].

Damasio, A.R. (1999). *The feeling of what happens: Body and emotion in the making of consciousness.* New York: Harcourt Brace.

Dennett, D. (1976). On the conditions of personhood. In A.O. Rorty (Ed.), *The identities of persons.* Berkeley: University of California Press.

Eichenbaum, H. (2002). *The cognitive neuroscience of memory.* New York: Oxford University Press.

Elster, J. (1985). *The multiple self.* New York: Cambridge University Press.

Epstein, M. (1995). *Thoughts without a thinker: Psychotherapy from a Buddhist perspective.* New York: Basic Books.

Gallagher, S. (1996). The moral significance of primitive self-consciousness. *Ethics, 107,* 129–140.

Gallagher, S. (2000). Philosophical conceptions of the self: Implications for cognitive science. *Trends in Cognitive Science, 4,* 14–21.

Greenwald, A.G. & Banaji, M.R. (1995). Implicit social cognition: Attitudes, self-esteem, and stereotypes. *Psychology Review, 102,* 4–27.

Hall, C.S., Lindzey, G. & Campbell, J.B. (1998). *Theories of personality.* New York: John Wiley & Sons.

Higgins, E.T., Klein, R. & Strauman, T. (1985). Self concept discrepancy theory: A psychological model for distinguishing among different aspects of depression and anxiety. *Social Cognition, 3,* 51–76.

James, W. (1890). *Principles of psychology.* New York: Holt.

Kolm, S.-C., (1985). The Buddhist theory of "no-self." In J. Elster (Ed.), *The multiple self.* New York: Cambridge University Press.

LeDoux, J.E. (2002). *Synaptic self—How our brains become who we are.* New York: Viking.

Markus, H.R. & Kitayama, S. (1991). Culture and the self: Implications for cognition, emotion, and motivation. *Psychology Review, 98,* 224–253.

Neisser, U. (1988). Five kinds of self knowledge. *Philosophical Psychology, 1,* 35–39.

Pigliucci, M. (2001). *Phenotypic plasticity: Beyond nature and nurture*. Baltimore: Johns Hopkins University Press.

Rochat, P. (1995). *The self in infancy: Theory research*. New York: Elsevier.

Sorabji, P. (2001). *Emotion and peace of mind: From Stoic agitation to Christian temptation*. New York: Cambridge University Press.

Squire, L.R. & Kandel, E.R. (1999). *Memory: From mind to molecules*. New York: Scientific American Library.

Strawson, P. (1959). Persons. In *Individuals: An essay in descriptive metaphysics*. London: Methuen.

Tellegen, A., Lykken, D.T., Bouchard, T.J., Jr., Wilcox, K.J., Segal, N.L. & Rich, S, (1988), Personality similarity in twins reared apart and together. *Journal of Personality and Social Psychology*, 54, 1031–1039.

Wilson, T.D. (2002.) Strangers to ourselves: Self-insight and the adaptive unconscious. Cambridge, MA: Harvard University Press.

Questions for discussion

1. O'Brien's reading leads us to think about living with apparently contradictory identities. What are some examples of other identities that involve "living a contradiction"? How would you study the experience of doing so?
2. The chapter examines the influence of ethnicity, sexual preference, and religion on the self. What other identities or statuses have an impact on our sense of who we are? Are some of these more salient for self-construction than others are? What makes them so?
3. The readings in this section raise questions about how and to what extent we choose identities or have them assigned to us by others. Some people argue that we can reject an unfavorable identity. What position do you take on this issue? What factors influence what we might call our identification with identities?
4. How has race/ethnicity, class, and gender shaped your family's history? How have these factors shaped your own identity? How does your identity affect your daily life? How does it affect your values, beliefs, and purpose? What impact do you imagine your identity will have on your future? On your economic prospects?
5. Do you think animals have selves, or are we just projecting identities onto them?
6. In your view, what does the possibility of animal selfhood mean for our treatment of them?
7. How does memory relate to the self? What does this imply for people who lose their memories? Do they have a sense of self?
8. Do you think further research on the self is important? Why or why not? What are some of the possible directions for future research on the self?

Further reading

Arluke, Arnold, and Clinton R. Sanders. 1996. *Regarding Animals*. Philadelphia: Temple University Press.

Damasio, Antonio. 1999. *The Feeling of What Happens: Body and Emotion in the Making of Consciousness*. New York: Harcourt Brace.

Irvine, Leslie. 2004. *If You Tame Me: Understanding our Connection with Animals*. Philadelphia: Temple University Press.

LeDoux, Joseph. 2002. *Synaptic Self: How Our Brains Become Who We Are*. New York: Viking.

Sanders, Clinton R. 1999. *Understanding Dogs: Living and Working with Canine Companions*. Philadelphia: Temple University Press.

Waters, Mary C. 2001. *Black Identities: West Indian Immigrant Dreams and American Realities*. Cambridge: Harvard University Press.

Wilkins, Amy C. 2008. *Wannabes, Goths, and Christians: The Boundaries of Sex, Style, and Status*. Chicago: University of Chicago Press.